Female Complaints

Female Complaints

Lydia Pinkham and the
Business of Women's Medicine

SARAH STAGE

W · W · NORTON & COMPANY

New York · London

LIBRARY OF CONGRESS CATALOGING IN PUBLICATION DATA

Stage, Sarah.
  Female complaints.

  1. Gynecology—United States—History—19th century.
2. Pinkham (Lydia E.) Medicine Company—History.
3. Pinkham, Lydia Estes, 1819–1883.   4. Advertising—
Drug trade—United States—History—19th century.
5. Women—United States—Social conditions.   I. Title.
RG67.U6S73   1979   338.7′61′615320973   78–14414
ISBN 0–393–00033–8

This book was designed by A. Christopher Simon

2 3 4 5 6 7 8 9 0

For my mother
ELIZABETH KIRCHNER STAGE

and my father
ROBERT ELLSWORTH STAGE

Contents

Illustrations following page 140

Foreword

Oh-h-h, we'll sing of Lydia Pinkham
And her love for the Human Race.
How she sells her Vegetable Compound,
And the papers, the papers they publish,
    they publish her FACE!

The year 1975 marked the hundredth birthday of Lydia Pinkham's Vegetable Compound, a patent medicine created to cure female complaints. Few proprietary remedies can boast a longer history. Lydia Pinkham, the woman who first sold the Compound in 1875 and whose face made the medicine famous, has become a part of American folk culture. For generations her picture appeared in the daily papers and on the druggist's counter with a regularity that inspired college men to sing in endless bawdy verses of Lydia and her famous face.

By the time I met Lydia Pinkham, she had gone respectable. Her oil painting hung on the wall of Radcliffe's Schlesinger Library, next to portraits of the library's donors in a room dedicated to America's outstanding women. On the floor, in packing cases, were the records of the Lydia E. Pinkham Medicine Company,

recently donated by her grandson after her heirs sold the medicine business. How Lydia Pinkham had arrived in such exclusive
company intrigued me.

It soon became clear that to understand Lydia Pinkham's place
in history I must approach her from several angles. Neither business history nor biography told the whole story. To account for
the spectacular rise and continued success of the Vegetable Compound it was necessary to explore the pervasive popular concern
with women's health in the late nineteenth century and the ways
in which both the medical profession and the patent medicine
manufacturer defined and dealt with female complaints.

Medical doctors would have us believe that all patent medicine
makers were knaves and all their customers fools. Yet to understand why women took Lydia Pinkham's Vegetable Compound
one must look closely at the options available to them. Not until
women could be convinced that the medical profession offered
safe, effective treatments which were accessible and economically
feasible would they abandon patent medicine. In the absence of
readily available, valid medical therapies the Vegetable Compound
made sense.

The Pinkham company spent millions of dollars in advertising
to convince women that the Vegetable Compound was safer and
cheaper than the treatments provided by physicians. Clearly the
profit motive lay behind Pinkham advertising copy, but however
self-seeking its purpose, the advertising mirrored in magnified
form popular dissatisfaction with the medical profession and its
treatment of women's diseases. Pinkham ads gave voice to sensational but frequently sound critiques of gynecology as it was practiced in the nineteenth and early twentieth centuries. The advertising also reproduced and reinforced conceptions of women and
women's health current in the culture. To trace Pinkham advertising is to view in microcosm changing attitudes toward women
and medicine.

The story of the company is itself a chapter in American social
and political history. The Pinkham concern weathered internal
schism, attacks by the muckrakers, and government regulation to
reach a sales peak of over three million dollars annually by 1925.

In the next two decades a long-standing family feud pitted Lydia Pinkham's children and grandchildren against one another in a battle for control of the company. The lengthy fight badly crippled the business. By 1968 when the family sold the company, the business had fallen upon hard times, not so much a victim of government regulation or advances in medicine as a casualty of changing styles and an advertising and marketing policy which had failed to keep pace with the competition.

The Vegetable Compound itself survived the company's demise to celebrate its centennial. Cooper Laboratories, a large, diversified pharmaceutical company, continues to make the medicine and sell it without fanfare to a clientele growing smaller each year.

As much a social as a business phenomenon, the rise of Lydia Pinkham's Vegetable Compound can tell us a good deal about women and medicine in the United States. The history of the Pinkham company and its product speaks to changes in the lives of American women, to changing cultural attitudes toward female sexuality, and to the prolonged failure of the medical profession to provide adequate treatment for women's physiological and psychological complaints.

S. S.

Williamstown, Massachusetts
June 1978

Acknowledgments

When one works for a long time on a book, as I have on this one, the debts of gratitude incurred mount up to a total impossible to account for in the space of an acknowledgment. The most obvious debts are monetary. I am grateful to the American Association of University Women for a fellowship which enabled me to begin research on this book and to Williams College for an assistant professor leave which expedited its completion.

For other less tangible, but no less valuable kinds of support, I am indebted to friends and colleagues at Yale and Williams, who have read and offered thoughtful criticism of parts or all of the manuscript in its various phases. Kai Erikson, Nancy Cott, David Musto, Leo Ribuffo, Cynthia Russett, Robert Dalzell, and the late George Rosen gave me the benefit of their critical reading. Abby Solomon, Warren Goldstein, Barbara Weisberg, Barry Kenyon, Ruth Nelson, and Joel Krieger fired my enthusiasm, aided in research, and offered helpful suggestions in editing and organization. And my students at Williams encouraged and challenged me by their lively interest in women's history.

The assistance of skilled archivists and librarians has made my work immeasurably easier. I especially wish to thank Jeanette Bailey Cheek, former director of the Schlesinger Library, for her interest and support. At the Schlesinger, Patricia Miller King, Eva Moseley, Barbara Haber, and Diane Dorsey provided valuable assistance. Oliver Field of the American Medical Association proved both cordial and helpful. And Lee Dalzell greatly facilitated my work at Williams.

My greatest debt is to John Morton Blum, who supported my interest in women's history and encouraged my study of Lydia Pinkham and her Vegetable Compound. His indefatigable energies as an editor and critic were matched only by his patience and kindness.

I wish to express my appreciation to the Arthur and Elizabeth Schlesinger Library on the History of Women in America, Radcliffe College, for permission to quote from the papers of the Lydia E. Pinkham Medicine Company and to the American Medical Association for permission to use materials from the Propaganda Department.

Female Complaints

The Woman
Behind the Trademark

Generations of Americans grew up with Lydia Pinkham. Her face, kindly yet abstracted, her gray hair drawn back into a braided bun, the solid respectability of black silk and white ruching, became as familiar as the daily newspaper or the neighborhood druggist's display where she advertised her Vegetable Compound for over eighty years. No advertising agent intent on creating the perfect grandmother could have done a better job. He didn't have to. Lydia Pinkham was authentic. And yet of the woman behind the trademark we know little. A few letters, a scrapbook, and a dog-eared set of cashbooks provide the only clues that help to separate the actual Lydia Pinkham from the advertisement of herself. Over the years the story of her life, like her famous photograph, has been continually retouched until the legend of Lydia Pinkham comes to us suspiciously cast in the language of a company advertisement. To discover the actual woman, we must place her against the social and intellectual landscape of nineteenth-century America and reconstruct her life by sketching in the background until the outlines of the woman emerge in relief.

Genealogical records provide the first clues. Born on February

9, 1819, in Lynn, Massachusetts, Lydia was the tenth of a dozen children in the family of William and Rebecca Estes. This prolific Quaker clan and their assorted kin counted themselves among the founding families of Lynn. When genealogy became fashionable, Lydia Pinkham's children traced their ancestry back to the thirteenth-century Italian house of Este. In the political intrigues of Dante's day, the Estes had been forced into exile in England where they remained for four centuries, until 1676, when Quaker Matthew Estes migrated to America. The penchant for political and religious dissidence which marked the Esteses' long history continued unabated in Lydia's family.[1]

Billy Estes, Lydia's father, began his career as a shoemaker, or cordwainer, in the late eighteenth-century when Lynn was already earning its reputation as "the city of shoes." During the War of 1812, Estes constructed a saltworks on the flatlands near his home, an investment which paid off handsomely and enabled him to escape the ranks of Lynn's independent shoemakers at a time when competition and repeated business depressions threatened to pauperize the cordwainers.[2] By the time Lydia was born, Billy Estes owned a substantial farm on the corner of Estes and Broad streets, ideally located in the path of the city's development. He became a gentleman farmer who made his fortune in real estate.

If, as some of the local reformers complained, Lynn Quakers too frequently lost their moral militancy when they achieved financial success, the pattern did not hold for Billy Estes and his wife. When the Lynn Friends refused to endorse the abolition of slavery in the 1830's, the Esteses joined the radical "Come Outer" faction, which left the meetinghouse in protest. Although Lydia was only in her teens when she put aside her Quaker dress, she always remained something of a Quaker in temperament, as evidenced by her distrust of ecclesiastical and secular authority.

Lydia's mother, Rebecca Estes, like so many other radical Quakers, turned to the writings of Swedish theologian Emanuel Swedenborg, and in her enthusiasm introduced Lydia and the family to his ideas. Swedenborg, an eighteenth-century scientist turned theologian, was viewed by many as a fanatical mystic. His claim to have been in communication with the angels led to his ridicule and persecution. In reality his theology was part of a broader reaction against the rationalism of his century. He sought not to reconcile religion to science, but science to religion—to get beyond the description of phenomena to first principles. American transcendentalists admired him because, as Ralph Waldo Emerson wrote, Swedenborg "saw and showed the connections between nature and the affections of the soul."[3]

Swedenborg's beliefs nicely suited the psychological needs of the nineteenth century. He insisted that he had visited a spiritual world—between heaven and hell—where men went after death. The dead, he promised, were not in the grave, nor did they await judgment before an angry God. Instead they were "resuscitated" after death and sent to "dwell in gardens where flower beds and grass plots are seen beautifully arranged, with rows of trees round about, and arbors and walks, . . ."[4] Friends and acquaintances, wives and husbands, brothers and sisters met and conversed in the spirit kingdom. Children passed immediately into heaven where they became angels attended by a loving angel woman. His description of the spirit kingdom served to allay fears of damnation and helped to create an afterlife with an appealing human dimension. To the many nineteenth-century men and women who lost their children and loved ones to disease and hardship, his message came as a soothing balm.

It was a short step from Swedenborgianism to spiritualism. Although Swedenborg himself had inveighed against meddling with the spirits of the dead, many of his readers, Lydia Pinkham among them, could see nothing wrong with establishing contact with a spirit world so benign. In the 1850's, when the Fox sisters of Rochester created a sensation with their spirit rappings, many prominent Americans embraced spiritualism or flirted with seances and spirit boards.

Swedenborg's theology met the social as well as the psychological needs of nineteenth-century Americans. He replaced the harsh features of Calvinism with the portrait of a God at one with man and the promise that all men could win a place in heaven through love of God and fidelity to duty. His was a commonsense salvation which contained in it the seeds of social reform. European Swedenborgians were among the first to champion the anti-slavery cause. By the 1840's, Swedenborg's American followers embraced not only anti-slavery but a host of seemingly disparate movements which they saw as flowing from the same "fruitful unity."[5] Temperance, vegetarianism, homeopathy, and Fourierism, as well as spiritualism, won their support.

Although Lydia Pinkham never joined the Swedenborgian New Church and never formally claimed adherence to its doctrines, Swedenborgianism seems to have supplied the philosophical framework which held together her own commitment to movements which included anti-slavery, temperance, and spiritualism. Without an understanding of Swedenborg, it would be difficult to perceive a fruitful unity large enough to encompass her varied interests.

Lydia Pinkham grew up in the forcing house of New England reform. As Emerson wrote to Carlyle, "We are all a little wild here, with numberless projects of social reform. Not a reading man but has a draft of a new community in his waistcoat pocket."[6] So, although the perimeters of her life were marked by Boston on the south and Bedford on the west, Lydia came to know a surprising number of the leading figures of her day. In the decades before the Civil War, Lynn provided a center seat for the drama of agitation and reform.

The social atmosphere of Lynn intensified the reform spirit. Unlike its wealthier neighbors Boston and Salem, Lynn prided itself on its working-class character. An editorial in the local paper boasted, "This is not a place for idlers and social parasites." The townspeople frowned upon aristocracy. Lynn boosters liked to claim that the town was "a well regulated republic in miniature," but in fact the disdain for everything that smacked of conservatism or elitism made it an exceptionally volatile community which one prominent abolitionist characterized as a "place of fearless discussion."[7]

The Estes household in Lynn served as one of the gathering places for anti-slavery leaders. William Lloyd Garrison, editor of the *Liberator* and one of the most hated men in America, counted Rebecca Estes among his friends and visited her when he spoke in

Lynn. Lydia Maria Child, popular author of *The American Frugal Housewife,* and her husband, David, editor of the anti-slavery *Massachusetts Whig Journal,* found themselves ostracized from Boston society because of their radical views and were glad to find welcome in the Estes house on Broad Street. The fighting ministers Wendell Phillips and Parker Pillsbury, the Quaker poet John Greenleaf Whittier (a distant relative by marriage to Rebecca Estes), and Nathaniel Rogers, editor of the *Herald of Freedom,* all frequented the Estes drawing room.

Down the street lived the Singing Hutchinsons, a colorful family who became the balladeers of temperance, woman's rights, and abolition. Abby Kelley, later one of the most effective speakers on the anti-slavery platform, taught at the local Friends' school. And on Union Street lived Lynn's most famous resident, the fugitive slave Frederick Douglass.

Small wonder Lydia gave her allegiance early to the anti-slavery movement. At the age of sixteen she joined the Lynn Female Anti-Slavery Society. Lucretia Mott, the Society's national founder, held a commitment to anti-slavery matched only by her belief in woman's rights. Abby Kelley, Lydia, her mother, and her elder sister were among the charter members of the Lynn group.

The Estes family and their friends to the contrary, anti-slavery was not a popular cause in the 1830's and 1840's. Abolitionist speakers often found themselves locked out of halls and churches and not infrequently met by angry mobs. On at least one occasion, an abolitionist orator had to seek protection behind the skirts of a cordon of Lynn girls. No doubt Lydia and her sister were among the group.[8]

The Estes family thrived on controversy. In 1842 Lydia's elder sister, Gulielma Maria (named for the wife of William Penn), was asked to leave the Methodist church because of her friendship with Frederick Douglass. The incident, recounted in the *Liberator* and the *Herald of Freedom,* began when Gulielma went walking with Douglass and took his arm. The Reverend Jacob Sanborn found her action scandalous. Summoning her to his study, he catechized her on her behavior. An indignant Gulielma scored him in kind for his bigotry. When the Reverend asked if she "was much acquainted with colored people," she responded "not as much as I hope to be," and asked him point-blank if he thought it a crime to associate with Negroes. The flustered minister blurted out, "I think them a different race—their features are different," and ventured that although he did not condone segregation, he thought when Negroes attended his church they should sit by themselves in the gallery. Sanborn brought the interview to a climax by putting to Gulielma the question, "Would you *marry* a colored man?" Color, she responded, would make no difference. She would look only on character. With that Sanborn dismissed her. Later he ordered her to come before the congregation and "confess that she had been imprudent in being in the company of colored men in the *manner* which she acknowledges, and promise that she will do so no more . . . or her connection with the Church must be dissolved." Gulielma scorned the invitation. At its next meeting, the Essex County Anti-Slavery Society resolved that the Methodist Episcopal church was not a church of Christ, but "a synagogue of Satan."[9]

Frederick Douglass remained a fast friend of the Esteses. Among Lydia Pinkham's few surviving possessions is a "Friendship Album" containing an entry written by Douglass in 1848 which begins, "My dear Friend, How unspeakably pleasant it is to meet old and dear friends after a long separation."[10] One story, probably apocryphal, recounted how Lydia once stood in the way of a conductor who threatened to evict Douglass to the Jim Crow car. Douglass resolutely refused to sit in the car reserved for blacks and Irish on the Boston and Lynn railroad. When an angry group of passengers tried to remove him, he clung so tightly to his seat that it was ripped from the floor.[11]

The segregation of public facilities extended to the churches, meetinghouses, and public halls. In 1842 the Lynn Lyceum barred the black speaker Charles Lenox Remond. Lydia and Gulielma Estes joined dissidents who boycotted the Lyceum and formed a new subscription lecture series under the auspices of a society called the Freeman's Institute. The group chose as its motto, "No concealment—No compromise."[12]

The following year the membership of the Institute, under the presidency of Douglass, elected Lydia Estes secretary. In her jour-

nal, she copied in her copperplate hand the constitution of the
club which provided, "No person shall be excluded from full par-
ticipation in any of the operations of the Society on account of
sex, complexion, or religious or political opinions."[13] The emphasis on sexual as well as racial equality distinguished the Freeman's
Institute and highlighted a significant aspect of the anti-slavery
movement.

The "woman question" touched off controversy in the anti-
slavery movement in the late 1830's. Garrison and Nathaniel
Rogers insisted that the women who formed the backbone of the
local societies should be allowed to hold national office. The notion that women should participate equally in the leadership of
the American Anti-Slavery Society disturbed not a few of the organization's male members. The controversy reached a climax at
the annual meeting in 1840 when Abby Kelley, with Garrison's
support, was elected to the business committee and Lucretia Mott
and Lydia Maria Child won places on the executive committee.
The more conservative delegates walked out, claiming that Garrison's insistence on women's equality clouded the anti-slavery issue
by raising an "extraneous novelty." The Bible, decorum, and social usage dictated that women remain silent in meetings. Led by
Arthur and Lewis Tappan, the faction soon formed the American
and Foreign Anti-Slavery Society, which excluded women from
its councils.[14]

The woman's issue gained its greatest notoriety the following summer at the World Anti-Slavery Convention in London.
America's representatives included seven women, among them
Lucretia Mott. The British rejected the women's credentials and
denied them seats on the convention floor. As one British clergyman explained, the admission of women would subject the convention to ridicule. When Garrison arrived a few days later and
heard of the episode, he refused his seat and joined the women in
the gallery. As far as he was concerned, a meeting which began by
barring the representatives of half the human race made a mock-
ery of its claim to be a World's Convention. His defection cast a
pall on the proceedings by robbing the convention of its most celebrated American delegate.[15]

Lydia Pinkham consistently backed the radical faction which

put woman's rights on a par with abolition. As the anti-slavery ranks split and regrouped throughout the 1840's, she took as her guide Nathaniel Rogers, the intransigent editor of the *Herald of Freedom*. The handsome Rogers and his family summered in Lynn where they enjoyed the Esteses' hospitality. Lydia admired Rogers so much that she later named a son after him.

In the internecine rivalries of anti-slavery, Rogers proved a demanding idol. Each split in the movement found him farther from the center. Early on he drew the rancor of many New England ministers when he attacked them for their moral cowardice on the slavery issue. A master of polemical prose, Rogers once described the clergy as having "an ear as deaf as an adder's to the wail of the American bondsman."[16]

In the end, Rogers' refusal to deviate from his principles led to his split with Garrison. When Garrison adopted as his war cry the slogan, "No Union with slaveholders," and called for the dissolution of the Union by political means, Rogers held fast to his belief in non-resistance and moral suasion. Rogers had always insisted that slavery was a "moral disease" that must be cured by moral and spiritual agitation. Political action, he argued, could not make the white and black man brothers. His uncompromising consistency so alienated his old allies that in 1845 they forced his removal from the *Herald of Freedom*. Sick in both body and spirit, Rogers went to Lynn where he spent the last year of his life. In the fall of 1846, he died at the age of fifty-two.[17]

In the meantime Lydia Estes had grown from a young girl to a young woman. She was strikingly tall for her day, standing five feet ten, with a spare build, solemn dark eyes, and auburn hair she wore drawn back in ringlets. Too tall and thin to be thought pretty, she may have suffered embarrassment over her gangling height, but she never slouched and is said to have carried herself with a calm composure. After graduating from the select Lynn Academy, she became a schoolteacher; her twenty-fourth year found her still in the classroom. During the spring of 1843, the Freeman's Institute absorbed much of her time, perhaps because there she had met Isaac Pinkham, a newcomer to Lynn.

Pinkham was a widower of twenty-nine with a five-year-old

daughter. Shorter and stouter than Lydia, he had fair skin, light brown hair, and quizzical blue-gray eyes. He dressed formally, always in black, from his Prince Albert coat to his boots and tie. Affable, kindly, but with no great mental power or personal dynamism, he seemed an odd match for Lydia when compared to the fiery Rogers she so much admired. After a short courtship, Lydia and Isaac married in September of 1843.

Isaac Pinkham lived on great expectations. The speculative fever of the 1840's made him discontented with a trade. Instead he moved from one enterprise to another in the hope of striking it rich. Isaac started out in Lynn as a shoe manufacturer, but increasingly he dreamed of making money as Lydia's father had—in real estate. Billy Estes set the couple up in a house on Estes Street which, like all of his holdings, lay smack in the middle of what promised to become the trading center of Lynn.

Shortly before Christmas in 1844, Lydia gave birth to her first son, Charles Hacker Pinkham. The increased responsibility, instead of steadying Isaac, made him more determined than ever to get rich quick through speculation. Before the next year was out, he gave up the shoe business and launched another enterprise. The Estes family must have watched with concern as the young couple struggled under the burden of Isaac's dreams.

It was during the following summer that Nathaniel Rogers made his last visit to Lynn. Lydia, pregnant with her second child, renewed their friendship and when the baby was born in July she named him Daniel Rogers Pinkham. The child lived only a year longer than his namesake. In 1847 the baby died of cholera infantum, a form of gastroenteritis which raged during the hot summer months and brought grief to scores of Lynn mothers. Lydia passed Rogers' name on to her next son, born a year later. The birth of a new baby seemed to punctuate each year. A picture taken during the period shows a pale and vaguely melancholy Lydia holding a baby on her lap.[18]

While Lydia took care of the growing family, Isaac Pinkham's fortunes continued to zigzag. He changed occupations as often as some people changed clothes. Produce dealer, kerosene manufacturer, trader, laborer, farmer, builder were among those he listed in the Lynn *Directory*. His real dream was to become a landed squire. When Billy Estes died in 1848, Isaac's ambitions knew no bounds. Although the estate was ample, it had to provide for a widow and ten surviving children. Isaac could hardly hope to fulfill his dreams on the couple's share. But even before the estate was settled, he began borrowing, buying, selling—moving his family eight times in a dozen years. He always seemed about to grasp success. Yet he so frequently overextended himself that the family found itself constantly out at the pocket.

During these bleak years, Lydia Pinkham, mourning the deaths of her friend Rogers, her father, and her infant son, not surprisingly turned to spiritualism for solace. The *Banner of Light,* Boston's spiritualist journal, supplemented the *Liberator* and the *Herald of Freedom* as regular reading in the Pinkham household. Lydia was not alone in her enthusiasm. Spiritualism swept the country in the 1850's. William Lloyd Garrison embraced it, as did Lydia's Lynn neighbors, the Singing Hutchinsons. And another Lynn resident, a Mrs. Mary Glover Patterson, better known in later life as Mary Baker Eddy, made a name for herself in local spiritualist circles. For a decade Mary Baker Eddy moved in and out of Lynn, once living on Broad Street in a house that had been part of Billy Estes' farmstead when Lydia was born. Their mutual interest in spiritualism may well have brought the two women together, but neither left a record of such a meeting.

In 1857 with the family fortunes at a low ebb, Isaac decided to quit the produce business and try his hand at farming. Lydia, pregnant again, removed the family which by now included three sons—William Pinkham had been born in 1852—to Bedford, Massachusetts, where a daughter arrived whom she named Aroline Chase Pinkham after her favorite cousin.

While in Bedford, Isaac Pinkham, perhaps smarting from a setback at the hands of an unscrupulous associate, set down in Lydia's journal a list of rules "To Secure Success in Business," which he ostensibly dedicated to his three sons but which read as if he were talking to himself. He wrote:

1. Make all your purchases as far as possible of those who stand the highest in uprightness and integrity. Men of character.

2. Enter into no business arrangements with anyone unless you are well satisfied that such person is governed by a strict sense of honor and justice.

3. Engage in nothing of business at arms length, and be sure you are well acquainted with whatever business you may engage in.

4. Be satisfied with doing well and continue well doing. A sure sixpence is better than a doubtful shilling, which motto, be governed by. . . .[19]

How well Pinkham himself held to these rules after leaving Bedford is debatable. But without a doubt, Lydia and her sons later violated every one of Isaac's prescriptions when they launched their patent medicine business.

In fact, if legend is correct, Isaac Pinkham's prodigality helped lay the foundation for the family's patent medicine success. Always free-handed as long as his credit was good, Isaac endorsed a note for a Lynn machinist named George Clarkson Todd. When Todd defaulted, Pinkham paid twenty-five dollars on the note. In partial payment Todd gave Pinkham the formula for a medicine. The recipe purported to cure female complaints—the catchall nineteenth-century term for disorders ranging from painful menstruation to prolapsed uterus.

Such cures were common. Lydia Pinkham lived at a time when housewives brewed home medicines as a matter of course. The therapeutic confusion of nineteenth-century medicine spawned a host of curative systems from homeopathy to the mind cure. With the doctor suspect, self-dosing became a logical and inexpensive substitute. Home doctoring claimed its own venerable tradition, but it received an added impetus from the reform spirit of the nineteenth century. A typical enthusiast like Lydia Pinkham embraced a wide series of reforms ranging from temperance to the Graham diet.

Lydia Pinkham kept a notebook labeled "Medical Directions for Ailments" in which she jotted down folk remedies. Some were commonplace. For dyspepsia she recommended Pleurisy root steeped in boiling water. Others were outlandish. One entry read: "A hog's milt procured fresh from the slaughter house split in halves, one half to be bound on the sole of each foot and allowed to remain there until perfectly dry, will produce relief and in many cases effect a cure of the complaint called asthma."[20] Her well-thumbed copy of John King's *American Dispensatory,* the most complete listing of pharmaceutical botanicals in its day, testified to her personal experiments with home remedies, quite apart from her supposed debt to George Todd. Whatever the source of the recipe for her female weakness cure, the medicine proved her most popular remedy. She brewed it on the stove and soon kept enough bottles on hand to give to neighbor women.

After three years in Bedford, Isaac Pinkham tired of farming and returned the family to the house on Estes Street. On the eve of Civil War, Isaac took up kerosene manufacturing. When the death of Lydia's mother brought the final division of Estes property in 1862, Isaac sold out his downtown holdings and moved his family to Wyoma, on the outskirts of Lynn, into a house with a roof so steep and sharp the neighbors called it the "Lightning Splitter." Pinkham hoped to buy the surrounding farmland and sell for a profit in what he anticipated would be a postwar real estate boom.

The coming of the Civil War did not affect the Pinkhams greatly. None of the boys was old enough to be conscripted, although Charles chose to enlist when he turned seventeen. His life had been particularly hard and perhaps he saw the war as a chance to escape the drudgery of the Pinkham household. As the eldest son, he had taken on a disproportionate share of the family's burdens. Before the war, he left high school to help support his younger brothers and sister. The only job he could find was in Cambridge, and he sometimes walked the eighteen miles to save car fare.[21]

The two younger boys, Dan and Will, fared better. They helped out by peddling popcorn and fruit, but they stayed in school. Both placed high in their classes in spite of the fact that they were so poor they had to borrow their schoolbooks. Dan won the silver medal in 1866 for "scholarship and deportment" and chose for his valedictory address a plea for Negro suffrage. Will followed four years later with a gold medal and a speech on the inevitability of progress. Lydia Pinkham had an especially close relationship with these two bright middle children. A well-educated woman for her generation, she delighted in their academic success and encouraged them by coaching them in Latin and declamation. Her journal for these years is laced with translations from Vergil, popular poems, and exercises invented to stimulate the boys' interest.[22]

After high school, Dan, the most resourceful and outgoing of the boys, determined to go West. Traveling through Missouri, Kansas, and into Indian Territory, he worked for a time as a cattle drover and later as a schoolteacher in Texas. During his adventure he contracted "fever and ague" which permanently damaged his health. Dan returned to Lynn in 1870, thin and hollow-eyed, but ebullient as ever. In 1872 he opened a grocery store in Wyoma which he soon turned into a forum for the political ambitions he had harbored since his days as class orator. At the age of twenty-two, he had already earned a reputation among local politicians as a young man to watch.[23]

Will, the handsome charmer of the family, possessed an intellectual bent. His friend and classmate, Will Gove, talked him into trying for Harvard and tutored him for the entrance examination. In the fall of 1872 the two friends took a walking tour of New Hampshire. Will Pinkham stayed on to teach at the Clinton Grove Quaker School. He hoped to enter Harvard the next year, but before he had completed his preparation the Panic of 1873 put an end to his plans.

On the eve of the Panic, the Pinkham family appeared to be prospering at long last. With real estate values soaring to dizzying heights after the war, Isaac Pinkham's property in Wyoma had more than doubled in value. He retired from the kerosene business and declared himself a builder in the next Lynn *Directory*, a claim he made good with the completion of Pinkham Hall, a business block with an auditorium on the second floor. In 1872 Isaac cashed in some of his profits and moved the family from the Lightning Splitter into one of the best houses in the Glenmere section of Lynn, complete with a fountain in the front yard and a grand piano in the parlor. For the first time since her marriage, Lydia Pinkham could afford a few luxuries.[24]

Behind the prosperous facade, Pinkham finances remained as

shaky as ever. The amiable Isaac endorsed promissory notes for more and more of his acquaintances. Money was easy, and he plunged into land speculation—buying, borrowing, and juggling his holdings by transferring chunks of his property into Lydia's name. Isaac did not worry about his indebtedness. Lynn had grown since Lydia's birth in 1819 from a village of 4,500 to a city of almost 20,000. Growth meant prosperity, or so Isaac Pinkham reckoned as he acquired more and more land.

What Pinkham had not counted on was a new national economy which inextricably tied Broad Street in Lynn to Wall Street in New York. On September 18, 1873, the banking house of Jay Cooke failed and within three months the financial panic touched off the most devastating industrial depression the country had seen. Credit froze, factories shut down, businesses folded, and wage workers faced a winter of starvation. Isaac Pinkham and thousands like him saw their speculative bubbles burst in their faces. Isaac's lands and buildings were mortgaged to the hilt. When the Lynn banks began to foreclose, they threatened to arrest those unable to pay their arrears. No longer a young man, Pinkham broke under the strain. When the bank officer arrived to arrest Isaac, he found him sick in bed. The family prevailed on the bank's attorney, who turned out to be a distant relative, to drop the suit; Isaac was spared the indignity of arrest and jail. But he never regained his vigor. He lived on until 1889, a diminished figure. His grandson recalled him as a feeble old man, rocking in his chair by the fire.[25]

The year 1875 found the family struggling together, with Isaac increasingly incapacitated. Dan's grocery store had gone under in the Panic. His liberality with credit led to bankruptcy. Will had given up his hopes of Harvard and taken rough work as a wool-puller. Together he and Charlie, who worked after his stint in the army as a conductor on the Lynn horse cars, pitched in to support the family. Aroline, who had graduated from high school with the predictable gold medal, helped pay her share by teaching school. The Pinkhams had given up their grand house in Glenmere and moved to a smaller home on Western Avenue.[26]

Facing hard times, if not actual destitution, the Pinkham family cast about for a money-making scheme and finally hit upon the idea of selling Lydia Pinkham's female remedy.

Always the hustler of the family, Dan was the first to see the possibilities of marketing his mother's female weakness cure. As the story later appeared in the local paper, the family was sitting around the kitchen one day in 1875 when a party of ladies from Salem drove up to the house and asked for a half a dozen bottles of Mrs. Pinkham's medicine. Generally Lydia Pinkham gave the medicine away, but sometimes she sold small lots, and, times being hard, she accepted five dollars from the Salem women. After they had left Dan blurted out, "Mother, if those ladies will come all the way from Salem to get that medicine, why can it not be sold to other people—why can't we go into the business of making and selling it, same as any other medicine?"[27]

Dan had a point. The newspapers were full of ads for remedies like "Wright's Indian Vegetable Pills," "Oman's Boneset Pills," "Vegetine,"and "Hale's Honey of Horehound and Tar." Lydia Pinkham at first demurred, but the boys' enthusiasm won her over. And so in the spring of 1875, the family, ignoring Isaac's motto of a sure sixpence over a doubtful shilling, launched their patent medicine business.

From its beginning the business operated as a family venture. Everyone contributed to the enterprise. Dan and Will provided the brains and sinew. Lydia made the medicine. Charles and Aroline turned over their wages to help pay for alcohol and herbs. And together Will and Lydia worked up advertising copy and put out a pamphlet called "Guide for Women." Even Isaac contributed. Sitting in his rocker, he folded and bundled the pamphlets for Dan to distribute.

Casting about for a name for the medicine, the family came up with "Lydia E. Pinkham's Vegetable Compound." Vegetable remedies, or botanicals as they were called, had gained wide popularity in the nineteenth century in reaction to doctors' indiscriminate dosing with mineral medicines like calomel. The straightforward name, "Vegetable Compound," proved a fortunate, if commonplace choice. When the government forced Pinkham competitors to change the names of their products to meet truth-in-advertising standards laid down in the twentieth century, the Pinkhams in this respect were above reproach.

Lydia, with Will's help, brewed the first batches of the medicine on a stove in the cellar. The original formula called for Unicorn root, Life root, Black cohosh, Pleurisy root, and Fenugreek seed macerated and suspended in approximately 19 per cent alcohol, for preservative purposes. Lydia Pinkham bought the herbs from local suppliers, measured her ingredients with kitchen measures, and after she had steeped and macerated the herbs, mixed them all together and dumped them into cloth bags through which the mixture percolated in much the same way that jelly was made. She then added additional alcohol to preserve the medicine, filtered it through cloth, and bottled it.[28]

The Pinkhams, like so many Lynn working-class families bent on self-improvement, were strict temperance advocates. Lydia and the children belonged to the local temperance society. When the boys were young they wore white ribbons on their coat lapels to indicate they had taken the pledge. Part of Dan's difficulty in the grocery business had stemmed from his insistence that the store sell only "dry goods," not rum or spirits. Yet the family saw nothing wrong with selling a medicine which contained enough alcohol to make it forty proof, stronger than table wine or sherry. Alcohol, as far as they were concerned, was a legitimate medicinal substance. When Lydia Pinkham came down with pneumonia in April of 1878, Will recorded in the "Medical Directions for Ailments" that she dosed with an herb decoction and "also took before each meal a teaspoonful of whiskey in two tablespoonfuls of milk."[29] Although Lydia Pinkham viewed the alcohol in her medicine as therapeutically valuable and necessary for preserving the Compound, she also made pills and lozenges for cases where alcohol might aggravate menstrual disorders. But taken as directed, three spoonfuls a day, the Vegetable Compound posed no threat to temperance, or so the Pinkhams argued when critics chided them.

With a Yankee passion for exact accounting, Lydia Pinkham kept cashbooks in which she recorded the first meager sales of the Vegetable Compound alongside the family's debts. In these ledgers something of the woman behind the trademark emerges. Family accounts she kept with unsentimental exactitude. Each child she charged for rent, clothing, and personal expenses, which could be written off by hard work. ("Daniel Pinkham, $311.32 balanced off by services.") Generosity occasionally prevailed. Next to one entry she noted, "A poor fatherless girl I promised to send six boxes for $3"—a discount from the normal price. In the back pages she collected remedies: "For consumption Pyrola and White-pine bark, equal parts of each, steep, strain. . . ."[30]

When the Lydia E. Pinkham Medicine Company officially organized in 1876, the Pinkhams, worried that Isaac's creditors might try to claim the profits of the business, named Will Pinkham sole proprietor because he was the only member of the family (besides nineteen-year-old Aroline) with no outstanding debts. Together Dan and Will carried on the burden of drumming up trade. Lydia remained in the background, making the medicine, answering letters, and writing advertising copy. The four-page "Guide for Women" began the first modest advertising campaign. Dan, who worked as a mail carrier, distributed the pamphlet on his rounds. Will joined him and together they covered the towns surrounding Lynn. Finally they tackled Boston. Riding into town on the ten-cent workingmen's train, they carried a few thousand circulars a day in knapsacks slung over their shoulders and worked door to door. Slowly their efforts began to pay off. Druggists who had at first been reluctant to stock the unknown medicine began to place orders. The Boston wholesale house of Weeks and Potter ordered a gross. But for a long time the Pinkhams counted themselves lucky if they could sell a bottle a day.

During the spring of 1876, Dan plunged full time into the medicine business. Packing a goatskin trunk full of circulars, he set off for Brooklyn to create a wider market for the Compound. In his mid-twenties by now and sporting a full beard, Dan was full of grit and not afraid of hard work. He took a two-dollar room on Willoughby Street and set out singlehandedly to advertise the Compound in Brooklyn, New York, and New Jersey. Borrowing pen and ink from the post office to save money, he wrote to his family almost daily and sometimes twice a day. His letters home, addressed "Fellow Doctors," captured the spirit of the early enterprise.[31]

"There is work enough around New York and vicinity to keep ten like me working from now to eternity," Dan wrote after he had taken a day to look around. "Send me another 100,000 pamphlets as I intend to do a 'Devil of a Business' here if possible."

Brooklyn proved more difficult than Dan anticipated. "There are more high toned people here in Brooklyn than I like to distribute among and the churches take up a little too much room," he complained. Because of the explicit wording of the pamphlet, which contained a reference to "Prolapsed Uterus" on its cover, Dan encountered difficulty getting women to read his pamphlet. Casting about for a more genteel ploy, he landed on a scheme to advertise and cut printing costs at the same time. "I believe a good way to advertise and a cheap way would be to get out small cards with this inscription on . . . and have them dropped around on parks and other places of resort, say, late Saturday night so people will pick them up on Sunday." He suggested that the family buy small calling cards and write on the back, "Try Lydia E. Pinkham's Vegetable Compound. I know it will cure you, it's the best thing for Uterine complaints there is. From Your Cousin, Mary, P.S. You can get it at P. Jackson's on Fulton Street." Anticipating his family's disapproval he hastily added, "They're all such darned frauds as that."

The more Dan contemplated his brainchild, the more enthusiastic he grew. The plan would foil the sharp-eyed rag pickers who too often got the pamphlets before women had a chance to read them. For a moment he fantasized littering the Chelsea beach with cards, then he realized the tide would wash them away. But he thought of other possibilities. "Before Decoration Day," he urged, "just try it and drop a few cards all through the Cemeteries around there and I'll bet it will sell a few bottles."

When after ten days Dan had put out more than 20,000 pamphlets only to discover that Jackson's pharmacy had sold but a dozen bottles of the Compound, he searched for another way to get sales started. The boy he hired to help distribute pamphlets gave him one idea. "His mother is a dressmaker and knows a good many sick women and has commenced to blow for the medicine," he wrote the family. "If you can send me that keg full of medicine I think it would be well for me to put it out in trial bottles here in Brooklyn and let her give it to parties she knows; if you can we can't lose much and I think it would be a grand good thing as it would get these Millinery Store keepers and Dress-Makers to guzzling it." Dan grew so impatient waiting for Will to send the medicine that he threatened to "buy some herbs and alcohol and make some medicine" himself. Will dutifully forwarded a keg of the Compound and Dan tried his experiment, which did not work as expected. "I haven't met with very good success on the trial bottles that I've given away," he confessed. "One of them made one woman a great deal sicker." Lydia, indignant, must have spoken her mind on the virtues of the Compound. A mollified Dan observed later, "I'm glad to hear the medicine is curing them up so well."

When it rained so hard that Dan was forced to "loaf for a spell," he paced his room trying to come up with ideas to increase sales. After one rainy weekend he wrote Will excitedly, "I think there is one thing that we are missing it on and that is not having something on [the pamphlet] in regard to Kidney Complaints as about half of the people out here are either troubled with Kidney Complaints or else they think they are." Dan suggested that Will change the copy on the front page of the "Guide" to include the new claim so that he could give the pamphlet to men as well as women. As he shrewdly noted, "[M]en have more money to spare these times than women." Will followed his lead and soon copy headed "Weak and Diseased Kidneys" appeared alongside claims that the Vegetable Compound cured uterine complaints.

When druggists showed some reluctance to display Pinkham posters and women refused to read the pamphlets because the explicit language embarrassed them, Dan countered the criticism by placing an ad "in a little religious paper that nobody but women read." The ad, he told Will, would give "a kind of religious tone to our Compound and get the good will of a few Methodists." More important, "if any publisher or editor refused to put our advertisement into their paper, [we can] show them this Pious Sheet."

Despite his machinations, business lagged during the summer. Dan became exasperated with the family, who kept him supplied with pamphlets but were maddeningly slow in sending money for his expenses. "For God's sake! Whose management is it that keeps me from having what I actually need?" he exploded after opening Will's latest letter and finding no money. "Now in consequence of your cussed judgment I shall have to loaf tomorrow and live upon a cracker diet." To prove he wasn't extravagant, Dan recited his expenses which totaled $1.55 a day, including the wage he paid his helper. "There is no use in writing," he lamented, "I actually can't spare 3¢ to buy a stamp with and cramp my guts. I have got to get a job at something else in order to keep my belly full. . . . I should think you either were all crazy or else thought I was getting my meals at free lunch establishments." (This last jibe could be appreciated only by an earnest temperance family like the Pinkhams, for of course a free lunch establishment was a saloon.) Angrily he concluded, "If it is necessary to wear a shirt two or three weeks at a time in consequence of the business not being good enough to have a clean one, I am willing to put up with that, but if it isn't good enough to supply me with food, then I want to get out of it."

By the next day Dan had cooled off. He wrote that his landlady, confident of the Pinkhams' success, had loaned him a dollar to carry him through. But, he warned, "I can't go it on my cheek much longer so hurry up with some money." "It beats all that everybody should say we are going to make a fortune," he marveled. "They seem to believe it, too."

In the meantime he sewed his shoes together every night and tried to keep his one suit clean. "This business is tough on clothing," he complained. "I'm beginning to look so confounded seedy that I feel as though I ought to go into the country pasting up posters." No sooner had he voiced the idea than he warmed to it. Everything in the city had been "advertised to death," he maintained. Why not get a horse and wagon and travel through the countryside peddling the Compound? "It seems to me," he predicted with some accuracy, "that cities and towns of less than

50,000 inhabitants are going to pay us the best." Dan never got his horse and wagon, although the time did come when Lydia Pinkham's face decorated barns and fences across the country.

Early in June, Dan came home for a stretch "to help recuperate on finances," and the Pinkhams put their heads together to figure out some way to make the business pay. Printers' ink was the lifeblood of patent medicine. Dan, with his eye for advertising, saw that clearly. But his ideas, like his plan to run a Pinkham poster the full length of the Brooklyn Bridge, cost more than the struggling company could muster. While Dan spent his time dreaming up ideas and haggling with printers to bring down the price of pamphlets, Will made a shrewder gamble. One day after he had collected eighty-four dollars for the last gross ordered by Weeks and Potter, he dropped by the office of the *Boston Herald* and inquired the cost of running the whole four-page circular on the front page. The *Herald's* manager quoted a price of sixty dollars and Will quickly struck a deal. When he returned home and told the family, they were incredulous. "That was like a thunderclap out of a clear sky," Lydia Pinkham recollected, "and we all sat down and had a good cry."[32] Will's expenditure struck the family as foolhardy. Sales of the Compound barely paid for the ingredients and the cost of printing up pamphlets. Will had thrown away sixty dollars on a single advertisement which would run for only one day.

In the long run Will's arithmetic proved sounder than the family's. The *Herald* reached a circulation of 50,000. To print and distribute that many pamphlets cost the Pinkhams almost a hundred dollars, not counting the labor the boys provided free. Newspaper advertising was not only cheaper but, as they soon discovered, it enhanced their credit. Within two days the *Herald* ad brought orders from three different wholesalers. The family skeptics were won over and soon hired an agent, T. C. Evans, who began a modest newspaper campaign.[33]

Dan returned to Brooklyn in the fall. Rested and full of new ideas, he determined to stick it out "till we either get rich or bust."[34] He worked himself relentlessly putting out pamphlets. "Send me 300,000 more," he ordered Will. No one he hired could keep up his demanding pace. "I've got sick of boys," he confided. "Other boys fight them too much." Next he hired a man for ten dollars a week, only to let him go because, as he put it to Will, "the cussed fool was too proud to work." Exasperated with hired help, Dan urged Will to send Charlie. "Tell Charlie to let the HRR job go to the Devil and be out here by Saturday morning," he urged. In November his older brother joined him and together they tramped the length of Manhattan shoving out circulars.

Dan liked having company and never tired of trying to induce the family to move to Brooklyn. He tantalized them with tales of exciting things to do (like hearing Henry Ward Beecher preach at Plymouth Church or attending the political rallies at Cooper Union). But the real advantage, as he saw it, lay in the opportunity to talk with druggists and patent medicine men. "I actually think if the whole family should move here the learning and sharpening of us all up during two years time would be worth thousands of dollars to us in this business which I think depends almost wholly on discernment, keenness, and knowledge," he insisted. "Hang it! We've got to reduce this advertising down to a science instead of so much brute force. . . ." Try as he might, Dan could never persuade the family to leave Lynn.

He returned home for Christmas and shortly after brought a guest from New York, the remarkable Charles N. Crittenton. Crittenton, a patent medicine dealer, later became something of a merchant evangelist who devoted the waning years of his life to rescuing "fallen women." In the 1890's, with the help of Frances Willard of the Women's Christian Temperance Union, he established National Florence Crittenton Missions in the United States and abroad.[35]

Crittenton seemed an odd friend for the free-thinking Dan, who once remarked that he would not mind church if "there's something else preached besides Come to Jesus gabble." Probably the druggist was more secular in the days when he met and took a fancy to Dan. He had come up the hard way himself, and he did not mind giving the younger man a hand, especially when he was peddling a product as promising as the Vegetable Compound. Crittenton's business gave the family its first break. Dan could tell other wholesalers, "Crittenton has got it, so you better hurry up. . . ."[36] Even better, Crittenton paid cash instead of taking the medicine on consignment. His money helped the Pinkhams over several bad stretches.

After Will's success with the *Boston Herald* ad, the Pinkhams turned more and more to newspaper advertising. They mortgaged their home on Western Avenue to pay for space in the papers. With newspaper ads replacing door-to-door advertising, Dan was free to stay home in 1878 and pursue his political ambitions. A major shoe strike had broken out during the summer. When the Republican mayor protected property by sending in police to break up strikers, the workingmen of Lynn responded by squaring off against the Republicans in the next election. A Workingmen's party ticket which included Dan Pinkham as representative to the state legislature triumphed in the fall of 1878. Dan quickly made a name for himself, and an odd one at that. His colleagues tagged him "The Fish-Ball Representative" after a speech he made in defense of the Lynn strikers. A Republican had argued that if the shoemakers could not live on their wages, they should cut their expenses. Dan countered hotly that they earned only twelve cents a pair for shoes they made. If his fellow representatives believed so firmly in cutting expenses, he suggested, they could cut their own salaries and live like the Lynn shoemakers, on fish balls instead of beefsteak.[37]

By the end of his first term Dan had built up an enthusiastic following. An ardent admirer of Ben Butler and the Greenback-Workingmen's coalition, he stumped the state preaching currency inflation as a cure for the plight of the workingman. No wonder his party was dumbfounded to see him deliberately throw away his chance for a second term. When the Republican opposition put forth an unpopular measure called the Civil Damage Bill, which would have prohibited the sale of alcoholic beverages in the county, Dan deserted the Workingmen's party to remain loyal to his temperance convictions. He voted in favor of the Republican measure. After the bill passed by a narrow margin, the *Lynn Examiner* vented its anger on Dan. "How does Dan Pinkham expect his mother to keep her roots and herbs without alcohol?" the paper queried. "That was a mean piece, Dan, voting prohibition; you were not elected for that, and next year you will be elected to advertise cures for female complaints at home."[38]

The antiprohibition forces made good the threat. In the next election, rum dominated politics. Dan faced a young unknown named Henry Cabot Lodge, who made it perfectly clear that, although he was a Republican, he would not oppose the repeal of his party's prohibition bill. In a bitter personal campaign the Pinkhams combined politics and advertising in broadsides headed "Republicans! Democrats! Workingmen!" which urged voters to support the Greenback-Workingmen's ticket, and promised in the same breath that sufferers from kidney complaints and dyspepsia could find relief by taking Lydia E. Pinkham's Vegetable Compound. Their efforts proved futile. Lodge began his long political career, with the backing of North Shore brewers and saloonkeepers, by defeating Dan Pinkham in a close race.[39]

Shortly after the election Dan returned to Brooklyn. Out of politics and able to devote his full mental energies to advertising, he hit upon the idea of his life. For three years Dan had searched for a gimmick that would put the Compound out in front of its competitors. During his first stay in Brooklyn he had noticed that "folks seem to be all tore up on home made goods," an observation which led him to suggest that they advertise the Compound as "The Great New England Remedy" and embellish the label with a picture of "a humble cottage." The family did not have money enough to alter the wrappers, so Dan's idea died stillborn. But he continued to ruminate and in 1879 came up with the idea of putting a picture of "a healthy woman" on playing cards with the caption, "She is now as healthy a woman as can anywhere be found/Having taken four bottles of Mrs. Pinkham's Compound."[40] When he came home for Christmas and saw his mother, he realized he had found his "healthy woman." At sixty Mrs. Pinkham was a dignified, handsome woman who possessed a benign motherly countenance. No better advertisement could be imagined. So, after a family council, Lydia Pinkham posed for the photograph which made advertising history.

The picture conveyed the whole Pinkham message. At a glance

it inspired confidence. The attractive woman, sagacious and composed in her best black silk and white lace fichu, appealed to her audience as an idealized grandmother, sympathetic and compassionate. Other advertisers had used pictures. The Smith brothers bearded faces appeared on the glass jars which contained their famous cough drops and in the newspapers Buffalo Bill Cody advertised his Wild West show. But no one had thought of using a woman and no one had used a portrait to such good effect. Lydia Pinkham not only identified her product, she came to embody it.

The picture ads did a good deal to authenticate the medicine in the eyes of the trade and the general public. Will Pinkham handled most of the business arrangements and as a result skeptical druggists and editors, doubting there was a real Lydia Pinkham, had taken to calling him "Lyddy." Once the picture ads appeared and Lydia's face graced the trademark, the Pinkhams had the last laugh. According to the company's agent, H. P. Hubbard, the picture "boomed the sales immensely." About six months after the ad began to run, the family refused an offer of $100,000 for the business and the new trademark.[41]

Lydia Pinkham soon became a national figure. Editors used the electrotype of her picture whenever they needed a photograph of a famous woman, be it Queen Victoria or actress Lily Langtry. Her ever-present face, staring from newspapers and drugstore displays, led Dartmouth men in the 1880's to parody in song:

> There's a face that haunts me ever,
> There are eyes mine always meet;
> As I read the morning paper,
> As I walk the crowded street.
>
> Ah! She knows not how I suffer!
> Her's is now a world-wide fame,
> But 'til death that face shall greet me.
> Lydia Pinkham is her name.[42]

Soon other college glee clubs picked up the song, embellishing it with infinite ribald verses. Sung to the tune of "Our Redeemer" and ending with the refrain—"Oh, We'll sing of Lydia Pinkham/And her love for the human race/How she sells her Vegetable Compound/And the papers they publish her face"—the Lydia Pinkham song became part of the American folk tradition.

Amused, and with a sharp eye to the advantages of free advertising, Lydia Pinkham clipped the songs, jokes, and anecdotes which played on her name and carefully pasted them in her scrapbook. A favorite went: " 'Oh, I've smashed my bottle of Lydia Pinkham's!' 'Aha! A compound fracture!' "[43]

By 1881 sales of the Compound amounted to almost $200,000 a year. Dan Pinkham, who had once written from New York that when he returned to Lynn he wanted to dress "as if I'd just bankrupted a Rainbow," lived to see the business established on a solid footing and his mother something of a national celebrity. But by the time he could afford a new suit, he was dying of tuberculosis. "Daniel sick in New York," Lydia Pinkham wrote in November 1879. "Recommended to take three of my Liver Pills, then steep one-half ounce of Pleurisy root and Bugle weed and one-half once of Marsh-mallows, taken one-half cup at a time three or four times per day." Dan returned home for Christmas "threatened with Pneumonia." His mother prescribed another dose of Pleurisy root and Bugle weed and resorted to the Indian treatment of "sweating" him with hot bricks wrapped in soaked flannel. "In two days he was decidedly better," she concluded. "Advised . . . to take when on feet again one or two bottles of Pierson's B[lood] Invigorator."[44]

When Dan's cough lingered on only to flare up a year later, Lydia Pinkham's letters took on a note of desperation. "If you have pain in your lungs I want you to come home immediately," she wrote. "Don't go to staying out there and running any risk. Dr. Mason can bring your blood in right condition in a month so that you won't have a cough or pain for years."[45]

In her anxiety Lydia Pinkham revealed her genuine faith in her own remedies, in patent medicines in general, and in Dr. Monica Mason, a local homeopath. But in the end she watched as her most trusted remedies proved futile. In the winter of 1880, Dan headed south, hoping to regain his strength. He returned home in the spring too weak to walk. Exhausted, he lay in bed reading from the spiritualist *Banner of Light* and trying his best to cheer the stricken family. Early in October, a month before his thirty-third birthday, Dan Pinkham died.[46]

The family scarcely had time to mourn his passing. A second shock followed almost immediately. Will Pinkham contracted consumption early in 1881, just months after his marriage to Emma Barry. The disease proved as quick in Will's case as it had been lingering in Dan's. By October, Will was too ill to attend his brother's funeral. His frantic wife moved him to California in December, but it was too late. Will died in Los Angeles less than two months after Dan, at the age of twenty-eight.[47]

Bright, energetic, and fired by the dream of success, the two brothers burned themselves out building up the business. The years of hard labor, long hours, and poor meals consumed their physical strength. Their work paid off handsomely. They lived to see the Compound selling not just a bottle a day, but over two hundred thousand bottles annually. But six years of hard work won them only six months of security. They died, in the words of one obituary, martyrs to the cause of the great business they helped to start.[48]

The double blow shattered Lydia Pinkham and sent her retreating further into spiritualism. Both Dan and Will had been spiritualists and their belief, coupled with her own, must have given her some solace. The local medium, a Mrs. Sanborn, became a frequent caller at the Pinkham home. Charles and Aroline, although they did not share their mother's faith in the spirit world, dutifully participated in the seances that were held each Saturday in the Pinkham parlor. Successful at long last, they could afford to humor their mother.

Two days before Christmas in 1882, Lydia Pinkham suffered a paralytic stroke. During her last months she felt very close to Dan and Will. Mrs. Sanborn came almost daily for private sessions. On May 17, 1883, Lydia Pinkham died at the age of sixty-four. Her funeral was held in the spiritualist manner as she had requested. Instead of lamenting her passing, the friends who gathered in the Lynn cemetery celebrated her reunion with her sons. At the close of the service her old friend John Hutchinson, last survivor of the

Singing Hutchinson family, sang the sad but hopeful refrain, "Almost Home."[49]

Lydia Pinkham combined a shrewd business sense with a penchant for reform—a penchant which led her from anti-slavery through a labyrinth of movements from temperance to the Greenback party. Without hesitation she would have placed her Vegetable Compound squarely in the reform tradition. Like many in her age she believed that women suffered needlessly at the hands of doctors. She offered her Vegetable Compound, as we shall see, convinced it was more effective and less dangerous than the treatments of the medical profession. Her advice to women who wrote to her was direct and commonsensical, drawing on the practical knowledge of diet, health, and exercise she had gained in years of domestic practice. Conviction coupled with the hustle and pitch of advertising when she proclaimed herself in banner headlines "Saviour of her Sex."

The glimpse we are able to get of the woman behind the trademark reveals an intelligent, sincere woman who possessed absolute confidence in the medicine she sold. It is unfortunate that in the years following her death, Lydia Pinkham became more and more a victim of her own advertising. The story of her life, like her famous portrait, has been touched and retouched until the actual woman has become obscured. Today she is remembered not as a reformer, but as a trademark—her legacy the benign countenance that sold millions of bottles of Vegetable Compound.

The Poisoning
Century

Lydia Pinkham's bias against medical doctors was rooted in the social, intellectual, and medical history of her century. Confidence in medicine reached its nadir during her lifetime. At her birth in 1819 doctors were already under fire for their indiscriminate use of dangerous therapeutic techniques. Physicians themselves spoke out against practices which made the nineteenth century, in the words of one practitioner, "the poisoning century."[1] By mid-century the public had, to an alarming extent, abandoned the established profession to patronize newcomers whom the regular doctors regarded as quacks. The rise of medical sects in the nineteenth century and the accompanying patent medicine craze which helped launch Lydia E. Pinkham's Vegetable Compound grew out of the public's increasing distrust of the therapies employed by orthodox physicians.

A letter written to Lydia Pinkham as late as 1881 testified to the medical confusion of the period and highlighted the failure of doctors to understand properly or treat effectively female complaints. "Dear Mrs. Pinkham," wrote the wife of an attorney, "I have been afflicted with a malady that my physician frankly tells me he has never met with before and I write to ask you the cause and what the cure [is]." The woman went on to describe her ailment:

It is an affection of the gums and the mucous membrane of the mouth—the gums turn white and a layer easily rubs off leaving them very red and angry—the inside of my cheeks and corners of my jaw are white and look and feel hot and parboiled and contracted—it has extended to my tonsils and seems to have started down my throat. . . . I have also womb trouble, constant pain in the small of the back. . . . I have [an] enlarged urethra, the mouth is wide open all the time large enough to admit a small bean, sometimes it gives me great trouble and agony and is then comfortable for a time. I sleep well and my appetite is good and I am regular in my bowels, but not strong, no endurance. . . .[2]

Lydia Pinkham answered confidently, "You have taken virulent poisons in the form of medicine that has caused disease of the mucous membranes." Diagnosing at long distance, she deduced that the woman suffered from mercurial poisoning brought about by overdosing with calomel. Similar cases of mercury poisoning persisted as long as physicians relied on heavy doses of the drug. Although the use of calomel decreased in the second half of the century, many old-fashioned doctors continued to prescribe the powerful cathartic. Taken over a length of time, the drug had a cumulative effect that could produce the type of symptoms the woman described in her letter.[3]

Impatient with "physicians who physic us to death," Lydia Pinkham advised the woman, "Bathe yourself all over every night in hot water. . . . Eat farinaceous food and broths. . . . Ride out and walk out; dig, use the trowel. When in the house sit by [an] open window (well protected) that you may inhale all the outdoor air possible."[4] For the womb trouble she prescribed the Vegetable Compound, but she took care to suit the medicine to the woman's symptoms. "Now about the Compound," she wrote:

I would not have you take my liquid for although there is only a sufficient quantity of alcohol in it to keep it, that little would be bad for you. My Compound in dry form is good for you; its cleansing and healing properties will benefit you.

She closed by urging her correspondent to "Take the Compound according to directions and let Doctors alone."[5]

Lydia Pinkham's advice made sense. Medicine for much of the nineteenth century, as one prominent physician lamented, was little more than "ineffectual speculation."[6] Physicians sought cures for diseases they could neither diagnose nor distinguish from their symptoms. Totally reliant on visible symptoms, doctors lumped diseases into categories (nosologies) on the basis of such gross symptoms as fever, skin eruptions, and swelling with the result that symptoms which exhibited a superficial similarity but differed widely in significance and pathogenesis were often grouped together. Therapies treated not specific diseases, but general conditions—dropsies, catarrhs, fevers. Because they were pressured to produce visible results, doctors resorted to bleeding, blistering, and purging—a therapy so aggressive it earned the name "heroic."

Heroic therapy found its staunchest American exponent in the person of Dr. Benjamin Rush of Philadelphia. The redoubtable Rush—writer, physician, and signer of the Declaration of Independence—personified the active approach to medicine. For Rush the sickroom was a battlefield where the doctor combated disease with an arsenal of powerful medicines. Rush banished nature entirely from the therapeutic process. "The death of a patient, under the ill-directed operations of nature, or what are called lenient and safe medicines," he told his students in 1801, "seldom injures the reputation or business of a physician. For this reason many people are permitted to die who might have been recovered through the use of efficient remedies."[7]

Rush's absolute confidence in his art found its basis, unfortunately, in theory rather than practice. Rush lived in an age of "medical systematists," men who hoped to systematize medicine as Newton had mechanics and astronomy. This passion for simplification and systemization led Rush to insist that all disease emanated from a single cause—hypertension of the blood vessels. "There is but one disease in the world," he announced to his class triumphantly. That one disease, "morbid excitement induced by capillary tension," accounted for symptoms as diverse as fever, diarrhea, and skin rashes. Reducing all disease to one cause, Rush then advanced a therapy to suit all situations. The advantage of his system was obvious. "We will suppose the Doctor to have a house consisting of one hundred rooms, each having a different Lock," he told his students. "Of course he must have an equal number of keys to open them—now I am capable of entering every apartment of my House with the assistance of a Single Key."[8] For Rush that key was the lancet. More specifically, he advocated depletive therapy (bloodletting and purging) to reduce capillary tension. In a lecture at the University of Pennsylvania, he exhorted his students, "Do hommage to the Lancet. . . . I say venerate the Lancet, Gentlemen!"[9] By the early nineteenth century, Rush had succeeded. The lancet had become the hallmark of the medical profession.

Bloodletting (phlebotomy), constituted the standard therapy for nearly every ailment from the 1790's until after the Civil War. Many doctors considered bleeding a routine part of their treatment for conditions ranging from pneumonia to hernia. Where the lancet proved too cumbersome, physicians used leeches. Amenorrhea (suppression of menstruation) they treated by placing leeches in the vagina or applying them directly to the cervix. More alarming than the frequency with which doctors employed bloodletting was the amount of blood they took. The dominant school advocated bleeding to syncope, or unconsciousness; others argued for a more quantitative measure. Rush, in extreme cases, called for the removal of four-fifths of the blood in the body. For the infant or the "patient who cannot be raised from his pillow without fainting," a noted physician counseled "recourse . . . to the juglars [sic] from which blood will flow when it cannot be elicited from the arms."[10]

The universal acceptance of bloodletting by doctors owed less to their adherence to Rush's monistic system than to the demonstrable effects bleeding produced in cases of fever. The pulse weakened, the flush gave way to pallor, and the patient perspired freely. Physicians mistook such symptomatic relief for cure. Neither doctor nor patient seemed to notice the anemia which resulted from frequent bloodletting. In fact bloodletting proved popular with patients who sought an active therapy without unpleasant aftereffects. Practiced moderately, bleeding constituted perhaps the least unpleasant of the heroic therapies.

Just as the doctor wielded the lancet to carry off "bad blood," so he dosed with harsh purgatives and emetics to clean out the stomach and bowels. Emetics produced immediate and often violent vomiting; purgatives, or cathartics, acted as potent laxatives. Calomel (chloride of mercury), a powerful cathartic, ranked with the lancet as "one of the sheet anchors of heroic therapy."[11]

Therapeutically useless, calomel broke down in the intestines into a virulent mercurial poison. Heavy doses produced a violent laxative effect followed by profuse salivation as the body attempted to throw off the drug. Continued doses destroyed the mucous tissues of the mouth, softened the gums, and led to the loss of teeth. In the final stages of mercurial poisoning "the upper and lower jaw bones exfoliate and rot out . . . in the form of horse shoes; parts of the tongue and palate are frequently lost."[12] Despite these visible side effects, doctors declared the drug "safe and gentle."[13] "Calomel to salivation," became as common in the medical vernacular as "bleed to syncope."

Indiscriminate overdosing led to attacks on physicians both in print and in song. Lydia Pinkham's Lynn neighbors, the Singing Hutchinsons, popularized the satiric ballad, "Calomel," which in dozens of variations stressed the greed and ignorance of doctors.

> Physicians of the highest rank,
> To pay their fees we need a bank,
> Combine all wisdom, art and skill,
> Science and sense in Calomel.

> When Mr. A. or B. is sick,
> Go call the doctor, and be quick;
> The doctor comes with much good will,
> But ne'er forgets his Calomel.

> .   .   .   .

> The man grows worse quite fast indeed,
> Go call the doctor, ride with speed:
> The doctor comes like post with mail,
> Doubling his dose of Calomel.

> The man in death begins to groan,
> The fatal job for him is done;
> He dies, alas! but sure to tell,
> A sacrifice to Calomel. . . .[14]

Blistering, or the use of skin irritants, provided yet another heroic therapy. By means of cantharides or tartar emetic plasters, the doctor raised a blister, or second-degree burn. When the wound suppurated, he viewed the pus as an indication that the infection had been drawn out of the system. The moxa and the seton, less common than the blister, worked on similar principles. Doctors placed the seton—a thread, horsehair, piece of lint or some other foreign matter—on open wounds and surgical incisions to promote infection because they believed the ancient theory that "laudable pus" signalled a sure sign of healing. The moxa, a coil of carded cotton, was placed directly on the affected area, then lighted and allowed to burn down to the skin. In cases of serious illness, doctors did not hesitate to add to the patient's suffering by employing such counterirritants. One doctor treated a typhus case by shaving the patient's head and applying upwards to thirty blisters.[15]

"The doctor came every day," observed a terse Ohio settler. "He purged, he bled, he blistered, he puked, he salivated his patient. He never cured him."[16] Skepticism of heroic treatment developed slowly but persistently throughout the first half of the century. Yet the public's prejudice against doctors inhibited therapeutic reform. The doctor remained a luxury to the great majority of Americans who called the physician only in serious cases that would not yield to folk remedies and self-treatment. Medical fees were high and as a result the doctor, once he was consulted, was under pressure to do something dramatic. No wonder physicians continued to use strong medicines and active therapies. "Perhaps the disposition to demand of the physician an active medication in all cases exists to a greater degree in this than other countries," observed a thoughtful physician. "We are preeminently an energetic and enterprising people, and therefore the bold 'heroic' practitioner is apt to meet with favor from the public."[17]

Insistence on active therapy did not preclude the development of alternatives to heroic therapy, but it did dictate that those alternatives themselves be active. Botanical remedies, no less dramatic in their effects than mineral preparations, provided the basis for the first successful assault on the heroic practice of orthodox physicians. Americans claimed a long tradition of botanical medicine. From the Indians, early settlers learned of native medicinal plants. Some, like Nathaniel Hawthorne's fictional Roger Chillingworth, schooled themselves in Indian lore; others merely pretended to a knowledge of Indian cures. The "root and yarb" doctor, lowliest practitioner on an occupational ladder that included almost any self-styled "physician," became a common village phenomenon. Frequently these root and herb practitioners were women skilled in domestic practice who, like Lydia Pinkham, developed a clientele among their neighbors.

By the beginning of the nineteenth century the botanic, or "empiric," actively challenged the competence of the medical doctor. Drawing on religious and patriotic themes, botanics skillfully played to the public's prejudices. "Must we go to Europe to import mineral poisons?" cried one. "No! never! the remedies are here; they are spread over the plains and mountains in abundance, they surround every cottage and bloom round every cabin door. . . ."[18] To buttress their claims, botanics pointed to two significant vegetable discoveries—quinine and digitalis. Quinine, an alkaloid extracted from cinchona bark, provided a legitimate example of a powerful and effective vegetable remedy. Peruvian Indians in the seventeenth century had discovered the therapeutic value of cinchona in the treatment of malaria. A native plant, discovered by native Americans, and successful in treating the country's most serious endemic disease, quinine seemed to support the botanics' claims. Digitalis, derived from foxglove and used effectively to treat certain heart diseases, provided still another example of the efficacy of botanical medicines.

Doctors who could claim either some formal schooling or apprenticeship training under a practicing physician looked down on the botanical practitioners as rash "empirics," and untrained charlatans. But it would not be wise to exaggerate differences in the outlook or the skill of the "regulars," as they called themselves and the upstart "empirics." The "regulars" were little more scientific or rational in their approach than their opponents. They, too, relied heavily upon crude empiricism. The limited medical knowledge of the period meant that the "regular" medical practitioners could offer patients few therapies superior to those of the empirics they so disdained. In practice they tended to cling to heroic therapy in the face of mounting public opposition to the dangers of calomel and bleeding and to respond to the financial competition of the botanics by ridiculing their class and educational background. At a time when politicians pitched their appeal to the "common man," the arrogance of the regular doctors became a weapon in the hands of their rivals.

Democracy combined with botanical empiricism in the early decades of the nineteenth century to produce Thomsonianism, a botanical sect that stood as a direct precursor to the development of patent medicines such as Lydia E. Pinkham's Vegetable Compound. Samuel Thomson, the sect's founder, popularized a patented system of botanical medicine designed to circumvent the regular profession (which he called the "mineral faculty") by enabling every man and woman to become a family physician.

In a *Narrative* of his life published in 1822, the New Hampshire farmer turned physician capitalized on the ridicule heaped upon him by regular doctors by emphasizing his common origins and the commonsense nature of his cures.[19] Thomson had become dissatisfied with the therapy used by regular physicians when his mother died. "The doctors gave her over," he wrote in his *Narrative,* "and gave her disease the name of galloping consumption, which I thought was a very appropriate name—for they are the riders, and their whip is mercury, opium and vitriol, and they galloped her out of the world in about nine weeks."[20] Disgusted with heroic treatment, Thomson studied with a local root and herb doctor. His accidental discovery of the medicinal qualities of *Lobelia inflata,* commonly called Indian tobacco, led to the development of the "Thomsonian system" of healing. One day when he was out mowing in a field, he cut a sprig of *Lobelia* and gave it to the man next to him, who ate it. Promptly the man began to perspire and vomit, and thinking Thomson had poisoned him, he struggled to a well to drink some water. According to Thomson, the man "threw off his stomach two quarts. . . . He afterwards told me that he never had any thing do him so much good in his life."[21] Here indeed was a vegetable emetic as powerful as the minerals given by regular doctors.

No sooner had Thomson discovered his remedy than the empiric turned systematist by propounding a theory of disease which rivaled Rush's monistic simplicity. "Heat is life, Cold is death," Thomson declared. The stomach acted as the furnace of the body, maintaining heat or life. Occasionally it became clogged and foul. This state, which Thomson likened to "a pipe clogged with soot," constituted disease. The cure involved cleansing the stomach and bowels and restoring the digestive powers, so that "the fire may burn free."[22] Thomsonian therapy consisted of steaming (a technique borrowed from the Indians) to raise the external heat and taking *Lobelia* to cleanse the stomach and promote free perspiration, cayenne to raise the internal heat, and vegetable tonics to restore digestion and strengthen the stomach. Active and immediate, Thomson's treatment had the added advantage of producing its results without the "pernicious and fatal effects of the mineral poisons."[23]

The regular profession indignantly labeled Thomson a "puke doctor" and a "steamer." A Rhode Island doctor brought Samuel Thomson to trial in 1809 for allegedly killing three patients with *Lobelia*. When the jury acquitted Thomson, his popularity spread as a result of the publicity.[24] The medical establishment then attempted to legislate Thomson out of existence through medical licensing laws and laws to suppress quackery. Harassed by the regulars, Thomson sought government protection. In 1813 he received a government patent which covered not only his medicinal discoveries, but his system of medicine as well. The patent granted Thomson complete ownership of a medical system which operated through the sale of family rights. The purchase of a right for twenty dollars entitled the holder to obtain from Thomson "a complete understanding of the obtaining, preparing and using of all such vegetables as are made use of in [the] system." In return the purchaser agreed "not to reveal any part of said information, to any person, except those as shall purchase a right. . . . under the penalty of forfeiting their word of honour, and all right to the use of the medicine."[25] In the *New Guide To Health or Botanic Family Physician,* Thomson spelled out his system for holders of family rights. Every person who purchased a right received a copy of the book and became a life member of the Friendly Botanic Society, which met to discuss Thomsonian treatment. He also made available a stock of medicine which could be purchased through Thomsonian pharmaceutical outlets.[26] As the movement grew, Thomson turned over the sale of rights to commissioned agents and moved to Boston where he installed himself in an office with an adjacent infirmary.

The Thomsonian movement flourished in the 1820's and 1830's, particularly in New England, western New York, and the South. Enthusiastic converts established Thomsonian conventions, medical societies, drug circulars, periodicals, pharmacies, infirmaries, and ultimately, against the wishes and philosophy of the sect's founder, Thomsonian medical schools. At the time of his death in 1843, Thomson claimed well over three million followers.[27]

Thomsonianism had particular appeal for women, who had to deal with childhood illnesses that all too frequently resulted in death. Eager for medical knowledge and barred from the conventional channels for receiving it, they took their training where they could find it. The family right system allowed women concerned with the health of their children to school themselves without confronting the sensitive issue of compromising their modesty by treating strangers.[28]

The success of Thomsonianism rested in part on public dissatisfaction with heroic practice and the high cost of medical treatment and in part on the egalitarian aspirations of farmers and mechanics who rankled at the elitism of the regular doctors. In the *New Guide,* Thomson sounded these themes repeatedly. He exhorted the people to think for themselves and to free themselves from the dominance of doctors. A thoroughgoing Jacksonian democrat, Thomson had a hatred of monopoly. By laying medicine open to the people, he hoped to tear away the veil of mystery which regular doctors used to shroud the nakedness of their art. Bold, ardent, and sincere, Thomson spoke out forcefully against the extremes of heroic therapy and the pretensions of medical orthodoxy. The movement he led provided cogent criticism of medical practice in his era and offered the public an alternative system of therapy no less valid scientifically and a good deal less harmful than heroic therapy.

The sect died out by the Civil War, a victim of internal dissension and the growing trend toward medical specialization. The greatest single beneficiary of Thomsonianism proved not the common man, but the patent medicine maker. Cashing in on popular prejudice against mineral medicines, patent medicine proprietors marketed a spate of vegetable preparations. Lydia Pinkham's Vegetable Compound stood as a direct heir of the Thomsonian tradition.

By the time Lydia Pinkham began marketing her Vegetable Compound in 1875, Thomson and his movement had been largely forgotten, pushed aside by more recent medical controversies that also played a role in the development and success of the Lydia E. Pinkham Medicine Company. By the 1830's, members of the regular profession had joined in the criticism of heroic therapy. Jacob Bigelow, a prominent Boston physician, delivered the first effective critique of orthodox therapy in 1835 when he presented a paper entitled "On Self-Limited Diseases." Bigelow argued that certain diseases, left to nature, completed their course without outside intervention. Although he acknowledged that it was difficult for doctors to "stand by as curious spectators to the natural history of disease," he pointed out that attempts to intervene boldly and dramatically too often left physicians unsure "whether the patient is really indebted to us for good or evil." Bigelow counseled caution and conservative treatment. "The physician," he warned, "can do little more than follow in the train of disease and endeavor to aid nature in her salutary intentions, or to remove obstacles in her path."[29]

Nature, banished by Rush from the sickroom, returned at the summons of physicians who had lost confidence in their art. Skepticism of heroic therapy received further encouragement from the significant research of what came to be called the "Paris school." French physicians working in Parisian hospitals during the first half of the nineteenth century adopted a clinical and pathological approach to disease. With great insight they attempted to correlate patients' symptoms with post-mortem findings. Their work marked a significant advance in the identification of disease, but it produced a skepticism toward prevailing therapy so pronounced that it was labeled therapeutic nihilism. The rejection of active therapies posed no problems for the French researchers, whose critics charged they were more interested in performing autopsies than in preventing them. Doctors who owed their livelihood to private practice treating sick patients found it difficult to accept the luxury of nihilism. What was the doctor to do? If, as Bigelow and the Parisians suggested, his therapies were useless or harmful, if his only contribution lay in smoothing a pillow or offering a glass of water, why call him at all? From the 1830's until the end of the century, orthodox physicians wrestled with precisely this problem.

Robert Grant, in his novel *Unleavened Bread,* dramatized the resistance encountered by doctors who sought to replace heroic therapy with more conservative treatment. Selma, the novel's shallow, silly heroine, becomes enraged at the doctor's passivity when he counsels rest and watchful waiting during her husband's fatal bout with pneumonia.

"Surely there must be some medicine—some powerful application which will help his breathing," she retorted, and she detected again the semblance of laughter in the doctor's eyes.

"Everything which modern science can do is being done, Mrs. Littleton."

What was there but to resume her seat and helpless vigil? Modern science? The word grated on her ears. It savored to her of medical tyranny, and distrust of aspiring individuality. Wilbur was now dying, and all modern science saw fit to do was to give him brandy and wait.[30]

Until modern science had something better to offer, conservative treatment was the best course. Yet one cannot blame Selma, or her thousands of real life counterparts, for feeling frustration at the poverty of medical science.

Homeopathy provided an effective way out of the therapeutic stalemate. Developed by German physician Samuel Hahnemann and introduced into the United States by his followers in 1825, homeopathy in theory advocated active therapy while in practice it allowed nature to take its course. Hahnemann's therapeutic system rested on the law of *similia similibus curantur*, or "like is cured by like." The name homeopathy derived from the Latin root *homeo*, or same. Hahnemann labeled orthodox medicine allopathy, from *allos*, or other. Intended as a pejorative term, allopathy became a generally used synonym for regular medicine.

Hahnemann, a trained physician, arrived at his system by observing that certain drugs produced in healthy patients the symptoms of disease, in mild form. After a series of tests, or provings, he concluded that drugs which produced certain symptoms in the healthy could be used to combat the same symptoms in the sick. As a corollary to the doctrine of similars, he developed the "infinitesimal dose." Because he believed medicines prescribed according to the law of *similia* aggravated the symptoms of the patient, Hahnemann prescribed the drugs in dilute doses. Yet he argued that the medicine gained in potency through the dilution, which he called dynamization. To dynamize medicine, Hahnemann took one part of a drug, added to it ninety-nine parts milk sugar, or alcohol and ground or shook the mixture in a prescribed manner. The result he labeled the "first potence." Optimum homeopathic dosage involved carrying the process to the thirtieth potency. When critics ridiculed the infinitesimal doses, Hahnemann argued that the diseased organism responded to doses which had no effect on the healthy.[31]

Detractors delighted in pointing out that if homeopaths followed the letter of Hahnemann's law, the Great Lakes would be drained to provide enough water for the dilutions. Oliver Wendell Holmes entertained the Boston Society for the Diffusion of Useful Knowledge in 1842 with two witty and biting lectures entitled "Homeopathy and Its Kindred Delusions." Homeopathy, Holmes insisted, was mere quackery akin to such historic frauds as the royal touch for scrofula and Bishop Berkeley's tar water.[32]

In the eyes of regular doctors, homeopaths offered their patients either too little or too much. Doctors who prescribed heroic doses laughed at the notion of infinitesimals, while therapeutic conservatives berated homeopaths for taking credit for cures effected by nature. "The homeopaths claim to war with almost unerring certainty against a tangible malady [by] feeding the patient upon thin air and a drop of water," chided one physician. "Let your medication be much or little," he scolded, "but don't delude your patient."[33]

The appeal of homeopathy lay precisely in its mild measures and pleasant-tasting medicines. Mothers particularly appreciated the homeopath's gentle treatment of their children. Frequently families employed a regular doctor for the adults in the household and a homeopath for the children. A common joke of the time ridiculed homeopathic practice by recounting how children gulped the tasty medicines on the sly. When their distraught mothers ran to the homeopath in fright, only to be told that they had no reason to worry, they did not know whether to be relieved or not.[34]

Neither ridicule nor censure prevented the spread of homeopathy. By the 1840's the popularity of homeopathic physicians constituted a threat to the regular profession so grave that it could be met only through organized resistance. Homeopathy provided the major impetus to the founding of the American Medical Association in 1847. The first order of business for the fledgling organization was the fight against the homeopaths. To discredit homeopathic physicians, the AMA adopted a code of ethics prohibiting its members from consulting with homeopaths. By depriving homeopaths of the courtesy of consultation, the AMA hoped to taint the rival sect with quackery.[35]

The zeal with which the AMA attacked homeopathy owed as much to financial as to scientific considerations. With their ranks already swollen by graduates of mail-order medical schools, the regulars could ill afford outside competition. Homeopathy, as an allopath remarked, was the "aristocracy of quackery." Its appeal to the intelligentsia and to the wealthy made it much more damaging economically to the regular profession than sturdy, working-class Thomsonianism. Indeed the list of men and women who supported homeopathy reads like a page from "Who's Who"—

Julia Ward Howe, Thomas Wentworth Higginson, Thomas Bailey Aldrich, Henry Wadsworth Longfellow, William Lloyd Garrison, Bronson and Louisa May Alcott, Daniel Webster, William Seward, James Garfield, and John D. Rockefeller.

Homeopathy's defenders were not backwoods democrats like the followers of Samuel Thomson, but men of learning and influence who argued cogently that the homeopathic sect, judged by the scientific standards of the day, was no worse than regular medicine. In fact homeopathic physicians, as E. L. Godkin pointed out in an editorial in *The Nation,* were frequently better trained than their allopathic brethren. On what basis, then, did the AMA presume to deny them the courtesy of consultation? Against Thomsonianism the regular physicians stressed their superior education. In the struggle against homeopathy, they found themselves supporting their less educated colleagues against their better trained rivals. A popular guide written in the 1880's counseled regular doctors to "give the right hand of fellowship to every regular . . . no matter what his misfortunes or how great his deficiencies," but to "refuse it to all irregulars, no matter how great their acquirements, their reputation, or their pomp."[36] In short, the AMA code of ethics worked not to raise standards in the regular profession but simply to quarantine homeopathy.

Such a quarantine proved necessary, not only to discredit homeopaths among potential patients, but to keep regular doctors in line. The lucrative practice of the homeopaths led many regularly-trained physicians to break ranks and join the rival sect. Many were simply fed up with the carnage wrought by heroic practice. Even when doctors did not desert allopathy entirely, homeopathy profoundly affected their practice. Increasingly doctors abandoned heroic therapy and acted on the advice of those who urged them to "follow the fashion of the day and give . . . the smallest and most pleasant dose that . . . safety will permit. . . ."[37]

Psychologically, however, homeopathy had a significant advantage over the therapeutic conservatism counseled by men like Jacob Bigelow. Homeopathy spared both the patient and the physician the anguish of helpless inactivity. The homeopathic physician, believing his remedies potent for good, prescribed with confidence. The patient swallowed his medicine believing in its potency. Thanks to Hahnemann's doctrine of the infinitesimal dose, homeopathy combined the psychological advantages of activism with the physical benefits gained by letting nature take its course.

The bitter and noisy battle between regular medicine and its rival sects, in which all parties sought to discredit one another, did little to further the public's confidence in medicine. Health fads which spurned doctors and medicines entirely gained a wide following between 1830 and the end of the century. In a sense the health and hygiene movements took their cue from homeopathy. As one wag observed in doggerel:

> The homeopathic system, sir, just serves me to a tittle.
> It proves of physic, anyhow, you cannot take to little;
> If it be good in all complaints to take a dose so small,
> It surely must be better still, to take no dose at all.[38]

Sylvester Graham, known today for Graham bread and Graham crackers, led a popular health movement in the 1840's which advocated precisely what the rhyme prescribed. Graham was born in 1794, the seventeenth child of a father over seventy years old. Unfortunately he did not inherit his father's robust health and longevity. A puny child, Graham suffered all his life from a delicate constitution and feared that he would contract tuberculosis. In search of health, he experimented with diets of all sorts until he hit upon the vegetarian "Graham diet."

As the grandson and son of New England ministers, Graham brought to the cause of diet reform a messianic vigor. Graham himself trained for the ministry at Amherst and preached for several years before he abandoned the pulpit for the lecture platform. He began his public career in the early 1830's as a temperance lecturer, but soon branched out to attack intemperance of all sorts. One of his associates estimated that alcoholism killed 50,000 annually, folly in dress accounted for 80,000, while "downright gluttony" destroyed 100,000. Americans, Graham warned, were headed straight for physical degeneracy. Overindulgence in foods like meat and white bread spelled "atrophy and death." The "laws of man's nature" demanded, according to Graham, a simple diet of fruits, vegetables, and unbolted whole wheat bread.[39]

Diet was of paramount importance to Graham because he located the source of all disease in the alimentary canal. "Debility, sluggishness, constipation, obstruction, and morbid irritability," he listed as "the principal roots of both chronic and acute disease." Medicine, he maintained, could not touch the source of disease and only "wears out life, impairs the constitution, and abbreviates the period of human existence." Graham counseled his followers to stay away from doctors and medicines. The best treatment for preventing disease lay in proper diet, fresh air, bathing, sensible dress, and sexual restraint. To those who maintained a strict regimen, Graham promised not only "health and longevity," but "prosperity in their vocations and pursuits of life."[40]

During the 1840's Grahamism attracted a large following. Graham boarding houses, Graham hotels, and Graham tables at schools and colleges testified to his growing number of disciples. His influence became so great that an angry mob of butchers and bakers attacked him when he lectured in Boston. Although Graham himself did not promulgate his system as an alternative to medicine, the extravagance of his claims led his followers to see in it a substitute for regular medicine. "I have seen nearly every form of chronic disease yield in a very short time to a correct diet and well regulated general regimen," boasted Graham, who had added the informal title of "Doctor" to his name.[41] Despite his disclaimers, it appeared that Grahamism was on its way to becoming a pseudo-medical sect.

Lydia Pinkham, growing up in Graham's home state during the peak of the movement, responded to Grahamism with enthusiasm. Her medical advice, with its emphasis on fresh air, bathing, exercise, and simple diet, owed much to Graham's teachings. But here, as elsewhere, she remained an eclectic. She never subscribed to the meatless diet. Her letters of advice recommended beef broth and fish, along with hearty portions of farinaceous food and fresh vegetables. Grahamism, like Thomsonianism, provided her with bits and pieces of information, ideas, and theories, which she collected in her bulging scrapbooks and adapted to suit herself.

By the Civil War the medical profession could no longer afford to ignore the mounting criticism of orthodox practice. The economic competition of the Thomsonians, homeopaths, and others led finally to a decline in the use of calomel, bloodletting, and blistering. Surgeon General William Hammond in 1863 lent his prestige to the anti-heroic cause by removing calomel and tartar emetic from the supply table of the Union army. Old-fashioned doctors continued to rely on heroic doses and venesection until well into the 1870's and 1880's, but on the whole the profession solved the therapeutic problems posed in the 1840's by replacing heroic therapy with new remedies made available by developments in pharmacology.[42]

Rejecting depletive heroic therapy, doctors rushed to the opposite extreme. Indiscriminately they prescribed drugs which were believed to "sustain the vital energy." A critic of bleeding and calomel endorsed opium and alcohol, observing, "Most physicians will agree in the statement that, when indicated as remedies, opium and alcohol sustain the vital forces. In this respect they are positively conservative."[43]

The new therapy shared with the old an emphasis on demonstrable symptomatic relief at the expense of sound treatment. Quinine, morphine, and alcohol in large doses produced side effects scarcely less harmful than calomel and tartar emetic. With the development of morphine, an alkaloid of opium, and the invention of the hypodermic syringe, addiction increased and became an all too common result of medical treatment. Alcohol constituted a therapeutic mainstay in the late nineteenth century. Prescribed first for its tonic effects and later for its supposed ability to kill germs internally, alcohol was usually administered as whiskey or brandy. Physicians recommended doses equivalent to five shots a day for adults and dosed children with amounts sufficient to cause drunkenness.

Indiscriminate drugging by the medical profession produced a climate of opinion ideally suited to the patent medicine business.

Already entrenched by the Civil War, the industry benefitted greatly from the therapeutic confusion of the century. Public education, coupled with the popular press, made possible widespread advertising, the lifeblood of the patent medicine business. When the Thomsonians pointed to the dangers of calomel, enterprising medicine vendors cashed in by advertising vegetable remedies with "no calomel" prominently displayed on the labels. In the post-Civil War period, alcoholic tonics and bitters and the more dangerous opiated preparations found a ready market among a public habituated to the use of such drugs by the medical profession. "The gulping is universal," moaned the *Western Journal*. "The propensity to be cheated is not confined to men or women, the old or young, the poor or rich, the unlearned or (we are sorry to add), the learned; but displays its workings in the weak-minded and credulous of all."[44]

Professional hand-wringing over the widespread use of patent medicines became a favorite pastime among physicians. Yet doctors quick to see the evils of patent medicines showed a remarkable blind spot when it came to the misuse of calomel, quinine, alcohol, morphine, and other dangerous drugs they used with abandon. In retrospect, it seems likely that medical doctors in the nineteenth century were responsible for at least as much promiscuous poisoning as the patent medicine vendors they attacked.[45] As long as orthodox physicians relied on dangerous drugs and ineffective therapies, Americans would continue to turn to medical sects and patent medicines.

The Age of the Womb

French historian Jules Michelet in his widely read *L'Amour* declared that each century had its own great malady—leprosy in the thirteenth century, plague in the fourteenth, and syphilis in the sixteenth. Writing in 1868, Michelet characterized the nineteenth century as "the age of the womb"[1]—an observation borne out by the century's pervasive concern with women's health. The popular medical literature of the period caricatured women as the victims of a host of female complaints. An emphasis on the morbid and the melodramatic—fallen wombs, hysteria, venereal excess—typified the style of the medical Jeremiahs whose articles on the "perils of American women" shared the pages of newspapers late in the century with testimonials for Lydia Pinkham's Vegetable Compound. Like all caricatures, the image of women purveyed in the literature distorted reality while roughly following its outlines. Women did suffer from female complaints, a variety of diseases and conditions that doctors did not properly understand and could not effectively treat. But the exaggeration of women's weakness so common in nineteenth-century writing resulted as much from social as from medical reality.

Under the impact of rapid social change, the conception of

woman and her role underwent a profound shift between roughly 1820 and 1880, the lifetime of Lydia Pinkham. Social instability, urbanization, and the grinding gears of a new industrial economy erased traditional patterns of life and created anxieties and confusions in the nineteenth century which were mirrored nowhere more clearly than in the attitude of the society toward women. Confronted with a new and unstable world, nineteenth-century man sought some touchstone, some link to a more settled past. In his search for stability, woman became a hostage imprisoned in her "proper sphere."

"[T]he inexorable opinion of the public carefully circumscribes woman within the narrow circle of domestic interests and duties, and forbids her to step beyond it," Alexis de Tocqueville observed after his visit to the United States in 1831.[2] Speaking as an outside observer, Tocqueville had no way of knowing that the restricted sphere he described was a recent phenomenon. Women in colonial America, although they drew their identity and rank from fathers and husbands, exercised their powers in productive labor both within the home and on numerous occasions outside it.

The constriction of woman's sphere which began in the late eighteenth century continued apace in the early decades of the nineteenth, precisely at a time when the need for traditionally female productive labor diminished. Homemade products like soap, cloth, and candles gave way to industrial goods. Immigration supplied domestic servants to take over household drudgery. With the advent of compulsory public education, children left the home to be schooled by paid professionals. Childbearing itself, long woman's premier occupation, declined in importance among middle-class families who began to limit the number of children they bore. Although industrialization brought with it opportunities for employment in textile mills and factories, industrial labor became taboo for middle-class women once immigrant workers entered the mills. By 1850 women composed only 13 per cent of the paid labor force. Within that limited group most found employment as agricultural workers or domestics.[3]

It would be wrong to imply that all middle-class women were idle in the home, although women's domestic occupations came to be confused with leisure. Industrialization redefined the concept of work. Increasingly men worked for wages in a system geared to time-oriented, not task-oriented work. In contrast women worked without pay in tasks like family care and household management which defied time orientation. Although women manufactured fewer household products than had their grandmothers, child care and housekeeping, including sewing, shopping, and often cooking and cleaning when domestic help was not available, remained demanding enough to occupy a married woman's time and deplete her energies. One has only to look at Lydia Pinkham's married life to recognize that the middle-class wife and mother was no pampered, idle toy.[4]

In addition to the very real work women performed in the home, increasingly they were called upon to play another, more symbolic role. As society became more and more unsettled, lines of social demarcation blurred. It became harder to tell who was who in the shifting social ranks of city life. Thorstein Veblen in *The Theory of the Leisure Class*, published in 1899, pointed to the burden placed upon women by the struggle to create and meet standards of "decency" imposed to bring order to the confused and transient social structure typical of a highly organized industrial community. Decency demanded that a wife remain at home as an emblem of her husband's earning power. The middle-class husband, according to Veblen, applied himself to work "with the utmost assiduity, in order that his wife may render him that degree of vicarious leisure which the common sense of the time demands."[5] In a treatise ostensibly on the physiology of woman, a medical doctor underscored Veblen's point. "Man's business is to earn money, hers to spend it," he intoned. "In love, is her true sphere of labor."[6] Yet the middle-class woman, as Veblen observed, acted only as a "ceremonial consumer." Her transformation from producer of goods to consumer, from diligent handmaiden to genteel female, marked no advancement in her personal freedom. "[S]he still quite unmistakably remains his chattel in theory," Veblen commented in his perceptive but typically hyperbolic style. "[F]or the habitual rendering of vicarious leisure and consumption is the abiding mark of the unfree servant."[7]

The need to restrict and codify woman's proper sphere intensified as women began to demand greater freedom. The "woman
question," as it came to be called, stirred controversy throughout
the century. The literature of the debate revealed, in part, a mis-
placed but evidently genuine desire on the part of men to shield
women from the realities of urban industrial life and its psychic
toll. Yet the men who eschewed the notion of woman's work outside the home engaged Irish domestic drudges and filled factories
and sweatshops with female operatives drawn from the "working
class." When men spoke of the need to protect women from the
contagion of the marketplace, they spoke of a particular class and
type of woman—the genteel female. She became his ward and
over her he exerted dominance with the conviction that he acted
in her best interest.

Goaded on by the exhortations of a culture that placed a pre-
mium on such catchwords as "rugged individualism" and "sur-
vival of the fittest," men labored under a staggering set of in-
ternalized demands—demands epitomized in the concept of the
"self-made man." Where men were weighted down with demands, women became weighted down with restrictions. Determined to be all strength, men saw in women all weakness. The
result was a strange and forced symbiosis in which middle-class
husbands battled in the immoral marketplace to ensure that their
wives remained at home to make of the home a redemptive counterpart to the world of grab and chance.[8]

The bifurcation of human attributes that became evident in the
nineteenth century, in which manhood became synonymous with
strength and womanhood with weakness, did not mark a new
departure so much as it exaggerated an ancient perception common in Judeo-Christian thought. Early arguments on women's in-
feriority drew support from the Bible. By the middle of the nineteenth century, the Bible began to lose its hold as a source of social
wisdom. Science, the new faith of the century, provided the
framework within which the social questions of the day were ex-
amined, dictated the terms and the idiom of the debate, and pre-
sumed to act as final arbiter. Much that passed for science remained subjective judgment decked out in pseudoscientific
jargon. The odd assortment of beliefs which paraded as "scientific

fact" was particularly apparent in the popular medical literature of the period.

Doctors took up the pen in the nineteenth century to produce a startling array of books ranging from standard medical texts to didactic treatises against sexual excess. Skilled surgeons, eminent teachers, doctors of dubious professional ethics, health faddists, and out-and-out quacks all authored volumes. Despite vast differences in the rank, ethics, and learning of the authors, the attitudes conveyed in the literature were strikingly similar—indeed sometimes identical. Often the wily quack, not much given to hard work of any sort, plagiarized whole chapters from the work of his more respectable brethren and added only the testimonials for elixirs and medical paraphernalia that appeared in the back pages.[9] To distinguish between the charlatan and the learned man of medicine on the basis of their literary accomplishments alone is to draw too fine a line between medical and pseudo-medical literature when both so frequently spoke the same language and mouthed the same ideas.

The constriction of woman's sphere apparent on the social level was paralleled in medical writing by a constriction in the field of vision which led doctors to focus, with obsessive concern, on woman's organs of reproduction. Michelet's characterization of the nineteenth century as the age of the womb, taken literally, reflected the contemporary preoccupation with woman's reproductive system and underlined the distortion of perception, which, by placing primary emphasis on the sexual organs, enabled men to view woman as a creature apart. The distinguished British physician Henry Maudsley concluded a discussion of woman's sexual organs in 1870 with the observation that "the forms and habits of mutilated men approach those of women." Maudsley warned his readers in rhetoric typical of the day, "While woman preserves her sex, she will necessarily be feebler than man, and, having her special bodily and mental characters, will have, to a certain extent her own sphere of activity."[10]

Viewing woman as a "mutilated male" enabled doctors to judge her unfit for the demands of the larger world and thereby justify her limited domestic sphere. Just as her sexual organs restricted her activities, so they dictated the pattern and purpose of her life. Her reproductive system came to be seen as a sacred trust, one that she must constantly guard in the interest of the race. The uterus, considered "the controlling organ in the female body,"[11] took on an importance which reduced woman to simply a vessel, an organ bearer. As one doctor put it, it was as if "the Almighty, in creating the female sex, had taken the uterus and built up a woman around it."[12] It became clear that the burden of carrying this "house within a house, engine within an engine," constituted a full-time occupation when doctors described the many ailments which could and did afflict women. Hippocrates' famous aphorism, "What is woman? Disease," was restated by doctors who dwelt ominously on the dangerous complexities of her sexual system.

The relationship between scientific ideas and social ideology has rarely been more obvious than in the way doctors used disease as a sanction to enforce traditional behavioral norms. Physicians hinted that women who attempted to enlarge their sphere of action would pay a heavy price—their sexual organs would rise up against them in retaliation. A Harvard physician writing in 1873 insisted:

Woman, in the interest of the race, is dowered with a set of organs peculiar to herself, whose complexity, delicacy, sympathies, and force are among the marvels of creation. If properly nurtured and cared for, they are a source of strength and power to her. If neglected and mismanaged, they retaliate upon their possessor with weakness and disease, as well of mind as of body.[13]

Advances in medical knowledge only furthered the mystification of the female body, as is evident in the curious way the medical profession interpreted new evidence of the relationship between ovulation and menstruation. For two centuries after Dutch physician Regner de Graff demonstrated the function of the ovaries, physicians continued to equate menstruation with evacuation. Following the ancient plethoric theory, they explained menstruation as the elimination of superfluous blood. The notion that the menses constituted a recurrent, natural bloodletting led some physicians to label the uterus "the sewer of all the excrements existing in the body."[14] Others took the monthly flow as proof of a certain female vitality, an excess of nutritive force. By the 1840's physicians had amplified their understanding of the function of the ovaries and the periodicity of menstruation. The plethoric theory at long last yielded to a clearer understanding of woman's sexual system. Yet the exaggerated emphasis placed on the periodicity of woman's organization led to the view that menstruation constituted a morbid state and that woman, by her very nature, was an invalid. "[I]n reality," wrote Michelet, "fifteen or twenty days out of twenty-eight (we may say nearly always) woman is not only an invalid, but a wounded one. She ceaselessly suffers from love's eternal wound."[15]

To understand how menstruation could be exaggerated and romanticized into an infirmity, one must examine the suppositions upon which nineteenth-century men regulated, or attempted to regulate, their lives. Self-reliance, thrift, and self-control constituted the canon of male virtues. In turn those virtues extended to encompass man's relationship to his own body. The medical manuals and purity literature of the nineteenth-century made it clear that in order to succeed, man must dominate not only his world but himself. Because nineteenth-century men viewed the body as a closed energy system, they believed that energy expended in one activity took away from another. From this assumption, they inferred that brain work robbed the body of vigor. Similarly, sexual activity supposedly sapped the body of vital energy by exhausting the nerves and depleting the system. Health lecturer Sylvester Graham gave voice to a widely held belief when he proclaimed that "the emission of semen enfeebles the body more than the loss of twenty times the same quantity of blood."[16]

Masturbation, known variously as "self-pollution," "the solitary vice," "self-abuse," or more euphemistically as "the vicious habit," became the bogeyman of countless young men who were told repeatedly that the act would result in softening of the brain, impotency, insanity, and paralysis. While men continued to masturbate and lived to tell of it, the gullible acceptance of the dangers involved seems universal. Literary critic and self-proclaimed rake

Frank Harris in his pornographic memoir, *My Life and Loves,* revealed a sincere belief in the dangerous consequences of "onanism." Describing one of his schoolmates, a "constant masturbator," Harris dwelt on his decline in a manner reminiscent of Sylvester Graham and his imitators.

The little fellow grew gradually paler and paler until he took to crying in a corner, and unaccountable nervous trembling shook him for a quarter of an hour at a time. At length, he was taken away by his parents: what became of him afterwards, I don't know, but I do know that till he was taught self-abuse, he was one of the quickest boys of his age.[17]

Harris overcame his own "vicious habit," by heroic self-restraint. He had little trouble holding himself in check during waking hours. But the Victorian code demanded unconscious as well as conscious control. Doctors warned against involuntary loss of semen which they diagnosed and treated as a disease under the label "spermatorrhea." Troubled by wet dreams, Harris determined to master his body. At bedtime he tied a whipcord around his penis. At the onset of an erection, he woke in pain and quickly doused with cold water to prevent seminal emission. The method worked so well he recommended it to his friends. Recounting the incident in 1925, Harris concluded with satisfaction, "I had conquered temptation and once more was captain of my body."[18]

Even in the marriage bed, men were exhorted to exert self-control. Graham counseled intercourse no more than once a month and warned of the dangers of sexual excess in a list of complaints that rivaled those mustered by any patent medicine salesman.

Langour, lassitude, muscular relaxation, general debility and heaviness, depression of spirits, loss of appetite, indigestion, faintness and sinking at the pit of the stomach, increased susceptibilities of the skin and lungs to all the atmospheric changes, feebleness of circulation, chilliness, headache, melancholy, hypochondria, hysteria, feebleness of all the senses, impaired vision, loss of sight, weakness of the lungs, nervous cough, pulmonary consumption, disorders of the genital organs, spinal diseases, weakness of the brain, loss of memory, epilepsy, insanity, apoplexy;— abortion, premature births, and extreme feebleness, morbid predisposi-

tions, and early death of offspring,—are among the too common evils
which are caused by sexual excess between husband and wife.[19]

Doctors vividly pictured the dangers inherent in sexual intercourse. During the sex act, wrote Dr. G. L. Austin, man "snatches
away from himself with violence a part of his being. It is the flesh
of his flesh, it is the blood of his blood which he gives." The vam-
pire imagery revealed a deep ambivalence in men's attitude toward woman. She, as sperm-absorber, not only sapped his powers
but grew stronger in the process. "The semen," Austin continued,
"does not fecundate the ovum of the wife, it fecundates the
woman." In this manner, "the wife derives many of the qualities
of character that she did not possess before marriage."[20] If, as Dr.
Augustus K. Gardner claimed in his popular book, *Conjugal Sins,*
"the erethism of the woman has no boundary," then indeed she
constituted a fearsome sexual adversary.[21]

The sexual anxiety spawned by such pronouncements proved
so strong that doctors had to reassure bachelors who feared that
marriage might prove beyond their physical powers. Fortunately
for their mates, women had no strong sexual feeling—or so the
doctors determined. Undeniably woman had the capacity to respond to sexual stimulation unrestricted by a set mating season.
But doctors insisted that far from making women sexually vora-
cious, the absence of a period of heat analogous to that found in
animals proved women's sexual indifference. "I should say that
the majority of women (happily for society) are not very much
troubled with sexual feeling of any kind," proclaimed British physician William Acton in 1857. What was good for society clearly
was good for women, or so Acton reasoned. In other editions of
his famous book, *Functions and Disorders of the Reproductive Organs,*
Acton changed his parenthetical aside to read, "happily for
them."[22] How conveniently woman's sexual nature suited man's
needs. Frigidity became a feminine virtue ordained by men's need
to conserve their energies and remain captains of their bodies.

The belief that men could control their bodies through force of
will became an accepted part of the nineteenth-century credo. Although most men flagged in their efforts to avoid "self-pollution"

or "conjugal sins," Frank Harris' testimony provides some insight into the university of the anxiety created by the doctrine of self-control. If man's attitude toward his body constituted a paradigmatic example of the power of mind over matter, what then of woman? The discovery of periodicity seemed to prove conclusively that woman's body was out of control. Men were the victims of an animal lust which could be controlled by force of will; women were the victims of a power so strong it could not be held in check by any degree of mental or moral exertion.

Harvard's Dr. Edward H. Clarke revealed the extent to which doctors interpreted menstruation by analogy to a male model when he adopted language frequently used to describe man in the grip of passion to explain woman's menstrual cycle. "The periodical movements which characterize and influence woman's structure for more than half her terrestial life . . . in their ebb and flow, sway every fibre and thrill every nerve of her body a dozen times a year. . . ." Menstruation and pregnancy, he concluded doubtfully, "are, or are evidently intended to be, fountains of power, not hindrances to it."[23] Clarke's ambivalence concerning the benignancy of woman's reproductive system found stronger statement in the writings of his Boston colleague Dr. Horatio Storer. Storer equated outright woman's weakness with her inability to control the periodicity of her sexual system. "In health, we find her still obedient to a special law," he wrote. "The subject here also, *we might even say the victim,* of periodicity, her life is one perpetual change, and these changes are still again subdivided."[24]

Woman, the doctors implied, could neither escape nor master her sexual system. Sexual function not only dictated the three great physical epochs of her life, punctuated by the onset and the cessation of the menses, but, because of its uncontrollable periodicity and seemingly inexorable demands, ordained that woman lead a life apart from man's world. Not simply the accidents or the diseases of her sex, but the normal exercise and functions came to be regarded as pathological. "The existence of this function [menstruation] alone," wrote Dr. Frederick Hollick, "makes it impossible for women—except in peculiar individual cases—to pursue the same avocations and follow the same mode of life as man."[25]

Of course, women were not the only victims of the medical profession's negative view of sexual function. Men's sexual systems received a close scrutiny in the nineteenth century, as is evident in the variety of quack treatments, the devices to cure impotency, and the tests for spermatorrhea advertised in the literature of the day, not to mention the lucrative trade of the "pox doctors" who specialized in the treatment of venereal disease. But as Dr. Mary Putnam Jacobi pointed out, "it is rare that [the sexual] influence [in men] has been regarded as 'limiting' in its nature."[26] Although doctors catechized their male patients on the hideous consequences of sexual excess or self-abuse, they believed that these dangers resulted from willful negligence or moral sin, never that they were consequent on what the doctors regarded as their "normal" (limited to be sure) exercise. Man, by right thinking and action, could dominate his sex; woman remained a prisoner of her sexual system.

In a society intent upon seeing women as inherently weak and infirm, it was not surprising that female complaints became common. "Every year I hear more and more complaints of poor health that is so very common among grown people, especially women," wrote Catharine Beecher in 1855 in her *Letters to the People on Health and Happiness.* "And physicians say, that this is an evil that is constantly increasing, so that they fear, ere long, there will be no healthy women in the country."[27] The conviction that women were less healthy, less robust than their mothers and grandmothers became a nineteenth-century commonplace. Nathaniel Hawthorne began *The Scarlet Letter* in 1850 with the observation that the Puritan dames of the seventeenth century, with their "broad shoulders and well-developed busts," were hardier than their descendants. "[E]very successive mother has transmitted to her child a fainter bloom, a more delicate and briefer beauty, and a slighter physical frame. . . ." Yet Hawthorne and other writers who decried the lack of vigor in the genteel female frequently did so in a tone that barely masked a boast. For if woman's frailty, on the one hand, was feared as a signal of decline and a threat to the race, on the other hand it was applauded as an emblem of progressive refinement and civilization. Hearty good health came to seem somehow crude, an indication, in Hawthorne's words, "morally, as well as materially" of a "coarser fibre."[28] The nineteenth century witnessed the creation of a new aesthetic type—the delicate, sickly heroine like Priscilla in *The Blithedale Romance*, "whose impalpable grace lay so singularly between disease and beauty."[29] The equation of physical decline with moral superiority led one writer to observe sardonically, "Illness is an achievement of culture."[30]

Behind the rhetoric of the decline of women's health could be glimpsed a curious ambivalence. Evolutionary optimism decreed that civilization marched forever forward. But writers in the late nineteenth century had not yet entirely abandoned the pessimism of Gibbon's decline and fall for the more sanguine progressivism of the social Darwinists. The juxtaposition of the two world views caused a profound sense of uneasiness as Americans viewed the rapid changes transforming society—changes both welcomed and feared. In a competitive industrial society which demanded aggressive optimism from its men, it became convenient, perhaps necessary, to externalize anxiety. By glorifying male strength and emphasizing female vulnerability and weakness, men projected their own very real fears and anxieties onto women.

Writers spoke endlessly of the "perils of American women." In a book of that title, Dr. G. L. Austin in 1883 spelled out in detail the manner in which the physical comforts of civilization could blight women. He cited "warm apartments, coal-fires, gas-lights, late hours and rich food" as factors which turned women into "helpless and confirmed invalids."[31] Another physician predicted that woman, by her very nature, would fall victim to the material progress elsewhere so highly touted.

The battle for life, for both sexes, is hard enough; but upon the sensitive and frail organization of woman, has upon the whole, been imposed the heaviest burden. . . . As civilization advances, as the refinements and luxuries of life are multiplied, and brought more and more within the reach of all,—the human organization, especially in woman, becomes more delicate and sensitive, and more liable to functional derangements and disorders, through the predominance of the nervous over the muscular system. Delicacy of body has hitherto been the penalty of a high civilization, and we see not why it should not continue to be so. . . . High civilization, and sophisticated and artificial habits, such as now generally prevail, are peculiarly damaging to women; . . .[32]

The allegation that civilization brought with it nervous disease received scientific sanction in 1879 when Dr. George Beard delivered before the Baltimore Medical and Chirurgical Society an address entitled "American Nervousness: Its Philosophy and Treatment." Beard claimed that evidence indicated nervous diseases were on the increase in the northern portion of the United States. Nervous weakness, he half-boasted, half-lamented, "is preeminently American."[33] Ostensibly Beard attributed American nervousness to the dryness and coldness of the climate, but his real message was that "neurasthenia," as he labeled the new disease, found "its one predisposing cause [in] civilization."[34]

In Britain, doctors viewed neurasthenia primarily as a "disease of brainworkers, and especially of those thus engaged who live under the stress of disadvantageous circumstances."[35] America, however, soon transformed neurasthenia from the occupational hazard of clerks and ciphers into a prestigious malady of bourgeois society—a malady which particularly afflicted the genteel female. Neurasthenia, in its myriad forms, became a fashionable disease, a badge of class and status. Women compared symptoms, physicians, and health spas. Perhaps the social acceptability of the disease allowed women to confess maladies which their mothers would have suffered in silence. The widespread claim to delicate or sickly dispositions led at least one physician to grumble, "It may be fashionable to be stunted, deformed, pale, feeble, and unsound; it may savor of delicacy to always be under the care of a physician; but to be healthy is certainly to be happier."[36]

Neurasthenia in women supposedly took on distinct sexual characteristics. Many doctors believed that women suffered all disease twofold because of mysterious sympathies connecting the womb with every other organ in the body. "It seems almost impossible," wrote Beard in a book entitled *Sexual Neurasthenia*, "for any woman to suffer from general neurasthenia without developing, sooner or later, primarily or secondarily, some trouble of the womb or of the ovary." Beard suggested that all women with symptoms of nervous exhaustion submit to examination by a gynecologist. "No treatment of these cases is regarded in any sense as scientific," he concluded, "where such examination is not made and where the proper local treatment is not employed."[37]

The role of the gynecologist and the definition of "proper local treatment," however, provoked heated controversy in the last half of the nineteenth century. Gynecology, or the treatment of women's diseases, originated as a special branch of surgery. America witnessed pioneer work in gynecological surgery—first in 1809 when Ephraim McDowell performed the first successful ovariotomy (without benefit of anesthesia) and again in the work of J. Marion Sims, whose practice in the 1850's won him the title, "father of American gynecology." The increasing emphasis placed on woman's sexual function in the middle and late decades of the nineteenth century gave added impetus to gynecological specialization.

Medical specialization, particularly in gynecology, had to overcome deep-seated prejudices. The medical profession initially balked at accepting specialists. With the market already glutted with doctors, established physicians feared that any division of their practice would cripple them economically. Furthermore, specialization smacked of quackery. In the first decades of the century, only charlatans advertised specialized cures. S. Weir Mitchell, the noted neurologist, recalled the time in Philadelphia when to specialize meant professional ostracism. Gynecologists found themselves especially subject to scrutiny because of the nature of their specialty and the treatments they promoted. In a society obsessed with the purity and gentility of middle-class females, many questioned whether women should consult a gynecologist in any circumstances. Dr. Charles Meigs in his well-known textbook, *Females and Their Diseases,* published in 1848, had boasted, "I am proud to say . . . that there are women who prefer to suffer the extremity of danger and pain rather than waive those scruples of delicacy which prevent their maladies from being fully explored."[38]

False modesty not only kept women from doctors, it encouraged physicians to sacrifice sound medical practice to the dictates of Victorian prudishness. An illustration in a nineteenth-century gynecological text shows a doctor examining a fully-dressed female patient by kneeling in front of her and, with his eyes averted, reaching under her skirts. Accepted standards of medical modesty permitted doctors to touch the female genitalia, but not to expose them to view—a procedure which helps explain numerous cases of misdiagnosis. Even after the introduction of the vaginal speculum in the 1850's, many doctors refused to employ the instrument because they feared it would sexually arouse their patients. British physician Robert Brudenell Carter claimed to have seen "young, unmarried women of the middle class of society, reduced by the constant use of the speculum to the mental and moral condition of prostitutes."[39]

Where Carter worried that women intent on sexual gratification would pursue unsuspecting physicians, women writers like Catharine Beecher feared that male gynecologists would take advantage of their patients. Beecher hinted broadly at the moral danger of gynecological treatments involving "daily mechanical operations, both external and internal" carried on behind "bolted doors and curtained windows."[40] Suffragist Mary Livermore spoke disparagingly of an "unclean army of gynecologists" who preyed on young women.[41] The implication that women might be debauched by unscrupulous physicians gained currency in the writing of medical men who opposed specialization. Dr. G. L. Austin insisted that any general practitioner could handle legitimate female ailments. "If there had been a race of gynecologists in the days of Molière," Austin observed dryly, "what sport he would have had with them!"[42]

Much of the censure directed at the gynecologist focused on local treatment, the use of nonsurgical techniques in treating female complaints such as displacements, leucorrhea, and prolapsed uterus. Because of its very accessibility, doctors frequently over-treated and maltreated the uterus. Physicians fretted over any deviation from what they considered normal. They insisted on treating displacements of the uterus with instruments in a vain attempt to bring the organ into its "proper" position. Leucorrhea, the generic term for vaginal discharges, received harsh treatments ranging from daily injections (douches) to cauterization by local application of nitric and chromic acid. "Thousands of women," according to one critic, "have been doomed to undergo the nitrate-of-silver treatment—their mental agony and physical torture were accounted nothing—in cases where soap and water and a gentle placebo would have been amply sufficient."[43]

Prolapsed uterus, or falling of the womb, constituted one of the most serious common female ailments in the nineteenth century. In *prolapsus* the ligaments supporting the uterus weaken, causing the organ to descend and, in some extreme cases, protrude beyond the vulva, dragging the vagina behind it. Poor obstetrics, which left the damaged perineum unsewn and weakened, accounted for many cases as did hard physical labor, repeated pregnancies, and poor diet. Yet doctors obstinately blamed tight lacing, sexual abuse, and such minor and outlandish causes as "singing, dancing, riding on horseback, and skating."[44] A tendency to attribute all pelvic pains to "prolapse" no doubt led to an exaggeration of the number of sufferers. As Catharine Beecher pointed out, many women suffering from ulceration or inflammation of the uterus received treatment for prolapse from doctors who had improperly diagnosed the malady and whose treatments aggravated the initial symptoms. Treatment consisted of manipulation, injections, and the use of intervaginal supporters called pessaries. By 1868 women could choose from over 123 different kinds of pessaries which ranged in size and complexity from a very simple plug to a device so complicated it could be worn only under a large hoop skirt. Surgical techniques, including the excision of the uterus, became common toward the end of the century.[45]

If the prying, poking, and prodding of the clinical gynecologist aroused the suspicion and the ire of the general practitioner and the public alike, the reckless operating which characterized surgical gynecology in the last decades of the century drew fire from critics both within and outside of the medical profession. Developments in antisepsis, anesthesia, and pathology moved surgery by late in the century from the periphery toward the center of medical practice. The glamour and prestige which came to surround the gynecological surgeon effectually eclipsed the "conservative" or clinical gynecologists who relied on local treatment. Sexual surgeons such as J. Marion Sims, Robert Battey, Thomas Addis Emmet, T. Gaillard Thomas in America and Spencer Wells and John Lawson Tait in Great Britain attained worldwide celebrity. Taught to view women's reproductive organs as the troublesome seat of disease, doctors frequently counseled surgery where less dramatic measures would have sufficed. Although many physicians were at first reluctant to extirpate the uterus, which they regarded with almost mystical reverence, they did not hesitate to sacrifice the ovaries. Ovariotomy became a fashionable operation in spite of a mortality rate sometimes as high as 40 per cent.[46]

Not only the diseased ovary, but the healthy, normal ovary fell prey to the sexual surgeons. In 1876 Dr. Robert Battey urged the removal of healthy ovaries as an effective treatment for menstrual complaints and such vague sexual disorders as "mania." Justifying his operation, Battey insisted that a healthy ovary might nevertheless be "viciously or abnormally performing its functions." By removing the ovaries, Battey hoped to "put an end to ovulation entirely" and thereby "to uproot and remove serious sexual disorders and re-establish the general health."[47] Clearly Battey viewed menstruation with it dangerous periodicity as the source of a variety of complaints which would be cured by removing the ovaries and thus inducing menopause. Yet in the cases he described, the results rarely seemed to merit the risk occasioned by surgery. Of his first ten cases, two patients died, six complained of their initial symptoms after they recovered from the operation, one failed to mention improvement, and only the remaining case Battey judged an unqualified success. The patient, a thirty-eight-year-old mother suffering from "threatening mania," became so tractable after the operation that the doctor noted with satisfaction "she now does unaided the house-work of her family."[48]

Despite its dubious benefits, doctors seized upon "Battey's operation" to treat a variety of sexual derangements ranging from painful menstruation to nymphomania. "We have reached the time," announced a physician scarcely ten years after Battey introduced the operation, "when the surgeon does not hesitate to take out the ovaries and tubes for a disease for which he can find no other means of cure."[49] The popularity of ovariotomy owed something to the fact that it was what doctors called a "young operation"—a relatively simple procedure which a young surgeon could master. At meetings of the American Gynecological Society, doctors boasted of the number of operations they had performed and displayed ovaries on platters to an admiring audience as specimens of their handiwork.

By the close of the nineteenth century, ovariotomy had led the way to further drastic gynecological operations. "After you have laid violent hands on the ovaries," reasoned one physician, "it matters not what becomes of the uterus."[50] Doctors evidently agreed, for by the 1890's hysterectomy, an operation rarely performed in the 1870's, had become commonplace. The more bizarre sexual operations, including female circumcision and the excision of the clitoris (clitoridectomy) which doctors sometimes recommended in cases of "nymphomania" or "excessive masturbation," continued to be performed well into the twentieth century, but with no great frequency.

Critics labeled gynecological surgery "mutilation" and charged that physicians performed unnecessary operations in order to pocket the high fees, mounting upwards to $1,000 for a single operation. Such complaints of malpractice disturbed the profession and led several prominent gynecological surgeons to warn their colleagues to practice more restraint. Jealous of their professional reputations, the sexual surgeons sought to take the scalpel away from incompetent or flagrantly dishonest practitioners. They rarely questioned the value of radical surgery as they practiced it themselves.[51]

For the most part, criticism of sexual surgery came from women who saw in male medical practice misogyny translated into medical treatment. Elizabeth Blackwell, America's first formally educated woman physician, campaigned vigorously against Battey's operation, which she characterized as "the castration of women."[52] Blackwell, who abhorred vivisection, fought sexual surgery on the grounds that doctors who experimented on live animals were simply extending their experimentation to female patients. Dr. Mary Putnam Jacobi, Blackwell's brilliant young colleague, shared her concern over reckless operating but warned that women physicians could not afford to substitute sentiment for science. Gynecological surgery, she reminded Blackwell, was often a legitimate and necessary form of treatment. "When you shudder at 'mutilations,' " she wrote Blackwell in 1888, "it seems to me you can never have handled a degenerated ovary or a suppurating Fallopian tube—or you would admit that mutilation had been affected by disease—possibly by the ignorance or neglect of a series of physicians before the surgeon intervened."[53]

The diseased ovary and the suppurating fallopian tube were all too familiar to Jacobi and the surgeons who treated women's diseases. But they did not, as so many doctors claimed, result from late hours, unnatural habits, brain work, or sexual excess. They resulted from venereal disease. Gonorrhea accounted for many of the commonest complaints that brought women to the gynecologist—vaginal discharge, backache, painful menstruation, abnormal uterine bleeding, incapacitating pelvic pain, and barrenness—not to mention blindness in newborn infants. In women the disease quickly spread from the vagina up into the uterus and the fallopian tubes and into the peritoneal cavity, causing sterility and frequently producing chronic invalidism. In such cases hysterectomy promised the only relief available.

Until late in the nineteenth century, physicians had no clear understanding of the nature or cause of the disease. Many doctors believed that gonorrhea was endemic in women. Vaginal discharges of all types they classified under the heading gonorrheal. Because doctors confused symptoms of minor infections with those of gonorrhea, they were slow to recognize that the disease was in fact venereal. One physician insisted that there were two kinds of gonorrhea, one venereal and one not dependent on sexual intercourse. "I do not say that there is no distinction," he told his students, "but only that the distinction cannot be made out by the practitioner so as to justify him, from his own inquiries into a case, in giving a decided opinion on the subject."[54] Behind the doctor's caution was concern for his patient's sensibilities—especially when that patient was a genteel female. Doctors showed a general disinclination to diagnose venereal disease in their wealthy female patients because to do so would be to point the finger at the women themselves or at their husbands.

The "pox doctors" who treated men for gonorrhea and syphilis often conspired with their patients to keep the nature of the illness from the men's wives and fianceés. Secrecy was the stock-in-trade of these physicians, who all too often came from the seamy underworld of medicine. But honest physicians, too, practiced the conspiracy of silence. Believing as they did that gonorrhea could be effectively cured, they had no reason to suspect that a man who refrained from sexual intercourse during treatment could later infect a woman. A course of treatment usually lasted for two or three months, during which time the initial symptoms disappeared. The doctor then declared his patient cured, free to marry or to resume sexual relations with his wife.

In 1876 German emigré Emil Noeggerath angered members of the newly formed American Gynecological Society by insisting that 90 per cent of sterile women suffered from gonorrhea contracted from husbands who often had been treated for the disease and pronounced cured by their physicians. Noeggerath pleaded with his colleagues to recognize that the disease might persist in men after the initial symptoms had subsided and thus be transmitted to their sexual partners. Latent gonorrhea in men, Noeggerath concluded, explained why so many healthy, blooming young women began to suffer from female complaints shortly after they married and why so many wives remained childless.

The leading figures in American gynecology proved neither ready nor willing to accept the implications of Noeggerath's research. In the remarks that followed his address, physicians sought to avoid the burden of male responsibility by insisting that gonorrheal infections in women resulted not from contact with a diseased partner, but from crowded city conditions, excessive masturbation, or exposure to the cold. Calm amid the often derisive criticism, Noeggerath remarked, "After [you] gentlemen have given five years or more of careful study to this question, I shall expect to hear more approval than I hàve done today."[55]

Noeggerath did not have to wait five years. In 1879 the German physician Albert Neisser succeeded in identifying the gonococcous under the microscope. Doctors soon learned to recognize and diagnose gonorrhea, which, as Noeggerath had predicted, retained its infective power long after its acute symptoms had passed. Until the development of sulfa drugs in the 1930's, physicians relied on prophylaxis, mercurial ointments, and antiseptic solutions to fight the disease. Since its symptoms often went undetected in women, it was difficult to catch and treat the disease before it spread through the reproductive tract. Gonorrhea continued to take a terrible toll on women's health and to account in part for the shocking incidence of pelvic surgery Blackwell and others so deplored.

The relationship between the genteel female and her physician became increasingly complex during the course of the nineteenth century. The medical profession itself underwent profound changes as it wrestled with sectarianism and struggled to replace invalid therapies with effective drugs and safer surgical techniques. In the middle decades of the century, the doctor, uncertain of his cures, frequently turned from a dispenser of medicine to a dispenser of advice. The rise of popular medical literature coincided with the increase in therapeutic nihilism.

As a guardian and counselor, the physician became something of a moral arbiter whose pronouncements, colored as they were by the cultural and class biases of the time, worked to buttress the status quo. Few physicians could resist the temptation to enlist biology in the fight against women's rights. Edward H. Clarke in *Sex in Education,* a polemic written in 1873 to prevent coeducation at Harvard, argued with conviction that women would ruin their health by undertaking serious study. Their wombs, he warned, would atrophy. With a few notable exceptions, doctors also denounced women's attempts to control their reproductive lives. Those who did offer contraceptive advice only increased the

chance of pregnancy. On the mistaken premise that woman's fer-
tile period occurred immediately before and after menstruation,
they counseled patients anxious to avoid unwanted children to
allow sexual intercourse only in the middle of the monthly cycle.
As the woman's rights movement gained momentum in the second half of the nineteenth century, many doctors became increasingly shrill. They dismissed feminism, whether social or political,
as unnatural, unhealthy, and undesirable. A host of physicians
used spurious biological arguments to relegate advocates of
woman suffrage to the ranks of "hermaphrodites."[56]

Doctors, it sometimes seemed, preferred weak women. Prevalent in the writing of several practitioners of the period is a strong
attraction to sickly women. Hollick, writing of chlorosis (a catchall
nineteenth-century ailment that combined the symptoms of anemia and mild hysteria), described its sufferers as "delicate and
sensitive, stricken by a disease from which they deeply suffer, but
which often leaves their beauty untouched, or even heightens its
attractions."[57] Doctors and laymen alike sentimentalized illness—
not cholera or smallpox, but diseases like pulmonary tuberculosis
where the lesions remain hidden—until the wan and wasted
woman became a perverse ideal of feminine beauty. Healthy
women drank vinegar and ate arsenic in an attempt to achieve the
pallor and blazing eyes of the tuberculosis victim.

The idealization of woman as invalid, as some writers have suggested, may have placed a potent weapon in her hand—a way to
dominate while remaining overtly submissive. The image of the
fashionable woman suffering a decline and taking to the couch, a
cliché of sentimental fiction, contained a grain of truth. Through
illness an unhappy wife could create some limited identity and
demand attention and affection from a husband too often absent.
"The idle, unoccupied, dissatisfied woman enjoys illness," a psychologist observed. "It is a distraction, a kind of occupation."[58]
Or, as others hinted, illness may have provided one of the most
convenient methods of birth control available to nineteenth-
century women. The delicate wife played on her husband's sympathy until she was excused from irksome sexual demands.

Physicians, suspicious that women used illness to gain their ends, treated patients suffering from neurasthenia and hysteria as adversaries in an elaborate psychological warfare. S. Weir Mitchell, the nation's leading specialist in nervous disorders, based his famous rest cure partially on the supposition that women were slyly malingering. The cure operated on the theory of reverse psychology. Women who took to the couch, he explained, should be forced to stay there. For a month or more, Mitchell confined his patients to bed and allowed them neither intellectual nor physical activity. "[The] rest becomes for some women a rather bitter medicine," he observed, "and they are glad enough to accept the order to rise and go about when the doctor issues a mandate which has become pleasantly welcome and eagerly looked for."[59]

Feminist theorist Charlotte Perkins Gilman was among a number of prominent women Mitchell treated for neurasthenia. Gilman began to suffer from nervous exhaustion shortly after her marriage in 1885. After the birth of her daughter, her depression became so intolerable that she agreed to undertake Mitchell's fashionable rest cure. In the face of her obvious ambivalence toward marriage and motherhood, Mitchell counseled her to give up all intellectual pursuits, devote herself exclusively to domestic duties and child-care, and "never touch pen, brush or pencil as long as you live." Under this regime Gilman, according to her own account, "came perilously near to losing my mind."[60] Sick of the treatment, she divorced her husband and resumed her writing career.

In a short story entitled "The Yellow Wallpaper," published in 1892, Gilman laid bare the helpless frustration of the female patient. Her narrator, an unnamed woman suffering from nervous disorders, is confined in an attic nursery decorated in disturbing yellow wallpaper. Forbidden any intellectual activity, she surreptitiously keeps a diary which, with chilling clarity, documents her descent into madness—a madness brought on by the patronizing mental cruelty of her doctor-husband.

John is a physician, and *perhaps*—(and I would not say it to a living soul, of course, but this is dead paper and a great relief to my mind)—*perhaps* that is one reason I do not get well faster.

You see he does not believe I am sick!

And what can one do?

If a physician of high standing, and one's husband, assures friends and relatives that there is really nothing the matter with one but temporary depression—a slight hysterical tendency—what is one to do?

. . . .

So I take phosphates or phosphites, whichever it is, and tonics, and journeys, and air, and exercise, and am absolutely forbidden to "work" until I am well again.

Personally, I disagree with their ideas.

Personally, I believe that congenial work, with excitement and change, would do me good.[61]

The enforced idleness of the rest cure which Gilman found so galling and which leads to insanity in her story was exacerbated by the god-like authority the doctor exerted over his patient. He alone decided whether she wrote a letter, read a book, saw her family, or so much as left her bed to urinate. Mitchell underscored the extent to which his cure duplicated, in exaggerated form, behavior patterns associated with the genteel female—submissiveness, idleness, passivity—when he observed that women made better patients than men. "With all her weakness, her unstable emotionality, her tendency to morally warp when long nervously ill," he observed, "she is then far easier to deal with, far more amenable to reason, far more sure to be comfortable as a patient, than the man who is relatively in a like position."[62] Men no doubt found it confusing and difficult to submit to treatment which called for behavior diametrically opposed to that which society defined as "manly." Women had only to overact a role already familiar and acceptable. The rest cure worked on one level to quell female rebelliousness by conditioning women to acknowledge and accept their subservience.

Surely in a society which idealized female invalidism, some psychological pressure pushed women to play out the role. Or less deviously, to internalize it. Surgeons repeatedly complained of healthy women who pleaded to have their sexual organs removed.[63] Yet to imply that the majority of sick women in the nineteenth century were either calculatedly shamming or neurotic would be to overlook the prevalence of legitimate female complaints in a period when medicine had few effective therapies to treat the most common vaginal infections, let alone the serious organic damage done by frequent pregnancies and poor obstetrics.

In 1875, at the height of "the age of the womb," Lydia Pinkham began marketing her Vegetable Compound. Women habituated to the popular concern with womb troubles provided a ready market for the medicine. But they were not simply gulled by the gray-haired lady on the medicine bottle. Lydia Pinkham offered her Compound in the belief that it provided women with a safe alternative to the therapies employed by medical doctors. Many women shared her conviction. Pinkham testimonials indicated dramatically women's dissatisfaction with regular doctors. A woman suffering from prolapsed uterus, leucorrhea, menstrual pains, or menopausal symptoms had little to gain from the interventionist therapies of the gynecologists. In cases of uterine and cervical cancer, pelvic inflammatory diseases, and ectopic pregnancy, doctors could and did save women's lives by resorting to surgery. But the high mortality rate that accompanied abdominal surgery in an era when doctors habitually operated in street clothes and without sterilizing their instruments gave patients good reason to fear operations.

In obstetrics, too, medical advances did not always spell improved care. The development of anesthesia in the 1840's eased women's labor pains. Anxious to avail themselves of the boon of anesthesia, women turned from midwives to male obstetricians, often with tragic results. The doctor who arrived to deliver the baby frequently carried, along with his chloroform or ether, bacteria from the autopsy table or the operating room. As late as the 1870's, doctors refused to recognize that they were responsible for spreading puerperal fever. Given the state of medical practice at the end of the nineteenth century, a woman suffering from female complaints might well have heeded Lydia Pinkham's advice and "let doctors alone."

Selling the Vegetable Compound

Lydia Pinkham began selling her Vegetable Compound in an era marked by medical controversy, public dissatisfaction with doctors, and an obsessive concern with woman's weakness—a climate ideally suited to promote the success of the Pinkham venture. Mrs. Pinkham's debt to the reform movements of her day was evident in the ingredients she chose for her medicine. An herbal remedy, the Vegetable Compound owed much to the popular health movements led by Samuel Thomson and Sylvester Graham. The original Pinkham formula called for:

8 oz. Unicorn root (*Aletris farinosa*)
6 oz. Life root (*Senecio aureus*)
6 oz. Black cohosh (*Cimicifuga racemosa*)
6 oz. Pleurisy root (*Asclepias tuberosa*)   for 100 pints
12 oz. Fenugreek seed (*Foenum graceum*)
Suspended in alcohol.[1]

In 1876 Lydia Pinkham registered her label and trademark with the United States Patent Office. Like most so-called "patent" medicines, the Vegetable Compound technically fell under the heading of a proprietary remedy. Only the name and trademark enjoyed government protection; the contents of the medicine remained secret. In black ink on bright blue paper, the label proclaimed "LYDIA E. PINKHAM'S VEGETABLE COMPOUND":

A Sure Cure for PROLAPSUS UTERI or falling of the Womb, and all FEMALE WEAKNESSES, including Leucorrhea, Painful Menstruation, Inflammation, and Ulceration of the Womb, Irregularities, Floodings, *etc.*

Pleasant to the taste, efficacious and immediate in its effect, It is a great help in pregnancy, and relieves pain during labor.

For All Weaknesses of the generative organs of either Sex, it is second to no remedy that has ever been before the public; and for all diseases of the Kidneys it is the Greatest Remedy in the World.[2]

The "cure-all" claims made for the Compound took their cue from John King's *American Dispensatory,* Lydia Pinkham's medical handbook. King, a medical doctor and professor of medicine, belonged to the Eclectic medical sect, a latter day offshoot of the Thomsonian movement. In the *Dispensatory,* King compiled all the known botanical medical agents into an alphabetical listing which included their descriptions, properties, histories, and uses. The claims for the Vegetable Compound and perhaps the basis for the formula itself came directly from King's book.[3]

Unicorn root was listed by King as having a tonic influence on the female generative organs and as being useful in the prevention of miscarriage. The herb could also be helpful in cases of chlorosis, amenorrhea (suppression of the menses), dysmenorrhea (painful menstruation) and inflammation of the uterus. "[I]n prolapsus of that organ," he remarked, "it is one of our best vegetable agents."[4] King recommended that Unicorn root be used in conjunction with Life root and Pleurisy root in the treatment of uterine diseases. Lydia Pinkham apparently took King's advice by incorporating the three herbs into her medicine.

Life root (commonly known as "Squaw-weed" and "the Female Regulator"), the second ingredient in the Compound, had, according to King, "cured several cases of amenorrhea."[5] It had also been observed to produce abortion, and King recommended it as a substitute for ergot, a frequently used abortifacient. Apparently neither King nor Lydia Pinkham worried about the conflicting action of Unicorn root, which supposedly prevented miscarriage, and Life root, which was believed to produce abortion.

Black cohosh the *Dispensatory* listed as effective in treating amenorrhea, dysmenorrhea, leucorrhea, and other uterine affections, as well as helpful in relieving the afterpains of labor. As for Pleurisy root, which took its common name from its use in respiratory diseases, King noted that "a number of cases of *prolapsus uteri* have been cured under the use of one ounce of Pleurisy root mixed with half an ounce of *Aletris farinosa* (Unicorn root)."[6] Fenugreek seed constituted Lydia Pinkham's only original contribution to King's suggested remedies for female weakness. King made no mention of it in the *Dispensatory.* Ordinarily used as a condiment in animal fodder, Fenugreek was reputed to act as a mild aphrodisiac.

King's descriptions of the therapeutic action of the botanicals found in the Vegetable Compound indicated that the label claims relating to female complaints, however exaggerated, were based upon medical opinion current at the time. Even the notion that a medicine taken internally could effect a cure for prolapsed uterus found some exponents among medical doctors. Confusion concerning the proper treatment for prolapse continued well into the twentieth century. Radical gynecologists, in what one doctor has described as "the dark ages of operative furor,"[7] increasingly resorted to abdominal surgery to shore up the ligaments supporting the uterus. Yet the procedure met with poor results. A less radical technique involved the closure of the vagina—a treatment which precluded sexual intercourse and childbearing. Pessaries and astringents, the stock-in-trade of the clinical gynecologists, proved equally futile in providing a "cure." Many doctors became disgusted with radical surgery and skeptical of painful local treatment. In cases of partial prolapse, they advised a simple treatment of soap and water, proper diet, and a regimen designed to strengthen the body. The Pinkham company's assertion that the Vegetable Compound could cure prolapse followed the current belief that medicines, by raising the general tone of the body, could effect cures. In her letters of advice, Lydia Pinkham conceded that cases of severe prolapse (where the uterus projected beyond the vulva) "cannot be relieved by medicine in any great degree."[8] The label and subsequent advertising copy, however, contained no such qualification.

Pinkham claims that the Vegetable Compound acted as a "specific" for female ailments did not square with the further promise that the Compound cured weakness in the generative organs "of either Sex," or with the boast that the medicine could cure kidney diseases. King's *Dispensatory* supported no such statements. They grew out of Dan Pinkham's advice. In May of 1876 he had written from Brooklyn, "I think there is one thing that we are missing . . . and that is not having something on the pamphlet in regard to Kidney Complaints. . . ."[9] With an eye to profits, the Pinkhams tacked on promises which would attract a wider market for the Compound.

Despite expanded claims, sales came in at a trickle. Since no personal sales force covered any given territory, sales of the Vegetable Compound depended entirely on the pulling power of advertising. From 1876 to 1883, the company spent the greater part of its gross sales revenue on advertising, as much as 78 per cent, or $172,478 in 1882.[10] To build up sales the fledgling company needed to advertise heavily in order to create a consumer demand and to convince druggists to carry the Compound. The hundreds of thousands of pamphlets which Dan and Will Pinkham "pushed out" were worthless if prospective customers could not obtain the Compound when they went to the drugstore. Newspaper advertising provided a way to coordinate demand and supply. Hungry for national advertising, newspaper publishers often accepted merchandise in payment for advertising space. The publishers acted as a sales force. They took the product and turned it over to local wholesalers and druggists who accepted it with the knowledge that they could count on a retail demand stimulated by the newspaper ads. Late in 1876, after Will Pinkham had achieved surprising results with his first ad in the *Boston Herald,* the company began a steady shift from pamphlets to newspaper advertising. While the Pinkhams continued to distribute the four-page "Guide for Women" and to utilize posters and illustrated advertising cards on a limited scale, the brothers realized the immense selling power that lay in advertising in the newpapers.[11]

Newspaper advertising in the Gilded Age offered the most promising route to success for the would-be medicine millionaire, but it often proved a trap for the unwary. The business of advertising in its primitive stages in the late nineteenth century provided a natural habitat for the devious, the unscrupulous, and the disreputable. With minimum capital and maximum guile anyone enterprising enough to print his name on a letterhead could solicit advertisements and bilk the unwitting advertiser. George P. Rowell, founder of *Printers' Ink* and a veteran of the push-and-shove days of early advertising, observed that advertising was "one of the easiest sorts of business in which a man may cheat and defraud a client without danger of discovery."[12]

The early advertising agent acted simply as a broker in space. With over eight thousand newspapers printed in the United States by 1876, few advertisers could afford the time away from their own business to learn the names and locations of the papers, much less check the circulation figures and bargain for advertising space. The agent took on those tasks. He accepted the advertisers' prepared copy and placed it in specified newspapers, or, more often, placed it in his own special list of newspapers. He received his pay not from the advertiser directly, but indirectly from the publisher in the form of a commission, usually 15–25 per cent of the cost of the advertising space.[13]

To secure the advertiser's business, the agent promised to get rock-bottom prices from the publisher. Although in theory, advertising space sold according to a set rate schedule, in practice the agent frequently enjoyed a buyer's market. From the publisher's viewpoint, unused advertising space constituted a distinct liability. If he did not sell his space before the paper went to press, he not only lost advertising revenue but had to pay the printer for the typesetting required to fill the space with reading matter. In such a situation the harried publisher threw away the rate card and settled for what he could get from the agent.

The vulnerability of the publisher acted to the economic advantage of the agent. The advertiser rarely shared in the good fortune. As a rule, advertisers had very little idea of the actual cost of space. It proved an easy job for the sharp agent to convince his client that the projected cost of an advertising campaign marked the smallest sum at which the requisite space could be secured. Most agents gave in to the temptation to make their profits as large as possible by getting from the advertiser all that he could be induced to pay and offering to the publisher as little as he could be forced to accept. The agent pocketed the difference and collected his commission as well. The plan led Rowell to protest that "it seemed hardly honest to charge $40 for a service in a paper that, although at its rates would amount to $75, yet in practice would commonly be secured at a gross price of possibly less than $25."[14]

Occasionally the agent got caught in the trap. When a publisher sensed that an agent had an iron-clad contract with an advertiser for space in his paper, he did not hesitate to dictate his own terms. "It was exceedingly unpleasant," observed Rowell, "to be mulcted $100 or more for a service for which we received less than $50, and which papers of equal value were generally willing to render for $20 or $25."[15] Wherever possible the agent stipulated in his contract with the advertiser that he reserved the option to substitute a comparable paper for the one contracted.

The tooth-and-claw practices which typified early advertising resulted in no small measure from the anomalous position of the advertising agent. He could hardly say for sure whether he was the agent and employee of the advertiser, working in his interest against the publisher, or whether he was the agent of the publisher, from whom he received his commission. In practice he tended to shrug off the question of loyalties and to expend his energies, in the words of one agent, "first, last, and always looking out for number one."[16]

The Pinkhams came in for their share of trouble with advertising agents before the business got on its feet. Dan Pinkham, who had the benefit of his seasons in New York to "sharpen" him, immediately grasped the problems which confronted the prospective advertiser. When Will wrote that he had contacted a New York agent about the possibility of placing Pinkham ads, Dan cautioned, "[T]hese Advertising Agents are hungry for business the whole of them and it seems to be full necessary for us to look out as sharp for them as they do for us."[17]

In the next ten years the company had occasion to act on Dan's advice in its dealings with Harlan Page Hubbard. By 1878 Hubbard already had earned a reputation among newspaper publishers and editors as a combination highwayman, blackmailer, and confidence man. In short, Hubbard beat the prices down so low that publishers could not turn over a profit. When the editor of the *Marblehead Messenger* complained to Will Pinkham that Hubbard's advertising did not pay, Will was smart enough to realize that the agent most unpopular with publishers was the best agent to hire. Will had grown dissatisfied with the company's current agent, T. C. Evans, who was too conservative for the Pinkhams' taste. Hubbard sounded like a good bet.[18]

Not long after he first heard of Hubbard, Will paid a visit to the agent's New Haven office and the two signed a contract. In return for the Pinkham account, Hubbard agreed to extend $1,000 in credit for three months and promised that if the first advertising campaign panned out, he would extend the credit. Hubbard planned his strategy carefully. He began by placing a ten-inch ad in "every paper worth using" in Connecticut and Rhode Island. After the first three months of saturation advertising, the Compound was selling well enough to pay the advertising bill, which amounted to over $4,000. Will Pinkham, pleased with the results, authorized Hubbard to open up new territories on further credit.[19]

Although the Pinkhams were gratified by Hubbard's success, they were not yet ready to grant him an exclusive contract. They continued to experiment with other agents. "You might as well get half or the whole of the advertising agents in the country on a string,"[20] Dan Pinkham advised. At Dan's prompting, Will visited New York early in 1880 and talked to agents at one of the city's largest advertising agencies, Dauchy and Company. Will and Dan were elated when the firm agreed to sign a contract for $10,000 worth of Pinkham advertising. But no sooner was the contract signed than the deal fell through. The conservative Dauchy company wrote to a Lynn bank for information on the Pinkhams' credit. The bank remembered only Isaac Pinkham's financial disasters, which so horrified the Dauchy agents that they quickly rescinded the contract.[21]

Shortly after the Dauchy affair, the Pinkhams turned over full control of their advertising to Hubbard. Whatever his faults, Hubbard was not afraid to gamble. But as the Pinkhams soon learned, Hubbard's easy credit came at no small cost. When advertising in 1879–81 did not produce sufficient sales revenue to pay expenses, Hubbard stepped in and demanded a share of the business in lieu of the money owed him. The Pinkhams, suspecting that Hubbard had engineered the deficit in order to get his hands on the business, were anxious to prevent the family concern from falling into his grasp. Charles Pinkham, who had taken over when Dan and Will became too ill to work, cast about for a solution to the company's problems. In March of 1881, Charles entered into negotiations with F.C. Cross of New Jersey in the hope that Cross would agree to back the company. Instead Cross offered to buy it outright. Charles, who had no intention of selling the business, used the offer to bargain with Hubbard for an extension of credit. Knowing he would be out in the cold if the Pinkhams sold the company, Hubbard yielded. In the future the Pinkhams dealt more cautiously with their agent.[22]

Not long after the trouble with Hubbard, the family officially organized the business as a partnership among the four Pinkham children: Dan, Will, Charles, and Aroline. After Dan's death in October of 1881, the three surviving partners reorganized under the name "Lydia E. Pinkham's Sons and Company." The family wanted to be sure that Isaac Pinkham's many creditors could not make claims on the business. Isaac and Lydia Pinkham, who had inherited Dan's share of the company, signed an agreement in which they turned over their share in Dan's estate to their three surviving children with the stipulation that Will, Charles, and Aroline would furnish them with "comfortable and sufficient support so long as they . . . shall live."[23] The Pinkhams left nothing to chance.

Lydia Pinkham's name and face had become so closely associated with the business that try as they might, the Pinkhams could not squelch the rumor that she owned the company. Isaac's creditors began to pressure her to pay her husband's debts. To dramatize her separation from the business, Lydia Pinkham took the Poor Debtor's Oath in the spring of 1882. The *Lynn Bee* reported that she arrived at the court house "riding in a magnificent coupé." Other papers picked up the story and embellished it until the story spread that the business had failed and that Hubbard had suffered great losses. The negative publicity distressed the family, but delighted Hubbard. It "made people talk," he said, and in the end worked practically like an advertisement, "as it convinced many that she was a real person instead of a mythical one."[24]

When Hubbard acted to reassure papers running Pinkham ads of the company's solvency, he inadvertently laid a trap for himself. In the summer of 1882, he circulated cards denying the failure of the Pinkham company and asking papers to publish a disclaimer. An editor at the *Chicago Mirror* scrawled across the card, "I will do nothing of the kind for this Hubbard is a thief and we are going to advertise him well." The writer went on to complain, "He beats us down to half our prices, and at the end of three months refuses to pay our bill. . . . He is a Daisy—and we will worry him for a fact!"[25] Similar complaints poured in to the Pinkham company on the cards Hubbard had sent out. Publishers recounted how Hubbard refused to pay his back bills and threatened to stop Pinkham advertising unless Hubbard paid up. Charles Pinkham became uneasy and suspicious.

Like most advertisers, the Pinkhams had no clear understanding of the advertising game. They simply assumed that Hubbard bought advertising space at the price he quoted to them and collected a 10–15 per cent commission from the publishers. In reality Hubbard followed the established practice of buying space by the column and selling it to the advertiser by the inch at a substantial profit. Often his commissions ran as high as 50 per cent. To further increase his profits, he collected interest on credit he extended to the Pinkhams at the same time that he let his own bills with the newspapers run for months and sometimes years.

Slowly it dawned upon Charles Pinkham that Hubbard had once again managed to place himself in a position to take over the company. By running advertising campaigns which ate up 72 per cent of gross sales revenue in 1881 and 78 per cent in 1882, Hubbard had contrived to get the company in over its head. At the end of 1882 he stood on the books as the company's largest creditor. Angered over what he considered Hubbard's excessive profits and panicked by the agent's hold on the company, Charles demanded an accounting. Hubbard indicated that the Pinkhams owed him some $42,500. Without flinching, Charles signed forty-three $1,000 notes to placate Hubbard and keep the business in family hands. He then threatened to place no more advertising unless Hubbard agreed to submit his newspaper contracts to the Pinkhams for approval.[26]

Relations between Pinkham and Hubbard cooled considerably during 1883. Charles kept a sharp eye on his agent. That winter he made a hurried cross-country trip to talk with publishers in an effort to discover if Hubbard had kept his promise to pay papers promptly and take only the commissions Pinkham allowed. The trip supplied him with enough evidence to prove that Hubbard had not lived up to his end of the bargain. Charles found himself in a delicate situation. He could not afford to fire Hubbard; he owed him too much money. Instead he cut advertising drastically to meet the payments on his notes to Hubbard and, armed with the information he had gleaned on his cross-country trip, he forced Hubbard to sign an agreement regularizing business practices. Under the terms of the agreement, signed on December 27, 1883, Hubbard wrote off over $6,000 and extended further credit of $4,000 on future advertising with the understanding that the settlement would "be considered as a healing of all differences which may have existed as to rates of commission . . . to the full satisfaction of both parties."[27]

From then on Charles Pinkham kept Hubbard on a tight rein. Hubbard's annual contract in 1884 stipulated that the agent submit monthly bills and take only a 10–12½ per cent commission. The Pinkhams also insisted that Hubbard open his books for inspection. After a dangerous apprenticeship, Charles Pinkham had learned to take Dan's advice and "look out sharp" for his advertising agent.[28]

Relations with Hubbard improved. In the summer of 1884, Charles asked the agent to handle a difficult problem for the family. After Will Pinkham's death in 1881, his share of the company passed to his recent bride, Emma Barry Pinkham. Her sudden death in 1882 left her interest in the company in the hands of her brother, Eugene Barry. When the company incorporated in September of 1882, forty-nine shares of stock went to Charles Pinkham, who became president of the new corporation. Another forty-nine shares fell to his sister Aroline, who had married her brothers' childhood friend Will Gove. Aroline turned over one of her shares to her husband so that he could sit on the Board of Directors. Eugene Barry held the remaining fourteen shares. The Pinkhams were anxious to recover the stock from him. Reluctant to approach Barry directly, Charles asked Hubbard to serve as an intermediary. In June of 1884 Hubbard obtained the fourteen shares and two months later they were reissued, seven to Charles and seven to Aroline. Hubbard's sharp trading in this instance worked to the Pinkhams' advantage. Barry settled for the face value of the shares ($1,400) and a cash settlement of $290.[29]

Back in the Pinkhams' good graces, Hubbard once again went to work selling the Vegetable Compound. By 1884 the company boasted that it spent almost $100,000 a year on advertising which covered every state and territory in the country as well as various provinces in Canada and parts of South America. Advertisements for the Vegetable Compound appeared in German, French, Spanish, Italian, Bohemian, Dutch, Swedish, Welsh, and Hebrew. In addition to newspaper advertising, the company sent out large quantities of circulars and pamphlets, sometimes at the rate of three tons a day, for distribution by druggists.

Pinkham advertising followed the prescriptions laid down by the successful patent medicine men of the period. With so many remedies clamoring for attention, the latecomer in the field found it necessary to resort to the eye-catching and sensational. Advertisers in patent medicines admitted that they pitched their messages in an exaggerated manner, but justified their action by pointing to competitors. "You are starting out on a long up-hill journey," advised an old-timer to a would-be patent medicine advertiser, "and [you] must write your advertisements to catch damned fools—not college professors." After a moment he added, "And you'll catch just as many college professors as you will of any other sort."[30]

Pinkham advertisements in the early years ran in eleven-inch single columns under scare headlines so that they would look like news stories. The headline, often taking up half the length of the column, caught the readers' attention and supposedly "tricked" them into reading the copy. A typical scare head consisted of one bold line followed by four to six sections, each in consecutively smaller type. "LIFE'S WOES," began one head. "THOUSANDS DYING ANNUALLY, From Causes to the World Unknown, While Other Thousands Are Being Restored to Health, Hope and Happiness by the Use of LYDIA E. PINKHAM'S VEGETABLE COMPOUND, The Positive Cure for Female Complaints." A more ingenious headline capitalized on a much discussed murder case: "A FEARFUL TRAGEDY—A Clergyman of Stratford, Conn., KILLED BY HIS OWN WIFE. Insanity Brought on by 16 years of Suffering With Female Complaints the Cause. LYDIA E. PINKHAM'S VEGETABLE COMPOUND, The Sure Cure for These Complaints, Would Have Prevented the Direful Deed." Occasionally the headline gave no hint of the copy to follow, as in the case of one headline which bore distinctive traces of the Pinkhams' early Greenback views: "THE EARLY DEAD. Thousands Heartlessly Immolated, On The Altar of Mammon."[31]

Conspicuously absent from the headlines, the explicit wording of the label with its reference to *prolapsus uteri* could be found in the copy which followed. Here in the fine print, graphic descriptions of female complaints introduced claims for the Vegetable Compound even more exaggerated than those spelled out on the label. The ads reeled off a list of painful symptoms, some so general that any woman could identify with them. Since headache and restlessness shared equal weight in the descriptive copy with prolapse, the ads led the credulous reader to conclude that the minor symptoms indicated uterine disease.

Female weaknesses so common to our best population, are generally manifested by the uneasy restless sensation of the patient. The stomach and nervous system are all sympathetically disordered in most diseases of the uterus. There is also a dull heavy pain constantly felt in the lower portions of the back, or a severe burning and sharp pain that is almost unendurable; a soreness through the loins, pubis or lower portion of the abdomen, and through the upper portion of the thighs; nausea in the stomach is of frequent occurrence; pain and giddiness in the head, a sense of confusion or weakness, and constant running from one or both eyes, sometimes follow as a sympathetic symptom of diseased uterus, and with the weakness of the muscles there is a constant bearing down pain, a pulling from the bowels that render [sic] it very painful to walk or stand for any length of time.[32]

The ideas which informed Pinkham copy came, for the most part, directly from the medical literature of the period. The notion that all diseases in women affected or emanated from the uterus found support in the writings of a popular medical writer, Dr. Frederick Hollick, whose well-known work, *The Origin of Life*, shared space on the Pinkham bookshelf with King's *Dispensatory*. Hollick, along with eminent physicians like George Beard and Horatio Storer, spoke of "mysterious and extensive sympathies" which "connected the womb with every other organ in the body."[33] Among the symptoms which Hollick looked for when diagnosing prolapse, he cited bearing-down pains, soreness in the abdomen, stomach disorders, and backache. The extensive list of symptoms incorporated in Pinkham copy drew from the medical record, as did the notion that uterine disease in large measure afflicted the fashionable, or, as the advertisement put it, "our best female population." Neither original nor unusual, Pinkham advertising copy simply appropriated commonly held medical opinion and put it to use selling the Vegetable Compound.

Elsewhere the copy gave way to the excesses typical of patent medicine advertising. Describing the benefits of the medicine, one advertisement claimed not only that the Compound acted in cases of prolapse to "strengthen the muscles of the uterus and lift it into place" (a cure which the copy declared "radical and entire"), but also that the Compound "permeates every portion of the system, and gives life and vigor." There followed a staggering list of claims:

It removes Dyspepsia, Faintness, Flatulency, destroys all craving for stimulants, and relieves weakness of the stomach. It will cure entirely the worst forms of falling of the Uterus, Leucorrhea, Painful Menstruation, Inflammation or Ulceration, Irregularities, Floodings, *etc.* For the cure of Kidney Complaints of either sex this Compound is unsurpassed.[34]

Again the Pinkhams seemed intent on widening their consumer market by inserting non-specific claims. Americans suffered collectively from poor digestion fostered by bad eating habits. By purporting to remove "Dyspepsia," "stomach weakness," and "Flatulency" the advertisement offered something for everybody as well as something for nothing. Men could benefit from the Compound, and women could improve their digestion while curing their female complaints.

More subtle claims were made between the lines. The spread of the opium habit after the Civil War created a market for "opium-habit cures," many of which contained the drug they purportedly acted against. The broad phrase, "destroys all cravings for stimulants," could be interpreted as a promise to cure addiction. Similarly, the promise that the Vegetable Compound cured "Irregularities, Floodings, *etc.,*" held a special meaning for readers seeking an abortifacient. Throughout the nineteenth century desperate women poisoned and mutilated themselves in their attempts to avoid the social stigma of unwed motherhood or the economic and physical burden of repeated pregnancies. These women needed only the slightest hint that a medicine might get them out of their predicament. Although the Pinkham company assumed an indignant tone when women wrote to complain that the medicine had not produced abortion, the indignation smacked of hypocrisy.

The rhetoric of the advertisements, with its repetitive emphasis on "constant bearing down pains," "dull, heavy pains," "severe burning and sharp pains," and "pain in the head," helped pioneer what came to be called the "pain and agony" pitch. When readers complained of the unpleasant detail and charged that the ads were designed to gull the healthy into believing themselves sick, the ad men countered by pointing out, "When a man reads a medical ad that tells him exactly what his symptoms are, he is more likely to believe that the man who made the medicine knew what he was doing." Patent medicine ads unabashedly appealed to the hypochondriacal on the theory that "most ailing people get a morbid satisfaction from reading vivid descriptions of the symptoms of their sickness."[35] One advertising text observed, "Most men are not at all satisfied to be sick and not have people thoroughly appreciate the fact."[36] Clearly the same held true for women as far as the Pinkhams were concerned.

Pinkham testimonials appeared to justify the pain-and-agony approach and worked to embellish it. Unsolicited letters in which women detailed their symptoms provided the company with valuable advertising copy. "I have been a sufferer for years from female weakness in the worst forms," began one woman, who went on to describe "pains in back and loins, great fatigue from walking, leucorrhea and frequent desire to urinate." Invariably the letters concluded on a satisfied note: "The Vegetable Compound has cured me of all my weakness. I am a different woman."[37] The best letters were turned over to Hubbard to be "worked up" for the newspapers. Some editing evidently proved necessary to pass the censorship of publishers. "It is hard to get publishers to accept such testimonials as we ought to print, on account of their being a little rank," the agent complained. "As long as they will take them, however, and they will sell medicine, we will put them out."[38] A few women also acted as censors by asking that their names be withheld or that their testimonials not appear in their local newspapers. Yet many women seemed to welcome the opportunity to describe their ailments, complain about their doctors, and share their experiences with sympathetic listeners.

Testimonials constituted a staple item for nineteenth-century advertisers. Often they put their own words in the mouths of prominent individuals to give their message more weight. Unfortunately for the Pinkham company, famous women showed an understandable reluctance to associate their names with a uterine medicine. Druggists had no such scruples. Early Pinkham advertisements relied heavily on druggists like Philo Jackson of Brooklyn, who testified, "Your Vegetable Compound gives universal satisfaction without exception. It is the best preparation I ever knew for Female Diseases." The testimonials provided free advertising for the druggists, while they helped stimulate trade. Medical doctors occasionally endorsed the Compound in print. "I shall continue to prescribe your Vegetable Compound," wrote Dr. John S. Carter of Erie, Pennsylvania. When doctors balked, the Pinkhams pressed their friends into service by the simple addition of a medical title. Thus J. M. Grosvenor, a druggist who sold the Compound, appeared in a testimonial as "Dr. Grosvenor."[39]

In their early advertising campaigns, Hubbard and the Pinkhams seemed anxious to legitimate the Vegetable Compound by masquerading Lydia Pinkham as a medical doctor. The ruse worked well because, as luck would have it, there happened to be a Dr. Pinkham who practiced in Lynn—Dr. Joseph G. Pinkham, a graduate of Long Island College Hospital. An early ad in the Lynn papers traded on the confusion created by the coincidence. The ad, which read like a news story, began by quoting "Dr. Pinkham of Lynn," to the effect that uterine troubles were especially prevalent among women factory workers. The text that followed drew heavily from Dr. E. H. Clarke's *Sex in Education.* Although Clarke had aimed his remarks on the baneful effects of menstrual periodicity at middle-class women seeking a college education, the ad extended his logic to deal with the condition of working women. For "those unfortunates who must struggle on with unremitting toil," and could not enjoy the "periodic remission which such eminent authorities as Dr. Clark [*sic*] declare that their nature demands," the ad recommended Lydia E. Pinkham's Vegetable Compound. "This remedy," the copy promised, "will remarkably relieve those who must still continue to overwork, and it will give them strength to continue their toil with comparative ease." The bogus news story ended with an unabashed plug for the Vegetable Compound by referring working women to "one of the most eminent of physicians, Lydia E. Pinkham of Lynn, Mass."[40]

The Pinkhams quickly tired of the ruse. Their copy in 1879 shifted ground dramatically. "We lose our respect for university honors, proud titles and gilded reputations, when they bring us no panacea for the ills which banish rest and sleep and threaten our very existence," one ad announced. "Then we may be forced to respect as a Deliverer even an UNTITLED WOMAN who has no higher ambition than to do good to others." The image of Lydia Pinkham as a symbol of the common people appealed to the family so much that when Hubbard began in 1879 to head Pinkham ads with Lydia's picture, the caption frequently identified her as "A Noted but Untitled Woman." Even as they ridiculed the ineffectual treatments of the regular doctors, the Pinkhams continued, often in the same advertisement, to seek the legitimacy of medical endorsement by proclaiming that "Physicians Use It and Prescribe It Freely." Some no doubt did. Patent medicines often found their way into the doctor's black bag during the period.[41]

The use of Lydia Pinkham's face on the trademark, beginning in 1879, served as a successful advertising ploy and added a personal touch to Pinkham copy. Advertisements inviting readers to "Write to Mrs. Pinkham," promised that she would personally answer all letters of inquiry at no charge. Soon letters came in at the rate of a hundred a month. Lydia Pinkham dutifully answered the correspondence until the last year of her life. When her health failed, the company established a special correspondence department to handle the mail. Mrs. Pinkham's death in 1883 presented the company with a serious problem. Hubbard worried that the postmaster might refuse to turn over to the company letters addressed to Lydia Pinkham. Searching for a solution, Hubbard approached Charles Pinkham to see if his wife or sister would be willing to appear in advertisements as "the new Mrs. Pinkham." Pinkham's secretary answered curtly, "The fact of the matter is that Mr. Pinkham does definitely prefer not to advertise either his wife or his sister as a professional adviser."[42] With wealth had come social aspirations which precluded either Jennie Pinkham or Aroline Pinkham Gove from appearing in company advertising. Fortunately for Hubbard, the postmaster allowed letters addressed to Lydia Pinkham to pour in to the factory. Ads continued to invite women to "Write to Mrs. Pinkham."

More than a few of the letters that women wrote to Lydia Pinkham found their way into Pinkham advertising as testimonials. In these letters, women spoke disparagingly of doctors and medical treatment. A standard line complained, "I have doctored for several years with no success." Disillusioned with expensive and prolonged treatments, women often attributed remarkable cures to the Vegetable Compound, as in the following letter:

My family physician told me that unless I obtained speedy relief I could not live. My own weak and distressed condition too truly echoed his words. Just at that time a friend handed me one of your pamphlets, for which I shall be ever thankful. Now my friends congratulate me on my changed appearance, which, I can truly say, is entirely due to the use of a few bottles of your Vegetable Compound.[43]

Similar invidious comparisons appeared throughout Pinkham testimonials. Not infrequently writers concluded "Your Vegetable Compound has done . . . more good than the medicine of many doctors for years."[44]

Women often displayed an outright fear of doctors' methods, as in the case of one woman suffering from complications arising from prolapsed uterus who wrote, "Dr. tells me I can have the trouble removed but thought I would write and ask you if the Compound would do it before I submitted to an operation with *Doctor's tools,* a thing I have not much faith in." "By all means avoid instrumental treatment for your trouble," the woman was advised. "Use the Compound as you have been using it —faithfully and patiently—and it will eventually work a cure. . . ."[45]

Where doctors simply diagnosed and treated, the Vegetable Compound promised to cure. "Physicians have been greatly perplexed in regard to treating female weakness, especially *prolapsus,* successfully," one ad observed truthfully. The copy went on to insist that the mechanical supports and pessaries employed by doctors in the treatment of displacements of the uterus had no more power to "cure" than "surgeon's splints mend broken bones or crutches cure the gout." Treatment, the advertisement declared, must be directed at the cause of prolapse. "With occasional exceptions," the copy reassured readers, "these diseases all have a common origin and may therefore have a common cure."[46] In such statements the company, intentionally or unintentionally, blurred the distinction between functional and organic disorders.

Behind the Pinkhams' advertising approach lay the common nineteenth-century idea that good health resulted from following the "Laws of Nature." Writers rarely spelled out the letter of those laws. Evidently anyone with common sense could perceive and follow them. Such thinking implied that doctors were not only unnecessary but—because of their propensity for meddling—downright dangerous. The Vegetable Compound, in contrast, acted "in harmony with the laws of Nature" and thereby led to good health. The Pinkham company urged women to leave doctors alone, take the Compound, and follow the "laws of Nature."[47]

If the secret of good health were so simple, why then did so many suffer? Pinkham ads answered positively that the fault could be traced to social changes following the Civil War. The pace of life had speeded up. No longer did women follow "natural" patterns. New occupations placed them on an unnatural schedule. More specifically, Pinkham ads blamed the businessman, who stalked through advertisements as the set-piece villain.

Thousands of cases [of uterine displacement] occur among young ladies employed in our fashionable dry goods, millinery and confectionery stores, where through the long day they are obliged to be constantly on their feet, even when the necessities of business do not require this legalized and systematic violence. The man of business will respect his own law, at whatever sacrifice to others, and so he yields nothing in the interest of humanity, but smiles complacently, and MURDERS WHILE HE SMILES.[48]

Nowhere did the advertisements directly blame American women for their poor health. Circumstances, not wanton neglect, caused their distress. Buried in the copy could be found a female complaint different from the sort cured by the Vegetable Compound.

How American women can have health is something not so easily understood—for look at the lives their circumstances require them to lead.

Every American woman in any of the great centres of society—in any of the large country towns, indeed—is expected to play a complex role of many duties, some of which are entirely incompatible with each other. She is to keep the house, and sometimes do the work of it, do the marketing, bear the children and rear them, and teach them to some extent, do all their sewing, do all their nursing and walk the floor at night with them if they are ill; she is expected to do, very frequently, the finer cooking, and often portions of the finer ironing; be sometimes a servant and always a lady. . . . And with all of this, if she is not exactly expected to do it, yet she frequently does add her mite to the pecuniary support of the family by outside labor of one sort or another. Under such circumstances, is it strange that the complaints that are peculiar to this class are becoming alarmingly prevalent?[49]

The copy implicitly indicted husbands, along with employers and doctors, for the suffering endured by women. The discrepancy between the myth of the idle woman and the reality of the over-worked middle-class housewife must have especially nettled Lydia Pinkham, who struggled for years to make do on Isaac's fluctuating fortunes. A resentment toward the ineffectual, incompetent male provider runs throughout Pinkham advertising copy in the late 1870's and provides perhaps the strongest evidence that Lydia Pinkham herself wrote the early ads.

The suspicion that men victimized women led logically to the conclusion that only women could be trusted. By 1883 Pinkham advertising openly expressed this new-found sense of sorority by proclaiming above each portrait of Lydia Pinkham, "Woman Can Sympathize With Women—Health of Woman is the Hope of the Race."

The Pinkham advertising pitch remained consistent throughout the 1880's, even after Lydia Pinkham's death. In modified form the same copy ran from 1883 to 1889. One reason for the repetition was Charles Pinkham's determination to get the business on a sound footing after the company's financial difficulties with Hubbard in 1883. Charles began by cutting advertising expenditures. He shortened the length of newspaper ads, eliminated magazine advertising entirely, and curtailed billboards and horsecar signs. During the summer months, which Pinkham considered the dull season, he reduced or eliminated newspaper advertising in all areas. Sales dropped, but profits increased as a result of the savings on advertising.

In May of 1885 Charles Pinkham instructed Hubbard to stop all newspaper advertising. "We will wait for a little harvesting," he wrote cryptically, "before we proceed."[50] By the end of the year Charles was able to issue the first dividend on Pinkham stock—$6,000 each for himself and his sister. At Thanksgiving dinner, Charles surprised Aroline by placing the $6,000 check under her napkin. Before he was finished, Charles Pinkham's "little harvesting" yielded enough money to pay for a new factory building in 1886, as well as netting profits which enabled both the Pinkhams and the Goves to move into grander residences.

Pinkham's retrenchment hurt Hubbard badly. Under the terms of his contract, the agent was authorized to place only three months' advertising at a time. To get the lowest rates, Hubbard contracted for a longer period. When Charles Pinkham cut back, Hubbard could neither pay for nor fill the space he had contracted. The agent gambled that publishers would not bother to sue him for his "short rates." This time he lost. At least one irate newspaperman took Hubbard to court. Hounded by newspaper publishers, he wrote Pinkham to enlist his aid. Charles Pinkham, who had paid off his debts to Hubbard, could afford to watch with equanimity the spectacle of the crafty agent harassed and finally cornered. Politely but firmly, Pinkham refused to lend Hubbard money. "So far whatever profit there has been in the business has gone to you and the newspapers," Pinkham pointed out. "If we had managed to 'salt down' a comfortable heap for ourselves we should now have something to lend." But, he concluded, "[S]hould we now try to steady you while our own feet are on such slippery places, the chances are good for a double downfall."[51] Without Pinkham's support, Hubbard foundered. "The International Newspaper Agency, H. P. Hubbard, Proprietor," soon went under.[52]

The ubiquitous Hubbard did not stay down for long. In 1886

he surfaced at the head of a new agency, "H. P. Hubbard and Company," with the Pinkham account intact. But Charles Pinkham's reluctance to commit the company to extended advertising placed Hubbard in an increasingly tenuous position. To save his own business, Hubbard pleaded with Pinkham to advertise more heavily. Charles stood firm. In 1888 he cut advertising expenditures drastically, from $78,000 the previous year to a mere $16,000. A desperate Hubbard queried, "What are you planning to do, milk the business?" Pinkham indicated his answer by virtually eliminating newspaper advertising. He spent the company's $7,550 advertising budget in 1889 on trade cards which featured a picture of his two daughters under the caption "Lydia E. Pinkham's Grandchildren." Hubbard's business failed again and he was forced to mortgage his home to pay his creditors. Relations between the agent and the company grew colder. In 1889 Pinkham severed all business connections with Hubbard.[53]

In the decade Hubbard spent selling the Vegetable Compound, he served the company well, despite his occasional double-dealing. Massive newspaper advertising successfully launched the business and made Lydia Pinkham a household name. In embryonic form the advertising themes emerged which would continue to sell the Compound for the next several decades. But by the 1890's the company had outgrown Hubbard. Advertising was coming of age and in its attempt to clean house, men like Hubbard became outmoded. Respectability became the order of the day.

Sensational Prudery

In the fall of 1889 a dapper young man named James T. Wetherald called on Charles Pinkham to solicit the Pinkham advertising account for the Pettingill agency of Boston. In stark contrast to Hubbard, Wetherald exuded respectability from the conservative cut of his suit to his scholarly pince-nez. The change in style appealed to Pinkham. Perhaps it flattered him. Lately ensconced in a big house on Western Avenue which boasted, in the words of a local society editor, "four acres of spacious gardens and lawns,"[1] Charles Pinkham had clearly outgrown Hubbard. Wetherald, with his smooth, almost unctuous manner suited nicely Pinkham's new-found sense of himself as "somebody."[2]

The meeting went well. Wetherald immediately came to the point. The Pinkham company had cut advertising to the bone for the past two years. Unless the company began advertising soon, he warned, the business would die out. Charles replied pointedly that he was willing to advertise "if I ever find an honest agent who can write the kind of copy I want." Evidently he liked what he saw, for by the close of the meeting Charles agreed to let Wetherald launch a modest campaign. Within months, Lydia Pinkham's face again appeared in the newspapers of New England.[3]

The Pinkhams' new agent worked to make himself indispensable. Long before 1900, when Wetherald officially left Pettingill to become a salaried advertising manager for the Pinkhams, he acted as a company man. Each Friday he took the train from Boston to Lynn where he consulted with Charles Pinkham on issues ranging from the design of the company's checks and stationery to marketing and price maintenance policy—matters ordinarily beyond the scope of an advertising agent. For nearly forty years, until his death in 1927, Wetherald masterminded Pinkham advertising with a skill and an eye for the sensational that made him a crucial factor in the success of the Pinkham medicine company.

If Pinkham had initially been drawn to Wetherald's style, style alone did not account for his appeal. J. T. (as he liked to be called) represented a new breed of ad men. In its coming of age, advertising rationalized its business methods. The calculating businessman, on the surface responsible and respectable, replaced the colorful huckster.[4] The new ad men had what Charles Pinkham would have called "tone." Tone inspired confidence. It reassured advertisers who had been burnt by unscrupulous agents in the past that times had changed; now they could deal with their agents as one businessman to another. But tone did not sell patent medicine. Wetherald learned to wear his respectability like the lacquer on his nails, in a thin veneer. At times he fretted over the unseemliness of selling a patent medicine for female complaints. In his more expansive moments he took pride in his craft. After all, it brought him the considerable material success which enabled him to join the best clubs and find his name listed in the *Boston Social Register*.

Wetherald's uneasiness reflected in microcosm the split between values and behavior which characterized his age. He, along with his society, experienced the discrepancy between the realities of the marketplace and notions of propriety as they were reflected in social pretension. In a society which worshipped material success, money made in patent medicine did not handicap social success for long. A popular anecdote of the 1890's poked fun at the hypocrisies and deceptions employed to circumvent social prescriptions. "Emma's papa is the man that makes ──────

Bitters," said a little girl to her mother aboard a European steamer. "We will be careful not to let her mother know that we know it," the girl's mother replied, "It might make her feel badly."[5] In the scramble for pecuniary success, the ends justified the means but not without leaving a twinge of embarrassment.

The nature of the Pinkhams' product aggravated the embarrassment by adding to it a sexual dimension. The lewd wink, the ribald laugh everywhere greeted mention of Lydia E. Pinkham's Vegetable Compound. Wetherald sold a product which by its very nature called into play his own and his society's peculiarly bifurcated view of sexuality in general and female sexuality in particular. The dominant culture purveyed conflicting images of woman epitomized in the discrepancy between the sentimental view of women as spiritual, sexless creatures and the common practice of referring to women as "the sex," as though their unmentionable reproductive organs defined them entirely. Wetherald, a true Victorian gentleman, shared the ambivalence and confusion of his age. Under his direction Pinkham advertising mirrored the impact of the genteel tradition on the themes Lydia Pinkham and H. P. Hubbard had developed in the 1870's and 1880's.

When Wetherald started placing Pinkham ads in January of 1890, he faced a difficult task. Ad men generally conceded that once a patent medicine had been allowed to die out for lack of advertising, sales could never be revitalized, no matter how much money might be lavished on a publicity campaign. Charles Pinkham's practice of cutting advertising to increase short-run profit had brought the company close to disaster. Sales revenue plunged in 1889 to an all-time low of $57,794, down from a high of over $260,000 in 1882. Wetherald laid his plans carefully. He began by advertising heavily in limited areas of New England. As sales responded, he gradually expanded the campaign, moving westward and southward, adding a few states at a time. In 1890 gross sales revenue rose over 10 per cent. Encouraged by the increase, Charles Pinkham increased his advertising budget from $25,950 in 1890 to $107,921 for 1891. The company went deeply into the red. The breakthrough came in 1893 when sales, topping the $200,000 mark, yielded a profit of $14,000. From 1893 to 1898, despite a nationwide depression, sales revenues rose each year and the company calculated its profits in six figures.[6]

"The versatile Mr. Wetherald," observed the editor of *Printers' Ink*, "showed that there are exceptions to all rules when he took hold of the Lydia E. Pinkham business, at a time when it was nearly dead, and raised the sales to a higher point than they had ever reached in the preceding time of its greatest popularity."[7] In the period between 1890 and 1899, Wetherald's advertising led to an increase of 2500 per cent in gross sales revenue. The ratio of advertising expenditure to sales revenue stabilized at around 44 per cent and allowed the company to turn over a profit amounting to roughly 23 per cent of gross sales revenue during the decade.[8] In an interview with the *Kansas City World*, Wetherald characteristically downplayed his own role in the company's spectacular recovery. The agent credited Charles Pinkham for his nerve and willingness to spend money freely on advertising. In Wetherald's words, Pinkham was "a natural born advertiser."[9]

Wetherald and Pinkham did not always agree on advertising policy. In some cases the agent's strategies initially encountered Pinkham's stolid opposition. Wetherald realized that the company needed to take dramatic steps if it were to pull out of the downward spiral occasioned by Charles Pinkham's profit-taking. By 1890 many women had forgotten the Vegetable Compound while others had never heard of it. To stimulate consumer recognition, Wetherald traded on the personality of Lydia Pinkham. His first series of ads featured trademark heads prominently displaying Lydia Pinkham's face. Skeptical readers chided the company for hiding behind a woman's skirts. "You doubtless are not aware," wrote one cynic, "that I know old 'Mrs. Lydia' is a young quack of the male sex."[10] An exasperated Wetherald, searching for a way to buttress the company's credibility, hit on the solution of animating the trademark. The disembodied face became attached to a historical personality in ads which portrayed Lydia Pinkham speaking directly about the discovery of the Compound. Implicitly Wetherald brought Lydia Pinkham back to life. Charles Pinkham balked. The agent countered by pointing out that the animated ads simply pictured scenes from Lydia Pinkham's life.

Nowhere did they directly assert that she was still alive. Ingenuously he argued that the company's invitation to "Write Mrs. Pinkham" could be supported if Charles would consent to advertise his wife as the manager of the correspondence department.

At Wetherald's prompting, the company built up its institutional posture by the conscious use of half-truths. Deception operated to salve conscience and at the same time to improve company credibility. In an animated ad from the 1890 series titled "A Life's Experience," an illustration featured Lydia Pinkham seated at a desk speaking to a woman identified as Mrs. Charles Pinkham.

My daughter, you have spent many years of your life in aiding me to complete these records. An analysis of every case of female disease ever brought to my attention is here; this will aid you in perpetuating my work. Here is a life's practice of a WOMAN AMONG WOMEN, and contains FACTS that cannot be found elsewhere! It is the largest collection the world has ever known.[11]

No such conversation ever took place. No such records existed, save for the random "Medical Directions for Ailments," kept by Lydia Pinkham in the early days of the business. Certainly Lydia Pinkham never attempted a serious "analysis of every case of female disease." Nor did Jennie B. Pinkham, Charles' wife, actively oversee the factory's correspondence department. The company employed a staff of some thirty women to answer letters and provided them with a standardized book of responses which they copied by rote.

The introduction of Mrs. Charles Pinkham into company ad copy was at once a concession to honesty and a shrewd ploy to quash readers' skepticism. Lydia Pinkham could not be expected to live forever. Sooner or later someone would get suspicious and investigate. The company's decision to introduce Mrs. Charles Pinkham anticipated the problem and provided a convenient explanation. The gullible reader who accepted the advertising at face value received the impression that Lydia Pinkham was alive and that Mrs. Charles Pinkham acted as her assistant. The more skeptical reader, who knew or suspected that Lydia Pinkham was dead, could take no credit for exposing a fraud. The company sidestepped such charges in a form letter developed in the 1890's:

You can not read our advertisements if you assert that we say that Mrs. *Lydia E.* Pinkham answers all letters. You will not find this in any advertisement. We say that Mrs. Pinkham does this and in this, we are correct; Mrs. Pinkham, the daughter of Lydia E. who was with her mother for many years before her death, does superintend all this correspondence. The general public understands this very well.[12]

Deception masked deception. The denial itself contained yet another distortion. Jennie Pinkham was the daughter-in-law, not the "daughter of Lydia E."—a lie the letter compounded by asserting that the present Mrs. Pinkham had worked with "her mother" for many years. (The observant reader might well have wondered how Lydia E. Pinkham's daughter could herself be a *Mrs.* Pinkham.)

Wetherald could not take full credit for creating the mythical Lydia Pinkham. From Hubbard he inherited the myth in skeletal form. J.T. took the bones bare and fleshed them out with a disregard for fact which would have surprised even Hubbard, who, while he continued to use Lydia Pinkham's picture on the trademark after her death in 1883, never tried to trick people into believing that she was alive answering letters in Lynn. In 1884 when Hubbard had asked permission to use Mrs. Charles Pinkham's name, he had received the curt reply that Charles did not wish to advertise his wife as "a professional adviser." In 1890 Pinkham went along with Wetherald's similar scheme in order to lend a narrow technical honesty to the "Write Mrs. Pinkham" ruse. The incident pointed to Wetherald's ability to sell his ideas as well as the Vegetable Compound. Where Hubbard scarcely dared, Wetherald succeeded. His respectability enabled him to draw the line of fraud just beyond his own deceptions.

Success bolstered Wetherald's influence. J.T. proved himself a consummate ad man. His approach to Pinkham advertising ran well ahead of his time. He insisted that Pinkham advertisements consist equally of straight sales copy and copy designed to establish institutional identity. Public relations, he realized (without giving it that name), could be as important as salesmanship. Saturation advertising in the 1890's again made Lydia Pinkham a national figure, thus heightening consumer recognition of the Vegetable Compound.

Wetherald supplemented institutional copy with what he called the "bill of fare," a listing of symptoms which the Compound purported to cure. He left no room for equivocation concerning the benefits of the medicine. Every complaint prevalent among women found its way onto Wetherald's bill of fare. To the already lengthy list of conditions and diseases which the Compound supposedly cured, Wetherald added nervous disorders. By the 1890's George Beard's diagnosis of "American nervousness" had become a commonplace. Men and women spoke of a "case of nerves" as they might have spoken earlier of measles or scarlet fever. The symptoms of nervous debility, ranging from sleeplessness to irritability, provided the patent medicine man with a grab bag of vague and non-specific symptoms which could be turned to profit. Among the conditions which the Vegetable Compound purported to alleviate, Wetherald listed "backache, faintness, extreme lassitude, 'don't care' and 'want-to-be-left-alone' feeling, excitability, irritability, nervousness, sleeplessness, . . . melancholy, or the 'blues'." These symptoms, the copy explained, were "sure indications of Female Weakness, some derangement of the Uterus, or WOMB TROUBLE."[13]

Medical opinion supported the assertion that nervous symptoms in women resulted from uterine troubles. The medical materialism of the nineteenth century which caused doctors to confuse psychological and somatic disorders led gynecologists to treat hysteria as an affection of the uterus. Doctors in the nineteenth century no longer believed the ancient theory that during hysterical attacks the uterus got loose and flew about the body, but they persisted in treating hysteria with gynecological measures.[14] Pinkham advertising, echoing medical opinion, promised that the Compound would treat hysteria at its source—the womb.

It gives the womb and uterus [*sic*] the necessary strength to throw off the diseases which burden it, the jangling nerves are quieted, the sufferer becomes a rational being again, and can re-enter society with no fear of making a sad exhibition of herself.[15]

Under Wetherald's influence the bill of fare also reflected a new concern with beauty which subtly shifted the emphasis of the advertising message from health as an end in itself to health as a means to greater physical attractiveness. Implicit in the shift was the Victorian notion that a woman's power came through her looks. The genteel female, passive and domestic, influenced the world only through her ability to manipulate men by using the one tool at her disposal—her person. "Because of her," gushed one ad, "thrones have been established and destroyed. The flash of her eye, the touch of her hand, and we have the marvellous power of woman, glorious in the possession of perfect physical health." Ads encouraged women to preserve or restore their beauty by taking the Vegetable Compound. The ugly woman, Pinkham advertisements hinted, had no one to blame but herself. "There is no secret about a woman's beauty; it all lies in the care she devotes to herself, to removing from her system all poisonous impurities, and keeping at bay those fearful female diseases. . . ."[16]

Wetherald exhorted at one moment and chided in the next. By associating unattractiveness with impurities and carelessness, he worked to induce guilt in women dissatisfied with their looks. Pinkham ads goaded women to action with the promise that the Vegetable Compound "cleanses, invigorates, and consequently beautifies, the form of woman. . . ." Women who ignored references to womb trouble, Wetherald reasoned, might respond to ads which sold the Compound as a beauty aid.[17]

Wetherald liked to think of himself as something of an expert in the field of women's medicine. He pored over the popular medical literature of the period as well as standard medical texts on women's diseases in order to bring to Pinkham copy the vocabulary and tone of a professional treatise. The Pinkhams' most successful competitor, Dr. R. V. Pierce of Buffalo, who ran an "invalids' hotel" and marketed a spate of remedies (including Dr. Pierce's Favorite Prescription for female weakness), boasted the authorship of a thousand-page medical guide entitled *The People's Common Sense Medical Adviser*.[18] Pierce's medical credentials nettled Wetherald, who himself aspired to playing doctor. In the 1890's the agent decided to issue "Lydia Pinkham's Guide to

Health, A Private Textbook." Competition with Pierce spurred
Wetherald to discover ever more esoteric diseases which the Compound could claim to cure. His triumph was coccygodynia, or
pain in the coccyx. Wetherald penciled in the margin of his manuscript to an 1890's textbook the boast,

This is an exclusive!
Pierce hasn't *ingenuity* enough to write up *this* disease.
It was the discovery of *Dr. Nott, 1844,* and the
disease is being rapidly developed by the *bicycle.*
We are *up to date.* [19]

Wetherald's haste to extend the list of symptoms and diseases
which the Compound could cure (as well as his broad construc-
tion of "up-to-date") led to a blurring of functional and organic
conditions. Pinkham copy reversed the doctor's tendency to see
all female complaints as organic and therefore warranting surgical intervention. Mrs. Pinkham, informed one ad, "never advises
an operation—the shock is too great to be borne by most
women."[20] The bill of fare unequivocally stated that the "Vegetable Compound would dissolve and expel tumors from the uterus"
and "check any tendency to cancerous humors." Operations were
not only dangerous but unnecessary and useless. "While an operation will remove the tumor, it does not remove the cause and
additional growths are as likely to form as ever."[21]

Women agreed, or so Pinkham testimonials indicated. Published testimonial letters reinforced the bias against doctors and
operations. One woman wrote:

Two years ago I was a great sufferer from womb trouble and profuse
flowing each month and tumors would form in the womb. I had four
tumors in two years. I went through treatment with doctors but they did
me no good, and I thought I would have to resort to morphine. The doctor said that all that could help save me was to have an operation and
have the womb removed, but I had heard of Mrs. Pinkham's medicine
and decided to try it, and wrote for her advice, and after taking her Vegetable Compound, the tumors were expelled and I began to get stronger
right along, and am as well as ever before. Can truly say that I would

never have gotten well had it not been for Lydia E. Pinkham's Compound.[22]

Not all the afflictions which troubled women could be treated with medicine or surgery. Doctors who argued that women endangered their lives by taking the Vegetable Compound instead of seeking medical treatment too often overlooked psychological factors. A significant number of Pinkham testimonials hinted at hypochondria, and sometimes mental illness. The Compound in these cases acted as a placebo and did less harm than the more rigorous therapies employed by doctors who had not yet learned to diagnose or to treat psychological problems effectively. Women found in Mrs. Pinkham an audience for their troubles. The invitation to write to Mrs. Pinkham may well have encouraged an atmosphere sympathetic to modern psychology. A testimonial letter written in 1914 underscored the psychological nature of many of the female complaints which women claimed the Compound cured.

I was troubled with pains and irregularities for sixteen years, and was thin, weak, and nervous. When I would lie down it would seem as if I was going right down out of sight in some dark hole, and the window curtains had faces that would peek out at me, and when I was out of doors it would seem as if something was going to happen. My blood was poor, my circulation was so bad that I would be like a dead person at times. I had female weakness badly, my abdomen was sore and I had awful pains. I took Lydia Pinkham's Vegetable Compound and used the Sanative Wash and they certainly did wonders for me. My trouble disappeared and I am able to work hard every day.[23]

Women submitted testimonial letters for many reasons. Some may have wished to "share their secret." Others expected to profit, although few received any substantial cash payment. The company preferred to pay women in kind by offering them free supplies of the Vegetable Compound. A man who wrote to ask what his wife's testimonial would be worth received the answer, "We will give her all the medicine she needs for her own use; beyond this we can make no further inducement."[24]

The Pinkhams pretended that women wrote for nothing, but they made it a point to include certain fringe benefits. Testimonial writers got a stipend to spend on stationery and stamps which enabled them to respond to letters of inquiry. When Wetherald began to feature photographs of the writers above their letters, he made sure that testimonial women received money to pay a photographer and allowed them to have one copy made for themselves. Each Christmas the company sent silver spoons embossed with Lydia Pinkham's face to testimonial writers. These small benefits attracted many women, especially during the hard times of the 1890's.

The company maintained extensive correspondence with its testimonial women, who were regarded as part of the family. They swapped recipes, exchanged Christmas greetings, and occasionally received homemade preserves and embroidered work from their "friends." But when poor black women sought to enter the Pinkhams' extended family, the company's business manager, Laura Hunt, responded in horror. Writing to Wetherald, Hunt noted indignantly that several testimonials would have to be dropped because photographs revealed the writers to be "colored women."[25] Not until much later did the company actively pursue Negro consumers by consciously including their testimonials.

Early in 1890 Wetherald decided that the time had come to increase the market for the Vegetable Compound by appealing to healthy women as well as women suffering from female complaints. An astute ad man, well ahead of his times, Wetherald realized that advertising should not simply meet needs, but create them. To appeal to healthy women he decided to expand the company's thirty-two page "Guide to Health" into a "Guide to Health and Etiquette." All women, he reasoned, wanted to know about manners and etiquette. The new booklet appeared under the authorship of "Lydia E. Pinkham of Lynn, Mass." In practice, Wetherald himself and sometimes Pinkham employees wrote the copy for this and subsequent booklets, which became standard Pinkham publications. Some 167 editions were published between 1893 and 1935. The "Guides," which expended only 10 per cent of the company's yearly advertising budget, had a significant impact on the market. Wetherald, a better student of human nature than of medicine, insisted on charging fifteen cents or two postage stamps for the early booklets on the theory that women would think the "Guides" more valuable if they had to pay for them.

Wetherald hoped to attract a wider consumer audience and at the same time lend tone to the Pinkham booklets by adding etiquette to the format. Previous pamphlets bore the words *"Prolapus Uteri"* in bold letters on the cover. The agent replaced the straightforward language with the more genteel mention of etiquette. The change in tactics irritated Will Gove, Charles Pinkham's brother-in-law. "I am afraid from what Arrie [Aroline Pinkham Gove, his wife] says that you have made a mistake on the 'Etiquette'," he wrote Pinkham. "If you have got the ordinary run of etiquette bosh in it, we ought all to be ashamed to put out such snobbish stuff, and it would need another medicine to go with it to cure people of sickness at the stomach."[26]

Pinkham ignored Gove's advice. The "Guide" ran split-page copy with descriptions of female diseases at the top and etiquette tips (such as advice on the proper dress for a garden party) at the bottom of the page. Yet the high tone set by Wetherald's emphasis on etiquette was undercut by the suggestive nature of the pamphlet's description in Pinkham advertising copy. Advertisements emphasized that the pamphlet contained "illustrations" and urged all "married women or women about to be married" to write immediately. Such language carried the same implications that the words "mailed in a plain brown envelope" conveyed to a later audience.

Elsewhere in Pinkham advertising Wetherald applied the same formula. The series of ads which ran from 1890 to 1894 indicated a distinct shift in style from the straightforward approach of the preceding decade. Overt references to female ailments diminished. Descriptive sales copy in newspaper ads hinted obliquely at menstrual pains, menopause, and prolapse by employing euphemisms like "that all gone feeling," "that nervous irritable feeling," and "pains, aches, and weakness." Instead of claiming that the Compound acted as a "Sure Cure for Prolapsus Uteri," Wetherald's copy read, "Lydia E. Pinkham's Vegetable Compound is the only Positive Cure and Legitimate Remedy for those peculiar weaknesses and ailments of our best female population."[27]

On the surface Wetherald's message seemed pitched to the genteel female—the upper-middle-class woman of leisure. Illustrations pictured well-dressed women, often in social settings which suggested considerable wealth. Yet Wetherald knew that the "best female population" rarely bought the Vegetable Compound. "People of the highest class employ physicians and seldom buy proprietary medicines," he conceded in an interview for the *Kansas City World.*[28] Although Wetherald believed that workingwomen constituted the chief market for the Pinkham medicine, he wrote only three out of a total of twenty-six ads in the 1890–94 series to speak directly to women worn out from working in stores, offices, factories, or at home. One of the ads pictured a seamstress collapsed at her worktable. "The Dress Is Finished. So Am I," ran the caption. The ad implied that the seamstress and the wealthy woman who employed her both suffered from female weakness, ". . . one under hot house culture, luxury and excitement, and the other through toil of necessity." Both women, the ad promised, could turn to the Vegetable Compound for help in meeting "the demands of society."[29]

By associating her problems with those of the rich woman, Wetherald attempted to flatter the working-girl. Subtly he reinforced his society's equation of female weakness with status. Here, as in the "Guide to Health and Etiquette," Wetherald employed a high-flown pitch to sell the Vegetable Compound to housewives and working women. Like Theodore Dreiser, whose Sister Carrie would later personify the woman Wetherald wished to reach, the Pinkhams' agent understood that shopgirls and overworked wives craved luxury and respectability, if not real, then vicarious. In the long run Will Gove was proved wrong. "Snobbish stuff" could and did sell the Vegetable Compound throughout the 1890's.

The image of Victorian womanhood that emerged from Wetherald's dramatized newspaper advertisements and in the copy of numerous guides for women emphasized all that was morbid and melodramatic in the genteel female. Women in Pinkham advertisements were worn out, nervous, irritable, and so sickly that they could neither work nor bear children. They dragged themselves about while in the background their husbands looked on with mingled despair and annoyance. Early advertising for the Compound had urged women to try the medicine for their own sakes; now copy hinted that the sick woman should take the Compound for her husband's sake. A woman's duty, one ad sermonized, consisted of making herself attractive to men. Good health became simply instrumental—something a woman needed to get and keep a man.

Increasingly, Wetherald portrayed women not as hapless victims ("immolated on the altar of mammon") but as complicitous in, if not responsible for, their own suffering. An 1893 Pinkham pamphlet caught the new spirit in its title, "Woman's Beauty, Peril, and Duty." Sickness, Pinkham copy proclaimed, "is often just as unnecessary as crime."[30] Woman's duty demanded that she follow the "laws of Nature" in order to preserve her health and the health of the race.

The assumption that any woman could be healthy by correctly perceiving and following the laws of nature struck at the popular belief that women were inherently invalids. But once good health became a woman's birthright, sickness became the badge of her personal failure. Pinkham advertisements held up the promise of good health to all women. At the same time they reproached women for bringing on their own suffering, either by neglect or by wanton violation of "Nature's laws."

To add to women's guilt, Pinkham ads distorted the meaning of health. "Normal" became synonymous with "painless" in Pinkham copy. Reasoning that "there is not an organ of the human body that, operating naturally, does not add to the vitality," one ad concluded that the natural function of a woman's reproductive organs should be entirely painless.[31] Another ad dismissed morning sickness, menstrual cramps, and pain during childbirth as "unnatural, unnecessary." Subtly Pinkham advertisements indicted women who suffered. When reality clashed with theory, as in the case of labor pains, Pinkham copy glossed the discrepancy by insisting, "Childbirth is a work of Nature and like all her works was intended to be readily an easily performed, but through one cause and another, Nature's kindly intentions have been over-ruled, and childbirth has become an ordeal through which women hesitate to pass."[32] Who or what had overruled "Nature's kindly intentions"? Implicitly the wording induced guilt and laid blame, in this case societal as well as individual. A later booklet made explicit the relationship between social change and physical deterioration in a tone reminiscent of the popular medical jere-miads of the 1880's. "It is when men and women forsake the 'Silent places' of Nature and crowd together in towns, forgetful of the ways of Nature," intoned the copy, "that they fall from the highest standards of physical welfare. . . ." The pamphlet con-cluded by reiterating what by now had become a standard line.

A perfect woman should experience no pain, but as such a woman is rare in modern civilization, the great majority suffer more or less pain during these natural functions—according to their distance from Nature's stan-dard of perfection.[33]

Wetherald's intent in these advertisements was threefold. First, he had to convince women that they *could* be well, a task he per-formed by confounding the woman-as-invalid stereotype of the nineteenth century. "Women," one ad observed, "appear to ac-cept pain as their natural destiny and systematically neglect any attempt at cure. . . ."[34] Pinkham copy insisted that ignorance, not natural frailty, lay at the root of women's ill health. Next Weth-erald had to argue that women *should* be well. Literature roman-ticized female invalidism. To counter its influence Wetherald in-sisted that men not only preferred healthy women, but were apt to abandon the invalid wife who took no action to cure herself. "A sickly, half-dead-and-alive woman, especially when she is the mother of a family, is a damper to all joyousness in the home, and a drag upon her husband."[35] Finally, Wetherald had to persuade women that Lydia E. Pinkham's Vegetable Compound offered the only effective remedy for female complaints. "Women should remember that a cure for all female diseases actually exists, and that cure is Lydia E. Pinkham's Vegetable Compound. Take no substitute," counseled one ad.[36]

Wetherald's natural desire to develop a wider market for the Compound by selling it to women who were not sick, but who could be induced to think they were, operated at cross-purposes from his need to convince women who were sick that they were not natural invalids beyond the reach of medicine. The interaction of these two conflicting strategies led to a tortured logic. At one moment Pinkham advertising insisted all women could be healthy, at the next it described in provocative detail general symptoms which supposedly pointed to womb trouble. The inconsistency did not trouble Wetherald. Where profit was concerned he subscribed to Emerson's dictum that foolish consistency was the hobgoblin of small minds. J.T. preferred to think big.

In spite of his opportunism, Wetherald did not lack conviction. A true Victorian, he shared his society's indignation at those "unnatural" women who ventured outside the sphere laid down for them by God, Nature, and, not coincidentally, by Victorian men. In newspaper articles written to promote the Compound, Wetherald, masquerading as "Dorothy Grey," discoursed on the woman question. He began by equating health with woman's traditional domestic role, a position which led him to view the woman who stepped out of that role as not only misguided, but sick. "Why is it that we cannot feel as our grandmothers did?" the author asked rhetorically. "The fact of the matter is that the trouble lies in our physical rather than our social condition."[37] At one stroke, by reducing suffrage to suffering, Wetherald put aside the question of equality for women.

I do wish that every woman who feels dissatisfied with her lot would realize that she is sick, and would take steps to make herself well. . . . Mrs. Pinkham's medicine will make a woman cheerful and happy, will make her more ready to meet the wishes of her husband, and once more will they realize the joys of home . . . woman will have found her true vocation—to be a devoted wife and loving mother.[38]

Women, according to Wetherald, were born for one purpose and one purpose alone—to become mothers. "If you never become a mother," he wrote, "it is in vain that you were born a woman."[39] Failure to bear children, he threatened obliquely, led to physical as well as emotional blight. He portrayed the childless woman as "disappointed, tinged with discord and probably ill-health."[40] His reverence for motherhood, which he viewed as a providential gift, made it unthinkable that a woman would deny what he chose to call the "normal privilege of womankind."[41] He preferred to ignore the ambiguous claims on the Compound label which could be interpreted as abortifacient (e.g., "dissolves and expels tumors, will cure irregularity, *etc.*.") and emphasize the way in which the Compound could "cure" barrenness and sterility. He reassured the childless wife, "have faith, persevere with the Compound . . . and remember that this simple, inexpensive course has brought the joys and jewels of motherhood to many who were as hopeless as you are."[42] His emphasis on the Vegetable Compound as a boon to motherhood presaged the later Pinkham claim, "There's a Baby in Every Bottle."

Wetherald must have experienced some discomfiture advertising Lydia E. Pinkham's Sanative Wash, an herbal douche. Throughout the nineteenth century, women douched to avoid pregnancy. The practice, recommended by Charles Knowlton in his pioneer work on birth control, *Fruits of Philosophy,* had become prevalent if not publicly acknowledged by the turn of the century.[43] Because it could be justified as a legitimate hygienic practice, douching provided a method of birth control which involved neither selling nor buying a device exclusively and overtly designed for contraceptive purposes. The Pinkham company, however, preferred to avoid the risk of prosecution under the Comstock laws, which prohibited the sale of contraceptive devices. Ads for the Sanative Wash referred the reader to a footnote which recommended Ruth Paxton's "Improved Fountain Syringe" available by mail for $1.50. The Paxton company existed on paper only. Sales of the fountain syringe brought in a revenue averaging $1,700 annually to the Pinkham company.[44]

Ads for the Sanative Wash recommended it for "falling or displacement of the uterus," for "ulceration or leucorrhea," and for personal hygiene. Wetherald emphasized the hygienic claims. In his Dorothy Grey column he advised daily douching as a means to "perfect cleanliness." He even promised that vaginal douching would eliminate menstrual cramps and clear up pimples. Such obsessive concern with female cleanliness led doctors who damned contraception to advise their patients to douche. As a result, many women who denied practicing birth control douched after intercourse because they felt dirty. Ads in 1903 for the Pinkham Sanative Wash urged women to "syringe the vagina night and morning," a regimen which practiced faithfully reduced the risk of pregnancy. Advertising for the Sanative Wash occupied so little space in Pinkham ad campaigns that it could easily be overlooked. Either the company preferred not to push the product, or realized that it would sell itself and the less said the better.[45]

Wetherald's Victorian sensibility warred perpetually with the exigencies of patent medicine advertising. Wetherald was not without social aspirations. A life member of Boston's Algonquin Club, he maintained a fashionable residence in Back Bay and a summer home on Beach Bluff, where he enjoyed the facilities of the exclusive Tedesco Country Club. Charles H. Pinkham, Jr., who served his apprenticeship in the advertising business under Wetherald, recalled J.T.'s dilemma:

Wetherald, the advertising man, wrote copy which sold Pinkham products; Wetherald, the club man, was often tempted to sacrifice "sell" for subtle innuendo. Every time a letter, criticizing the propriety of his advertising copy, was received in Lynn, Wetherald became disconsolate. . . .[46]

During the 1890's complaints came in so often that the company developed a stock response. In a typical letter written in 1897, a prominent woman criticized Compound advertising as "immoral" and appealed to the Pinkhams as "fathers, husbands, and men of honor" to discontinue the offensive ads. The company couched its reply in belligerent, self-righteous language:

We do not think any *pure minded* woman would find any cause to blush or be offended at any advertisement through which so much good is being done, and as for the menace to the youths of our country, I do not believe there is one in 500 who has ever been hurt morally by reading the ads that we print. . . . You say that you could get the signature of thousands against our ads. I think we could produce the signature of many more thousands of grateful women who had they not read our ads and had not our ads been printed *just as they were*, would today, either be in their graves or total wrecks. . . .[47]

Distressed by mounting criticism, Wetherald toned down offensive language and pictured happy, healthy women in his 1899 advertising campaign. "I do not believe in picturing pain and agony," he told an interviewer. "Give people the happier side of life—there is enough pain and agony anyway."[48] Typical of his new resolve were ads with the headings "Women Who Earn Their Living," which pictured a robust and smiling salesgirl; "Woman's Devotion to Home," which hinted only vaguely at "female ills"; and "A Happy Mother's Gratitude," a testimonial ad in which a Texas woman thanked Lydia Pinkham for the birth of a healthy baby girl. The 1899 series offered a marked contrast to earlier ads which featured the headlines "A Prisoner in Bed," "No Woman Can Be Happy," "That Bearing-Down Feeling," and "Mrs. Pinkham Talks About Ovaritis."

Pinkham sales dropped 4 per cent in 1899—the first sales decline in the decade since Wetherald had taken over the Pinkham account.[49] Dismayed, he assessed the results of his "health and happiness" campaign. The company had cut its advertising budget for 1899 some 6 per cent as an experiment to see if sales volume could be maintained at a lower advertising cost. Possibly the advertising cut prompted the decline in sales. Wetherald could not be sure. Anxious to reverse the downward trend, he returned to the "pain and agony" pitch, this time writing ads more sensational than his earlier copy. His brief flirtation with "genteel" copy had taught him that to advertise effectively he must sacrifice sensibility.

Wetherald concentrated on a hard-hitting campaign designed to stimulate sales. He doubled and tripled the size of his ads in 1900 and 1901, until they occupied as much as eighty inches on a newspaper page. Dramatic pictures of miserable, sick women dominated the advertisements. Drawing on a time-tested ad from the 1889 series, "I Am Not Well Enough to Work," he came dangerously close to parodying his earlier style in an illustration depicting a wretched-looking woman being turned out by a mustachioed employer. Smaller, single column ads ran under bleak boldface heads like "Women Who Have the Blues," "Facts For Sick Women," "Painful Periods," "I'm Simply All Worn Out," "A Hospital Case," and "Social Tragedy—Women Who Brave Death for Social Honors."

Sensationalism and prudery came together in the dominant theme of Wetherald's new campaign, "Only a Woman Can Understand A Woman's Ills." Pinkham advertising in the 1870's and 1880's had featured trademark ads with Lydia Pinkham's picture under the caption "Woman Can Sympathize With Woman." Wetherald seized on this theme and combined it with another Pinkham standby, "The Doctor Did No Good," to produce a message which played to the prudishness of his audience. An exaggerated sense of modesty and decorum informed the new Pinkham copy.

Do you want a strange man to hear all about your particular disease? Would you feel like sitting down by the side of a stranger and telling him all those sacred things which should be known only by women? It isn't natural for a woman to do this; it isn't like her, isn't in keeping with her finer sense of refinement.[50]

"Every *true* woman," one ad insinuated, "appreciates the horror of relating her private disorders to men." Not content to hint at horrors, Wetherald refurbished the Gothic archetype of the evil doctor with allusions "to the inquisitive and indelicate examinations of the physician [and] the experiments of the young practitioner."[51]

Nineteenth-century gynecology drew serious and justifiable criticism from those within as well as those outside of the medical profession. Often Pinkham advertisements voiced legitimate complaints against harsh local treatments and radical operative practices. Certainly, as one ad proclaimed, some doctors did have "a perfect craze for operations."[52] Women were well-advised that it was "not necessary to remove the ovaries when one is suffering from painful menstruation."[53] But Wetherald did not stop there. Pinkham copy exaggerated its case by arguing that no decent woman would consult a doctor or submit to surgery.

The false modesty encouraged by Pinkham advertisements reached ludicrous proportions. Ads which equated true womanhood with the sort of prudishness which kept women from doctors made it necessary for Wetherald to reassure the women who wrote to Mrs. Pinkham, "Men NEVER See Your Letters." "No Boys Around," began one ad with a hushed urgency. "All letters are received, opened, read and answered by women only."[54]

The company's exaggerated assurances provoked at least one reader to satire:

The cuts in the Pinkham booklet present to us an Adamless Eden. The very office boy is a girl. The bird in the weathervane is unmistakably a hen. . . . It is unfortunately necessary to hire a few men in the bottling room, but they have all outgrown the riotous passions of youth, and I am told that they are forbidden, on pain of death, to read the labels. I do not believe the story that, in her eagerness to respect the modesty of her afflicted sex, Mrs. Pinkham will not ship goods on trains that carry the mails.[55]

Lydia Pinkham would have appreciated the joke. The sensational prudery of Wetherald's advertising distorted her message. Her advice to women had been candid and fresh. She had urged them to break stifling traditional patterns—to get more exercise, to bathe more often, to dress sensibly. Her distrust of the medical profession came from her conviction that physicians over-treated women with harsh drugs and radical surgery. She advised women to leave doctors alone not because she feared for their modesty, but because she feared for their lives. Wetherald took her ideas and twisted them into the clichés of Victorian gentility. Pinkham advertising reflected the curious blending of prurience and prudery characteristic of Victorian culture. The success Wetherald enjoyed testified to his peculiar ability to absorb and reproduce the attitudes of his society. As a Victorian gentleman, he subscribed to the meretricious gentility of his age. As a patent medicine man, he learned how to make that gentility pay off in advertisements which boosted Pinkham sales to a million and a half dollars a year.

"Up to our Necks in Trouble"

"We are up to our necks in trouble," the Pinkham business manager confided early in 1900.[1] As the year wore on the statement assumed the ring of prophecy. The sudden reverses which baffled the company in 1900 reverberated throughout the decade. Success had caught up with the Pinkhams. The spectacular growth of the company during the 1890's had obscured fundamental problems both within the company and in the patent medicine business as a whole. Discords within the family and increasing pressure for the regulation of patent medicines—problems easily overlooked in the expansive atmosphere of the late nineteenth century—became paramount in the opening years of the twentieth.

With the year 1900 barely underway, the company faced trouble on three fronts. The most serious threat came from a bill before the Massachusetts legislature which would require patent medicine makers to divulge their secret ingredients by printing the contents of their medicines on the labels. Similar bills had been introduced sporadically throughout the 1880's and 1890's in state legislatures and in the Congress. Repeatedly patent medicine interests in alliance with newspapers dependent on patent medicine advertising had worked behind the scenes to prevent passage of legislation inimical to the drug companies.

To counteract the threat of regulation, the patent medicine men, under the leadership of the Pinkhams' old friend Charles N. Crittenton, had formed the Proprietary Medicine Manufacturers and Dealers Association in 1881. When Congress proposed a 4 per cent tax on patent medicines to raise money for the Spanish American War, the Proprietary Association succeeded in limiting the tax to 2½ per cent. After the war, the trade association turned its attention to combating efforts at regulation. Whenever a restrictive measure threatened to come before a state legislature or the Congress, lobbyists from the Proprietary Association acted quickly and decisively to prevent its passage.[2]

Charles Pinkham at first viewed the efforts at regulation as unpleasant annoyances. But by the late 1890's annoyance turned into alarm. Year after year the swarm of bills persisted and grew larger. No sooner would a bill be defeated in one state than another would appear in a different legislature. Congratulating a Minnesota druggist on the defeat of a patent medicine bill in his state, Pinkham wrote, "Almost every state has had the same fight this year. It keeps me pretty busy looking after such Bills."[3]

An early and active member of the Proprietary Association, Charles recognized the advantages of organization and soon joined other prominent New England proprietors (among them J. C. Ayer of Ayer's Sarsaparilla and Dr. F. E. Greene of Greene's Nervura) in forming the Article Club, an organization designed to coordinate marketing and lobbying tactics on the regional level. At monthly meetings the New England manufacturers planned strategy. The Massachusetts bill of 1900 provided the first test of strength.

In the midst of the legislative battle, a second blow fell on the company. Philadelphia police arrested eight men hired to hand out Pinkham pamphlets and jailed them on the charge of distributing "obscene literature." In the 1870's Pennsylvania had passed its own version of the federal Comstock law, designed to ban "obscene, lewd, or lascivious" printed matter as well as "medicines or articles" intended for preventing conception or procuring abortion. In the eyes of some of Philadelphia's strict matrons, the Pinkham literature with its reference to prolapsed uterus, menstrual disorders, and leucorrhea violated the spirit of the purity law. At their bidding the mayor acted to suppress the offending pamphlet.[4]

Charles Pinkham responded by sending Wetherald to Philadelphia to negotiate the release of the men. The agent handled the situation with his usual aplomb. Anxious to avoid a court battle, he moved behind the scenes, using his influence with the local newspapers to get the charges dismissed. A tactful reminder of the thousands of dollars the Pinkham company spent on newspaper advertising proved sufficient to enlist the aid of Philadelphia publishers in the fight against city hall. Publicly Wetherald defended the medicine, arguing that it was not intended or advertised as a contraceptive. Nor was Pinkham literature obscene. The plain language used to describe symptoms was necessary "in order to make the different women, many of whom are ignorant, realize and understand just what their illness is. . . ."[5] The combination of public relations and pressure worked. Not long after Wetherald's arrival, Philadelphia papers announced the mayor's decision to release the distributors and drop the case.

When, less than a month later, another arrest occurred in Wilkes-Barre, the Pinkham company began to suspect an organized campaign against them in Pennsylvania. "It seems strange that after all these years that we have been putting out just this very same kind of manuscript, that they have just come to the conclusion that it is obscene," commented Laura Hunt, the company's business manager. "Surely there is a moral and an immoral side to this question and it seems very easy for one to see that we have been on the moral side of this for a great number of years."[6] Pennsylvania authorities evidently disagreed. Reluctantly, Charles Pinkham decided to discontinue pamphlet distribution in the state.

At the same time that the company found itself on the wrong side of the law in Pennsylvania, Charles Pinkham was working with Pinkerton detectives and police to track down drug counterfeiters operating in the state. Patent medicine counterfeiters stole or duplicated the bottles of popular remedies, filled them with some cheap concoction (usually stale beer), and sold them in phony wrappers to druggists and consumers. Proprietors detested counterfeiters, who not only lost them money, but jeopardized trade by driving away customers put off by the inferior preparations carrying the well-known labels. That the practice flourished, in spite of elaborate precautions, testified to the popularity of patent medicines and the profits to be made.

In February of 1900, an alert druggist in Scranton spotted several dozen counterfeit bottles of the Vegetable Compound. He warned the company of the counterfeiter, a man named Howells, who sold bogus bottles of Peruna and Paine's Celery Compound in additon to the Pinkham medicine. When Samuel B. Hartman of Peruna called in Pinkerton detectives, Charles Pinkham agreed to collaborate in the investigation and to share expenses. After a three-month search, Pinkerton agents tracked the counterfeiters to Cleveland where they were arrested, fined $350, and sentenced to eighteen months in prison. Pinkham's game of cops-and-robbers proved as expensive as it had been exciting. The company's share of the Pinkerton tab came to over $7,000.[7]

These three incidents which vexed the company during the early months of 1900 caused little serious damage. Pressure from the proprietary interests stymied the Massachusetts patent medicine bill; Wetherald's influence kept the company out of court on the obscenity charges; and Pinkerton detectives efficiently landed the drug counterfeiters behind bars. But in the aggregate, the unrelated events took on the character of an imbroglio in which the company saw itself pitted against hostile forces on all sides. Midyear found Charles Pinkham engaged in a fight with wholesale distributors who violated their contracts by selling to cut-rate outlets and by substituting their own private preparations for the Vegetable Compound. To make matters worse, sales fell for the second straight year.

Illness and death in the Pinkham family added to the nightmare quality of the year. Calamity stalked the Pinkhams in 1900. January found the eldest boy, Arthur, home from college with his leg in a cast. A month later one-year-old Daniel nearly died of pneumonia. Jennie Pinkham, who was pregnant with her sixth child, wore herself out nursing the sick boys. Charles worried that she might lose the baby and in March he took her to Florida for a rest. While they were away, Jennie's sister died following an attack of appendicitis. The couple cut short their vacation to return for the funeral. A few months later Jennie Pinkham's father died unexpectedly. By now the Pinkhams were exhausted and distraught.[8]

The strain of business and family worries began to take its toll on Charles Pinkham. For years he had suffered from rheumatism. In April the pain became so severe that he could not sit at his desk without bolstering himself with pillows. The doctor diagnosed his condition as "severe rheumatism in his back, caused by weak heart action brought on by heavy smoking," and recommended rest. When Charlie failed to improve, the physician grew alarmed and insisted on a trip to a health resort in Michigan. Jennie had just given birth to a baby boy, named Charles Jr., and Pinkham was reluctant to leave. But in September, at the urging of his physician, he headed west to take the healing baths. In spite of the treatment, his condition steadily worsened. By the time he returned home, his legs were paralyzed. Doctors attributed his suffering to "anemia of the brain" caused by overwork. In fact Pinkham was dying of kidney disease—a sad irony in light of the Compound's claims to cure all kidney troubles. During the last days of his life, he was wracked by paroxysms so strong it required three men to hold him in his bed. On November 10, 1900, he died at the age of fifty-six.[9]

For the Lydia E. Pinkham Medicine Company, Charles Pinkham's death came as the tragic climax to what had been on every level an unpropitious year. "Everything looks very dark and dreary ahead," wrote Laura Hunt. "It almost seems as though we could not do without him."[10] Pinkham had been the backbone of the business. In the early years of the company he had played a secondary role compared to Dan and Will. But when the burden of the business fell on his shoulders after their deaths in 1881, he showed he was both resourceful and responsible. He guided the company through the difficult days of the 1880's and proved more than a match for the company's crafty agent, H. P. Hubbard. In the nineties, thanks to Wetherald's effective advertising, he brought the business to new heights. In the face of mounting difficulties, the company badly missed his experienced leadership.

To add to the company's problems, Pinkham's death triggered a power struggle within the family which raged intermittently for the next half-century, several times threatening to tear the business apart. For years a family feud had been brewing between the Pinkhams and the Goves. The Gove side of the family, Aroline Pinkham Gove and her husband Will, had little to do with the business. Will Gove, who had been Will Pinkham's best friend, married Aroline in 1882 and the couple moved to Salem where Gove set up a law practice. Charlie Pinkham remained in Lynn and ran the company single-handedly. The Goves, more from inclination than oversight, shared only in the profits.

The inequity of the situation had not escaped Charlie, who complained that he was making his sister "immensely rich" and getting "nearly nothing" for his services. The Goves each made $1,000 a year for their minimal duties as secretary and treasurer of the corporation. As president and general manager, Charles Pinkham made only $5,000. In 1896 he wrote Aroline a long letter, spelling out his grievances and asking for a salary increase. Aroline responded in a fit of pique. Charlie's salary, she insisted, was "good pay." He could look to dividends "for the big money." She accused him of "putting on airs" and trying to take more credit than he deserved for the company's success. As for the complaint that the Goves contributed little to the business, she responded, "The fact is you preferred to do everything yourself as if there was nobody else to be consulted."[11] Charlie Pinkham had stirred up a hornet's nest. In the end, he got his raise, but only at the cost of creating bad blood between the families. Aroline Gove was not the kind of woman to forgive a slight.

After Charles Pinkham's death in 1900, Will and Aroline Gove moved quickly to seize control of the company and drive out the Pinkham heirs. However precipitous, their action was perfectly legal. Stock in the corporation had been divided equally between Charles and his sister at the time of the company's formation in

1882. Each held fifty-six shares. Aroline had transferred one share to her husband so that he might qualify to sit as secretary on the Broad of Directors. Charlie's death left the Goves in control of the Board. They promptly called a directors' meeting and elected Will Gove president and general manager of the company. Then they drove to the Lynn factory to announce their takeover. Arthur Pinkham, Charles' eldest son home from Brown for his father's funeral, recalled his aunt's words as she announced the coup:

For years your father ran this business and I suppose you think you are to run it now. Mr. Gove is the new President and General Manager and will remain so for a good many years to come. You, Arthur, will never have anything to do with this business; neither will your mother.[12]

Mrs. Gove spoke precipitously, as she often did. The Pinkhams proved tougher adversaries than she anticipated.

Charles Pinkham's death left Jennie Pinkham a widow with six children, one barely two months old. Grief-stricken and in poor health, she seemed no match for the Goves. In an act of gratuitous insolence, Aroline and Will Gove put up for sale a stable Charles Pinkham had maintained on company property. Horses had been Pinkham's one vanity. Ever since his youth he had coveted fast horses and fancy rigs. In a curt note to Jennie, Will Gove announced that he was selling the stable and asked if she wished to buy any of the items for sale. When she objected to the prices Gove quoted for the carriages and horses which her husband had considered his property, Gove replied that he had found them bargains and had purchased most of the items himself.[13] The spite Aroline and her husband displayed left Jennie Pinkham helpless and confused. In desperation she wired Arthur to leave school and come home.

It was not the first time a Pinkham had given up college plans to look after the business. Like Will Pinkham, Arthur had dreamed of attending Harvard. His ambition since childhood had been to become a doctor, and he had planned to enroll in Harvard's medical school after his graduation from Brown. When his mother's urgent summons came in the middle of his junior year, he swallowed whatever remorse he might have felt and headed home to take care of the family.

Arthur took control of the situation with a decisiveness remarkable in a twenty-one-year .old. He realized that the law offered the Pinkhams no recourse. A stockholders' meeting would only result in stalemate; each faction controlled the same number of shares. To wrestle control from the Goves he would have to force them to negotiate.

The Pinkhams had two important assets—Mrs. Pinkham's name and Charles Pinkham's reputation in the patent medicine industry. Arthur determined to use both as leverage against the Goves. He ordered the Lynn postmaster to deliver the thousands of letters addressed to "Mrs. Pinkham" to his mother and not to the Pinkham factory. Then, in a brilliant move, he went into competition with the company his father had spent years building. During summer vacations, Arthur had worked around the factory, where he learned the manufacturing process. With the help of loyal Pinkham employees who had been fired when the Goves took over, Arthur set up a "laboratory" in his backyard and began to manufacture the Vegetable Compound. Copyright protected the trademark, not the formula of the medicine. Arthur could legally duplicate the Pinkham Compound as long as he gave it a different name. Jennie Pinkham took the first letter of the names of each of her children and arrived at the name "Delmac". Early in 1901 Arthur ran a full-page ad in the local paper introducing the Delmac Liver Regulator. Its label featured a picture of Charles Pinkham, known by druggists across the country as the manufacturer of the Pinkham medicine. As a final touch, Jennie Pinkham wrote an enthusiastic endorsement which she signed "Mrs. Pinkham."[14]

In February, Arthur called on Will Gove and invited him to sample the Delmac Regulator. One taste and Gove capitulated; the medicine was indistinguishable from the Vegetable Compound. After several weeks of negotiations in which Wetherald acted as go-between, the Pinkhams and the Goves reached an agreement. In return for the written promise that she would refrain from marketing products which competed with those manufactured by the Lydia E. Pinkham Medicine Company, Jennie Pinkham gained a seat on the Board of Directors. She also became manager of the correspondence department with a salary of $5,000. The newly constituted Board then elected Arthur Pinkham vice-president and secretary of the company. Arthur's strategy had worked; four months after the Goves' takeover, the Pinkhams had regained a voice in the company's management.[15]

During the next decade the business foundered. Will Gove turned out to be a poor administrator. A Harvard-trained lawyer, Gove took little interest in the company and spent only a few days a week at the Lynn plant. Increasingly the burden of the company's management fell to Wetherald. In 1900 he had left the Pettingill advertising agency (which failed shortly after) to become the Pinkham company's general advertising agent under a ten year contract at a yearly salary of $15,000. The contract, signed before Charles Pinkham died, guaranteed a continuity badly needed when the Goves took over.[16]

The years from 1899 to 1910 were anxious ones for Wetherald. Sales suffered a protracted decline. Try as he might, J. T. could not reverse the trend even by spending over half of the company's gross sales revenue on advertising. In 1900 he spent $770,250 (63 per cent of sales) on his advertising campaign. Sales dropped again. In the 1890's each increase in advertising expenditure had resulted in a comparable sales increase. Now Wetherald found it necessary to reduce advertising spending to keep it in line with decreasing sales. Between 1903 and 1908 sales fell off by 68 per cent, or more than $430,000.[17] Poor management alone could not explain the decline, nor could advertising content, which remained consistent with patterns established in the 1890's. Wetherald had only to pick up *The Ladies' Home Journal* or *Collier's Weekly* to find the explanation.

Cyrus Curtis, the crusty publisher of *The Ladies' Home Journal*, disapproved of patent medicines, a distaste his editor and son-in-law, Edward Bok, shared. Both men aimed to raise the public's standards, to make *The Ladies' Home Journal*, in Bok's words, "a magazine of uplift and inspiration . . . that would give light and leading in the woman's world."[18] In 1892 Curtis closed the pages

Yours for Health
Lydia E. Pinkham

The Pinkham house, *right,* and factory in 1879.
Lydia is standing in the doorway.

Schlesinger Library, Radcliffe College

Isaac Pinkham, Lydia's husband.

Lydia Pinkham, age twenty-five, with baby Charles.

Schlesinger Library, Radcliffe College

Dan Pinkham dreamed of a poster to span the Brooklyn Bridge.

LYDIA E. PINKHAM'S VEGETABLE COMPOUND.

THE GREAT EAST RIVER SUSPENSION BRIDGE.
CONNECTING THE CITIES OF NEW YORK & BROOKLYN.

Daniel Rogers
Pinkham, the hustler
of the family.

William H. Pinkham.
He gambled on
newspaper advertising.

The 1879 photograph that became the trademark.

Lydia's grandchildren appeared on this 1889 trade card. *Right,* another example of early Pinkham advertising.

A FEARFUL TRAGEDY.

A Clergyman of Stratford, Conn.,

Killed by His Own Wife.

Insanity Brought on by 16 Years of Suffering With

Female Complaints the Cause.

Lydia E. Pinkham's Vegetable Compound,

The Sure Cure for These Complaints,

Would Have Prevented the Direful Deed.

"HOW OLD I LOOK, AND NOT YET THIRTY!"
Many women fade early, simply because
they do not take proper care of themselves.
Whirled along in the excitements of fashionable life, they overlook those minor ailments
that, if not checked in time, will rob them of
Health and Beauty. At the first symptom
of vital weakness, use

LYDIA E. PINKHAM'S Vegetable Compound

The roses will return to your cheeks, sallow
looks depart, spirits brighten, your step become firm, and back and head aches will be
known no more. Your appetite will gain,
and the food nourish you. The Compound is
sold by all Druggists as a **standard article,**
or sent by mail, in form of Pills or Lozenges,
on receipt of $1.00.

For the cure of **Kidney** Complaints,
either sex, the Compound has no rival.

Send two 2-cent stamps for Mrs. Pinkham's
beautiful 88-page illustrated book, entitled
" GUIDE TO HEALTH AND ETIQUETTE."
It contains a volume of valuable information.
It has saved lives, and may save yours.

Lydia E. Pinkham Med. Co., Lynn, Mass.

An advertisement from 1890.

Schlesinger Library, Radcliffe College

Schlesinger Library, Radcliffe College

Suffering women look to Mrs. Pinkham in these ads from the turn of the century.

Schlesinger Library, Radcliffe College

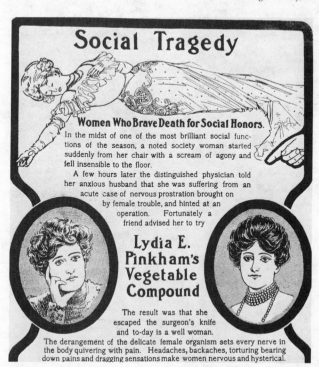

An early label for the Vegetable Compound, *left*, enumerated female complaints. A later bottle listed only the ingredients.

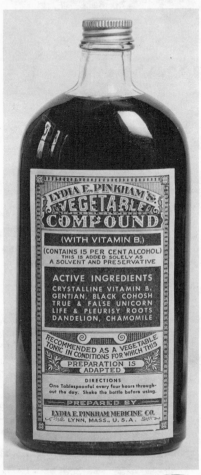

"The Touch." An illustration from a nineteenth-century gynecological

Charles Hacker Pinkham ran the business
after the untimely deaths of Will and Dan.

Jennie Pinkham, his wife.

The new Pinkham factory, 1886.

James T. Wetherald, Pinkham adman who exploited the pain-and-agony pitch.

Aroline Pinkham Gove seized control of the company in 1900.

, cure the d,
blame the woman,
embarrassing to detail some
.ptoms of her suffering, even to ...
.mily physician.

It was for this reason that years ago Mrs. Pinkham, at Lynn, Mass., determined to step in and help her sex. Having had considerable experience in treating female ills with her Vegetable Compound, she encouraged the women of America to write to her for advice in regard to their complaints, and being a woman, it was easy for her ailing sisters to pour into her ears every detail of their suffering. * * * * * *

No physician in the world has had such a training, or has such an amount of information at hand to assist in the treatment of all kinds of female ills.

This, therefore, is the reason why Mrs. Pinkham, in her laboratory at Lynn, Mass., is able to do more for the ailing women of America than the family physician. Any woman, therefore, is responsible for her own suffering who will not take the trouble to write to Mrs. Pinkham for advice.

This Advertisement of "Lydia Pinkham's Vegetable Compound" was Printed on June 27, 1905 (About Two Months Ago).

MRS. LYDIA E. PINKHAM'S MONUMENT in Pine Grove Cemetery, Lynn, Massachusetts. Mrs. Pinkham Died May 17, 1883 (22 Years Ago).

The "Tombstone Photo" as it appeared in *The Ladies Home Journal*, 1905. The question was, who answered the mail?

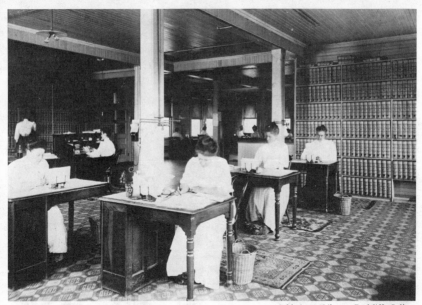

The correspondence room, 1907. "Men NEVER see your letters." The files along the wall contained thousands of letters asking Lydia Pinkham for advice.

Arthur Pinkham, Aroline's nephew, left college to fight the Goves.

Will Gove, president of the company from 1900 to 1920, proved to be a poor administrator.

Lydia Pinkham Gove in 1926. She was the first commercial passenger to fly coast-to-coast.

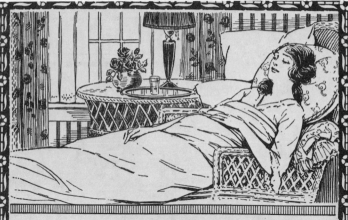

Nervous Breakdown

"I am so nervous it seems as though I should fly"—"My nerves are all on edge"—"I wish I were dead." How often have we heard these expressions or others quite as extravagant from some loved one who has been brought to this state by some female trouble which has slowly developed until the nerves can no longer stand up under it. No woman should allow herself to drift into this condition without giving that good old-fashioned root and herb remedy Lydia E. Pinkham's Vegetable Compound a trial.

Read the Letters of These Two Women.

North East, Md.—"I was in ill health four or five years and doctored with one doctor after another but none helped me. I was irregular and had such terrible pain in my back, lower part of my body and down each side that I had to go to bed three or four days every month. I was very nervous, tired, could not sleep and could not eat without getting sick. A friend asked me to take Lydia E. Pinkham's Vegetable Compound and I am sorry I did not take it sooner for it has helped me wonderfully. I don't have to go to bed with the pain, can eat without being sick and have more strength. I recommend your medicine and you are at liberty to publish my testimonial."—ELIZABETH WEAVER, R. R. 2, North East, Md.

Minneapolis, Minn.—"I was run down and nervous, could not rest at night and was more tired in the morning than when I went to bed. I have two children, the youngest three months old and it was drudgery to care for them as I felt so irritable and generally worn out. From lack of rest and appetite my baby did not get enough nourishment from my milk so I started to give him two bottle feedings a day. After taking three bottles of Lydia E. Pinkham's Vegetable Compound I felt like a new woman, full of life and energy. It is a pleasure to care for my children, and I am very happy with them and feel fine. I nurse my baby exclusively again, and can't say too much for your medicine."—Mrs. A. L. MILLER, 2633 E. 24th St., Minneapolis, Minn.

Nervous, Ailing Women Should Rely Upon

Lydia E. Pinkham's Vegetable Compound

LYDIA E. PINKHAM MEDICINE CO., LYNN, MASS.

A testimonial advertisement, 1920.

"THE WHISPERING CAMPAIGN THAT NEVER STOPPED"

One woman tells another how to go "Smiling Through" with
Lydia E. Pinkham's Vegetable Compound

Pinkham advertisements from the 1930's and 1940's.

Schlesinger Library, Radcliffe College

The fictitious Ann Pinkham replaced Lydia in this 1952 pamphlet, *right*.

A Woman's Guide to Health

By ANN PINKHAM

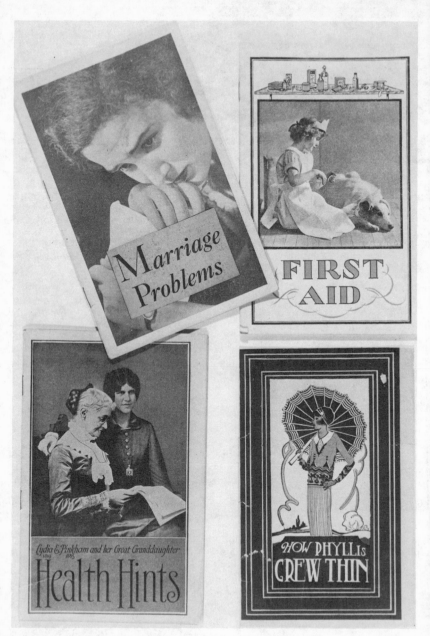

Pinkham pamphlets over the years.

Arthur Pinkham quaffing the Vegetable Compound. He sampled each new batch.

Cooper Laboratories bought the company in 1968 and moved the plant to Puerto Rico.

of the *Journal* to patent medicine advertising. "Our first consideration," he wrote, "is the protection and welfare of our readers."[19] The publisher's paternalism found expression in the didactic writings of his editor, who throughout the nineties took occasional jabs at patent medicines. Bok found it ironic that women active in the Women's Christian Temperance Union habitually doctored with alcoholic nostrums, and he told them so.

In 1903 *The Ladies' Home Journal* accelerated its attack on the patent medicine industry. The previous year Dr. Harvey Washington Wiley, chief chemist in the Department of Agriculture's Bureau of Chemistry, had captured national attention with his dramatic experiments with the effects of food adulteration. Thousands of Americans followed in the popular press the trials of Wiley's "Poison Squad," twelve young men who volunteered to test on their systems the effects of the preservatives and adulterants in everything from milk to catsup.[20]

The House of Representatives reacted to the publicity by passing a food and drug bill for the first time. Only the strongest pressure from lobbyists kept the bill from the floor of the Senate. On the state level, North Dakota, at the prompting of state chemist Edwin Ladd, wrote into law a drug measure which forced patent medicines to list their ingredients on the label. Rather than give up their secrets, the medicine makers with the support of the Proprietary Association, boycotted the state. The increasing agitation for food and drug regulation made patent medicine exposés good copy.[21]

Bok heated up his campaign against patent medicines in 1904 after Dr. Ray Vaughn Pierce of Buffalo, Lydia Pinkham's chief competitor, sued *The Ladies' Home Journal* for libel. Bok had printed what purported to be the secret formulas of twenty-seven nostrums. Dr. Pierce's Favorite Prescription (a female remedy), he listed as containing alcohol, opium, and digitalis. Pierce promptly sued, claiming that the medicine contained neither opium nor digitalis. Chemical analysis supported Pierce's contention. Bok had carelessly printed ingredients supplied by an outdated analysis made by the Massachusetts Board of Health. In the interim Pierce had changed his formula. Faced with a $200,000 libel suit, the editor hoped to buttress his defense by proving that Pierce's medicine had formerly contained the dangerous ingredients. He engaged Mark Sullivan, a young Harvard lawyer turned journalist, to track down an old bottle of the Pierce Prescription. Sullivan failed to produce the evidence Bok needed and the magazine lost its suit. An unsympathetic jury awarded Pierce only $16,000 of the $200,000 he had demanded. Bok emerged from the fray the moral victor, his appetite for exposé whetted. Sullivan's search, although it had not unearthed the bottle Bok needed, had yielded enough material on the patent medicine business for a half-dozen stories. Eagerly Bok printed them.[22]

"How the Private Confidences of Women are Laughed At," "Why Patent Medicines are Dangerous," "The Inside Story of a Sham," "How the Game of Medicine Advice is Worked," and other titles equally sensational appeared regularly in *The Ladies' Home Journal* from 1904 to 1907. The magazine guided readers through the sordid world of phony doctors, adulterated drugs, faked testimonials, and quack hospitals. Working undercover for Bok, Sullivan had advertised in the want ads for men experienced in the drug business. When they responded, eager for work, they bragged to him of the tricks of the trade. Sullivan learned the formulas, the business practices, and the lobbying tactics of the patent medicine industry.

He found in the minutes of the Proprietary Association mention of the notorious "red clause" used to muzzle the press and turn the papers into a lobby against patent medicine regulation. Patent medicine proprietors, who spent an estimated $40 million a year on advertising, wrote into their contracts with newspapers the clause, "It is hereby agreed that should your state, or the United States Government pass any law that would interfere with or restrict the sale of proprietary medicines, this contract shall become void." The insertion of the clause had been customary procedure at the Pinkham company since the 1890's. Other patent medicine companies, adopting the practice, called the newspapers' attention to the clause by printing it in red ink. The J. C. Ayer Company elaborated on the scheme by reserving the right to cancel advertising in the event "any material detrimental to the J.

C. Ayer Company's interest is permitted to appear in the reading columns or elsewhere in the paper." Frank J. Cheney, the president of the Proprietary Association, frankly acknowledged the benefits of the red clause and recommended it to the members of the patent medicine industry. The strategy, he noted, saved the organization a good deal of money by shifting the burden of lobbying from the proprietors to the papers.[23]

Sullivan's exposé of the collusion between the Proprietary Association and the press, which he titled, "The Patent Medicine Conspiracy Against Freedom of the Press," Bok thought "too legalistic" for *The Ladies' Home Journal.* He recommended it to Norman Hapgood, editor of *Collier's Weekly,* who bought the piece for $700 and incorporated it into his magazine's attack on the patent medicine business, a hard-hitting series entitled "The Great American Fraud."[24]

The first of ten scathing articles written by Samuel Hopkins Adams for "The Great American Fraud" series appeared in *Collier's* in October, 1905. Adams combined a scientific background with his skills as a crime reporter to produce a masterpiece of muckraking journalism. "Gullible America," he announced in his introduction, "will spend this year some seventy-five millions of dollars in the purchase of patent medicines. In consideration of this sum it will swallow huge quantities of alcohol, an appalling amount of opiates and narcotics, a wide assortment of varied drugs ranging from powerful and dangerous heart depressants to insidious liver stimulants; and, far in excess of all other ingredients, undiluted fraud."[25] In support of the assertion he mustered hard evidence—chemical analyses which revealed the dangerous drugs opium and acetanilide in so-called harmless preparations; death certificates which showed that testimonial writers died from the diseases they claimed patent medicines had cured; contracts between proprietors and newspapers which indicated their collusion in the fight against food and drug legislation. Adams named names, cited frauds, and quoted formulas with a fearlessness that came from careful research. Caught in the light of his harsh scrutiny, the patent medicine makers squirmed uncomfortably. Of the 264 medicine companies and individuals attacked, only two initiated libel suits. Unwilling to take the magazine to court, proprietors showed their muscle by withdrawing advertisements. "We spoke out about patent medicines," reported *Collier's,* "and dropped $80,000 in a year."[26]

The steady barrage of criticism leveled at patent medicines hurt business. Pinkham sales revenue fell as much as $100,000 a year at the height of the campaign against the "Great American Fraud." The company proved an easy target for the muckrakers. When Mark Sullivan learned that Lydia Pinkham had been dead for more than twenty years, he found a friend with a camera and headed for the Pine Grove Cemetery in Lynn. *The Ladies' Home Journal* ran the photograph of Lydia Pinkham's tombstone next to a reproduction of a current Pinkham ad, which read: "Mrs. Pinkham, in her laboratory at Lynn, Mass., is able to do more for the ailing women of America than the family physician. Any woman, therefore, is responsible for her own suffering who will not take the trouble to write to Mrs. Pinkham for advice." Bok called the simple juxtaposition "one of the most effective pieces of copy that the magazine used in the campaign."[27]

Sullivan's photograph destroyed the "Write Mrs. Pinkham" ruse which Wetherald had so elaborately constructed. The company responded in tones of wounded innocence that it had intended no deception, that it had published several advertisements indicating that the Mrs. Pinkham who answered women's letters was not Lydia Pinkham, but her daughter-in-law. The explanation fell flat. Too many women had trusted their letters to the kindly face on the label. Tricked into believing that they wrote to Lydia Pinkham, they were no less angry when they learned that another Mrs. Pinkham answered their mail. If, indeed, she did. Samuel Hopkins Adams penetrated the correspondence room and reported accurately that paid typists answered the mail by filling out form letters. Of Jennie Pinkham, who lent her name to the company's strategy, he wrote: "What sense of shame she might be supposed to suffer in the perpetration of an obvious and public fraud is presumably salved by the large profits of the business.[28]

Publicly discredited, the company was thrown on the defensive.

Sullivan's tombstone photograph, which caught the company squarely in one deception, led many people to reason that it must be guilty of others. The muckrakers did not make fine distinctions, nor did they encourage their readers to do so. In an article entitled "How the Private Confidences of Women Are Laughed At," Edward Bok alleged in boldface type, "NOT ONE IN A THOUSAND OF THESE LETTERS EVER REACHES THE EYES OF THE 'DOCTOR' TO WHOM THEY ARE ADDRESSED." Instead, they passed through the hands of "young men and girls" who enjoyed the "spicy" bits and sometimes took the letters home to show to friends and families for amusement. Bok went on to say that when the patent medicine company finished with the letters, they were frequently sold for a few cents a name to firms in other lines of business to add to their mailing lists. Not just the names and addresses, but the letters themselves, "with all their private contents," were sold. "This is the true story of the 'sacredly confidential' way in which these private letters from women are treated!" Bok concluded.[29]

The accusation made Pinkham ads, with their promise that "Mrs. Pinkham regards every letter as a Sacred Message," appear ludicrous. When the Pinkham company began reassuring women in 1900 that "men never see your letters," their copy inadvertently anticipated, possibly encouraged, the charges Bok later made. A Pinkham booklet in 1901 asked rhetorically. "[H]ow would it be when some boy opens the letters, steals time to read a few before they are handed to some other boy-clerk to distribute (and probably read) around the office. . . . It makes one almost indignant to think how light and trivial these serious matters are so often regarded."[30] The Pinkham company, the ad continued, was never guilty of such outrages.

Bok's rhetoric virtually duplicated Wetherald's. He drew the same picture, stating it as fact, and concluded with equal indignation: "Pretty story, is it not? The story of a business that thrives on violating the most sacred confidences of girls and women—confidences which a man with even a pretense of decency or spark of manhood would respect as he would his mother's name or his wife's honor, yet here are made capital of, ridiculed and laughed at as 'spicy' reading!"[31]

Few readers stopped to ask if the practices Bok attributed to the anonymous "Doctor" accurately described Pinkham policy. In fact they did not. Mark Sullivan, who gathered the facts for the story, later exonerated the company in his autobiography. Describing the Pinkham company as a firm "which had altogether higher standards than much of the industry," he stated, "It solicited letters but did not sell them."[32] Sullivan was only half right. A letter dealer inquiring after Pinkham correspondence in 1896 received the response, "We have never sold a copy of any names received by us and should not sell a copy of the original letters that we receive asking for advice." But, the letter continued, "We are receiving about two hundred letters daily from women asking for a book which we issue. These names we feel at liberty to sell. . . . How much are you willing to pay per 1,000?"[33]

In "The Inside Story of a Sham," a companion piece to Bok's article, Sullivan explored the way in which patent medicines obtained testimonial endorsements. He conceded that companies rarely paid cash to testimonial writers. The common practice was to hire a "testimonial broker" who procured the letters at a fixed rate. The broker Sullivan interviewed charged seventy-five dollars for the endorsement of a Senator, forty dollars for a Congressman. Women could be induced to lend their names for the cost of a photograph or an allowance for answering letters of inquiry.[34]

Testimonials made up the stock-in-trade of Pinkham advertising. Appended to every ad was a letter praising the effectiveness of the Vegetable Compound. "We never pay for our testimonial letters," the company insisted. "Most of our friends are so grateful for the good that they have received by the use of the medicines, that they are glad to tell their friends of it."[35] Once again the company stretched the truth. A few women who drove hard bargains did receive cash payments for their testimonials. And in addition to the many who received free medicine, postage allowances, or money to have their photographs taken, the company also employed a few brokers. The New York testimonial agent doubled her profits by selling the same endorsements to the Pinkham company and its southern competitor, Wine of Cardui, until the company caught up with her game.[36]

To allay the growing skepticism toward testimonials, Wetherald adopted the gimmick of offering a reward to anyone who could prove that a testimonial was not "genuine." A boxed notice beneath each ad promised that $500 would be paid "to any person who will show that the above testimonial is not genuine, or was published before obtaining the writer's permission."[37] Wetherald had nothing to fear. The testimonials he printed were genuine, in the sense that he could produce documentary evidence to show that women had actually written the letters and given their permission to the Pinkham company to use them. Whether or not the testimonials were honest, or informed, or accurate, was another matter.

Once he obtained written permission to use a woman's testimonial, Wetherald did not hesitate to rework the letter. Many needed to be edited to correct the mistakes which testified only to the writer's poor spelling and grammar. Others were touched up to make them more dramatic. Laura Hunt forwarded a batch of testimonials to Wetherald with the remark, "In glancing these over, I saw a great many of them that could be changed, perhaps made a little stronger. . . ."[38]

Reporters like Sullivan and Adams who took the trouble to trace testimonial writers occasionally found them in the cemeteries. Samuel Hopkins Adams called his readers' attention to a Doan's Kidney Pills testimonial which ran for over a year after the writer had died of kidney disease. The Pinkham company tried to avoid such carelessness. In at least one instance, though, the family of a deceased woman threatened legal action to remove her testimonial from the papers. The company responded imperiously, "Family threats really have no terror for us. We always discontinue the publication of a testimonial upon the death of the writer."[39]

Testimonial writers who sincerely felt they had benefited from a patent medicine, according to Mark Sullivan, generally took one which contained cocaine, morphine, or alcohol. The purchaser had no way of knowing the medicine's ingredients. An inadvertent addiction could easily develop (as it could and did from drugs administered by physicians). In some cases, medicine manufacturers consciously sought to make their customers addicts. Drugs containing opium and cocaine assured manufacturers a steady business. As one patent medicine man put it, "You want to get up a medicine that's full of dope, so the more they take of it, the more they'll want."[40]

The alcoholic tonics and bracers, although not physically addictive, worked on a similar principle. They appealed to a male audience seeking a substitute for whiskey (in dry states like Maine and Kansas, Peruna with 28 per cent alcohol and Hostetter's Bitters with 44 per cent enjoyed a brisk trade) and more subtly, they appealed to a female audience innocent, or presumably innocent, of their alcoholic content. Mark Sullivan detailed a typical case:

> Suppose a woman, for example, feels tired, depressed from domestic overwork. She is simply tired and needs rest. But in that condition she sees an ad of a certain "medicine" that exactly reflects her condition and feelings. She buys a bottle, takes it, feels better, and is perfectly willing to say so and does, and she does it very often from honest gratitude. But what has made her feel better? Purely and simply the exhilaration of the alcohol . . . in the "medicine" she has taken. She would have felt precisely the same change for the better if she had taken whiskey or brandy. . . .[41]

Perhaps. But social morés prohibited genteel women from drinking. Men adjourned for brandy and cigars; women for coffee or tea. The woman who would never knowingly touch liquor, as well as the woman who would never want it known that she did, drank alcohol in the form of "medicine."

After polling fifty members of the Women's Christian Temperance Union, Bok reported that thirty-seven regularly took patent medicines which contained from 12 to 30 per cent alcohol. And they did not hesitate to endorse alcoholic medicines like Lydia Pinkham's Vegetable Compound in newspaper testimonials. The Pinkham company made it a practice to cultivate good relations with the WCTU. Upon hearing that their competitor, the litigious R. V. Pierce, had sued the temperance organization, Laura Hunt remarked, "We think it is rather better to pat these people on the back than to sue them." To prove the point, Charles Pinkham turned over his home and grounds to the young women of the

Lynn WCTU for their annual lawn party in 1899. Not long after, the Pinkham company ran a testimonial for the Vegetable Compound written on WCTU stationery by an officer in the local chapter.[42]

Samuel Hopkins Adams joined Bok in chiding the WCTU for the naiveté of its members and pointing to "the whiskey cures that furnish quiet joy to the temperance trade." Alcoholic tonics, he alleged, led women to "unconscious drunkenness." "The drinker doesn't want to get drunk," he observed, adding that "at least she doesn't know that she wants to get drunk."[43]

When exposure and ridicule threatened to dry up the WCTU trade early in the 1900's, the Pinkham company took steps to reassure women that they could drink the Compound in good conscience. A two-page rebuttal to charges brought by *Collier's* and *The Ladies' Home Journal* ran in the spring of 1906 under the heading, "The Truth, The Whole Truth, And Nothing But The Truth." The ad dismissed as "foolish talk" comparisons of the Compound and alcoholic beverages. It explained that the alcohol in the medicine, which equalled "about 18 per cent," represented the smallest amount capable of preserving the medicinal ingredients. "A woman must be well nigh insane to drink a whole bottle of Pinkham's Compound at once," the copy continued, adding with peculiar logic, "She would have to do this to get as much alcohol as she would from a glass of liquor containing the same per cent of alcohol."[44] When all arguments failed, the company reminded teetotalers that the Vegetable Compound came in pills and lozenges as well as in liquid form.

Wetherald's efforts to deflect criticism made it politic to appropriate the rhetoric of the muckrakers and use it to his own advantage. In the "Guide to Health" he warned women that they lived in "an age of quackery," and counseled them to avoid "body and soul killing quack nostrums." At the same time he attacked the medical profession by labeling their practice "the legitimate quackery of the old school." Physicians, he noted, were not required to reveal the contents of their prescriptions. Why, then, should proprietors be forced to divulge their formulas? Adroitly, Wetherald turned attacks on patent medicines into a conspiracy against freedom of choice. The muckrakers, he implied, acted as tools of doctors who wished to legislate a therapeutic monopoly.[45]

Wetherald did not get specific in his charges, but surely no one could deny that the American Medical Association worked as actively for food and drug legislation as the Proprietary Association worked against it. Harvey Washington Wiley later cited "the medical profession, the American Medical Association with 140,000 members," as one of the chief influences upon Congress.[46]

By the spring of 1906, the publicity generated by the muckrakers goaded Congress into action. President Theodore Roosevelt somewhat belatedly swung his support to the movement for food and drug reform. His annual message, delivered in December, 1905, called for a law "to regulate interstate commerce in misbranded and adulterated foods, drinks, and drugs."[47] The next day Senator Weldon Heyburn of Idaho reintroduced a pure food and drug bill, which for four years he had tried unsuccessfully to bring to the Senate floor. Conservative Senate Republicans, led by Nelson Aldrich of New York, had consistently blocked debate on the measure. With Roosevelt's backing and the support of the AMA (as well as vigorous endorsements from the General Federation of Women's Clubs and the Consumers' League), the Heyburn bill could no longer be tabled. The Senate passed the bill on February 21, 1906.[48]

The bill went to the House, where its opponents hoped to keep it locked up in committee. There it would have died, had not Upton Sinclair's *The Jungle,* with its account of filthy conditions in Packingtown, resuscitated the pure food and drug debate. Seizing the opportunity created by the public outcry for reform, Congressman James R. Mann, a doctor from Illinois, enlisted the aid of Samuel Hopkins Adams and chief chemist Harvey Washington Wiley. Together the three men drafted a measure much tougher on patent medicines than the Senate bill. In June, Congress passed the bill and sent it to a conference committee which further strengthened the sections dealing with patent medicines. President Roosevelt signed the Pure Food and Drugs Act, popularly called "Dr. Wiley's law," on June 30, 1906.[49]

The federal food and drug law, which took effect on January 1,

1907, stipulated that all proprietary medicines involved in interstate trade meet certain standards of purity and that information printed on the label, box, or package be accurate and true. Unlike the North Dakota law, the federal bill did not require patent medicines to list their ingredients on the label, but it did require the declaration of certain dangerous ingredients including cocaine, opium, morphine, heroin, chloroform, alcohol, *Cannabis indica,* chloral hydrate, and acetanilide. If a company chose voluntarily to indicate that its medicine contained other substances, it had to be able to prove that they were present in the amounts specified. A misbranding section banned from labels statements "false or misleading in any particular." In short, the law left the patent medicine manufacturer to determine what he wished to say on the label, but demanded that whatever he said be the truth. Except for the stipulation requiring proprietors to list certain dangerous drugs, the law gave the manufacturers a choice—either keep quiet or tell the truth.[50]

"Let the label tell" had been the slogan for the pure food and drug campaign. Under the new law proprietors hastily amended their labels, and the additions and subtractions told a good deal. Lydia Pinkham's Vegetable Compound confessed for the first time on its label that the medicine contained "18 Per Cent Alcohol," intended "solely as a solvent and preservative." Gone was the promise that the Compound provided "A Sure Cure for Prolapsus Uteri." The new label read simply "For Prolapsus Uteri." Gone, too, was the phrase "for all diseases of the kidneys it is the greatest remedy in the world." A new modesty prevailed. Instead of saying that the Compound was "a great help in pregnancy," the new label "recommended" it as "a good help"; instead of promising to cure prolapse "and all female weaknesses," it simply listed "other female weaknesses." The company eliminated the claim that the medicine could cure "all weaknesses of the generative organs of either sex." The changes, some obvious, some more subtle, altered the tone more than the message. Consumers had to squint closely to see the difference.[51]

As Mark Sullivan pointed out, "let the label tell" was a fine slogan, but only if the buyer bothered to look. The effectiveness of the patent medicine provisions of the Pure Food and Drugs Act depended on the public's willingness to assume responsibility. Predicated on the characteristic progressive assumption that publicity, not prohibition, led to reform, the law did not abolish harmful medicines; it merely ensured honest labeling. *Caveat emptor* remained the rule of the marketplace. Adams put it succinctly:

[I]f you intoxicate yourself with raw alcohol in the form of "female remedies" or "catarrh cures," or play fast and loose with your heart by dosing yourself or your family with morphine or *Cannabis indica,* or chloral, you do so with your eyes open, and the responsibility is upon yourself.[52]

In the long run the patent medicine manufacturers proved more astute judges of human nature than the reformers. They fought the Pure Food and Drugs Act, but once it was enacted, they learned to live with it and to turn it to their advantage. Frank J. Cheney, president of the Proprietary Association, predicted the impact of the law. "People generally will reason . . . that preparations which come up to the requirements of a congressional enactment must be all right, or, certainly, that they are not harmful or dangerous."[53] What consumer would trouble to read the fine print when the label carried the heading "Guaranteed Under the Pure Food and Drugs Act"?

The guaranty clause of the law provided patent medicine manufacturers with a perfect device for deception. Wiley assigned a guaranty serial number to any patent medicine whose proprietor promised that the medicine met the standards set down in the law. If the Bureau of Chemistry later found the manufacturer in violation of the law, the guaranty protected the druggist who had sold the medicine. The presence of a guaranty on the label of a patent medicine did not mean that the government certified the effectiveness or the safety of the medicine. "It should be distinctly understood," Wiley warned the drug-makers, "that the filing of a guaranty and the securing of a serial number does not in any way mean that the Government guarantees your product."[54] Nevertheless the ambiguity created by the word "guaranty" made it possible for patent medicine proprietors to twist enforcement into endorsement. Patent medicine manufacturers had only to display the device on their labels. Customers who saw the official serial number and the phrase, "Guaranteed Under the Pure Food and Drugs Act," automatically assumed that the product had federal approval. Not until 1914 did the government call a halt to the hoax by abolishing the guaranty system.[55]

Advocates of the Pure Food and Drugs Act like Edward Bok, who predicted that the law would deal the patent medicine industry a blow from which it could never recover, ought to have known better. Nothing in the law touched patent medicine advertising. The injunction to tell the truth applied only to the label, package, and package inserts. On signboards, in streetcars, and in the pages of newspapers and magazines, patent medicines could claim with impunity to cure cancer, restore lost youth, or resurrect the dead. Samuel Hopkins Adams provided a useful rule-of-thumb: "Subtract the statement on the label from the claims made in the advertisements, and the difference is the lie."[56] How many Americans followed Adams' advice remained problematical. Patent medicine advertisers counted on the pulling power of advertising to lure customers to the drugstore. They gambled that once there the customer would not bother to read the label. As Adams later admitted, the law "aimed at the wrong side of the bottle."[57] The real damage was done in newsprint.

Pinkham advertisements reflected the general trend in patent medicine advertising following the passage of federal regulation. At first the company seemed confused and cautious, but as time passed, ads became bolder, more belligerent. Ads in the 1907 series assumed a defensive posture. The company continued to urge women to write to Mrs. Pinkham, but took time to explain that she was Lydia E. Pinkham's daughter-in-law. The vague, unattributed remark that the Vegetable Compound was "acknowledged to be the most successful remedy in the country," replaced former "Sure Cure" claims. A customer applying Adams' formula to Pinkham advertising would have noticed that advertisements continued to offer the Compound as a kidney cure after the law removed the claim from the label. And, in addition to the uterine complaints printed on the label, the ads listed a string of ailments from dizziness to tumors with the promise that the Compound would provide relief. Wetherald's ads capitalized on the Pure Food and Drugs Act by omitting reference to the alcohol in the Compound while insisting that the medicine, "made only from roots and herbs," contained "no narcotics or other harmful drugs."[58]

The "Bottle Books" which the company distributed in its packages came under the jurisdiction of the law. Changes in the copy after 1906 indicated a grudging concession to current medical opinion. In place of the flat assertion that the Vegetable Compound cured all female complaints, the copy equivocated. "There are a few incurable cases," the text admitted, "in which surgical operations are absolutely necessary, but with rare exceptions we believe that our Vegetable Compound will cure when a cure is in any way possible."[59] Pamphlets mailed to women and therefore outside the range of the drug law, took a different tone toward the medical profession. "Most doctors are of little service in so-called chronic cases," the booklet complained. "They try all sorts of experiments; sometimes they send you to the city to some 'specialist' who may help, or may merely try more experiments; and they may want to get a surgeon to cut you up."[60]

As the company became more confident of the limitations of the law, Wetherald's advertising assumed its old aggressiveness. In 1909 he used testimonials to make sweeping claims. Women recounted how the Vegetable Compound had dissolved tumors, cured uterine diseases, and saved them from the knife. By 1910 Wetherald felt confident enough to launch a counterattack. He sent twenty-eight reading notices to newspapers carrying Pinkham advertising with the instructions that the two-inch squibs appear disguised as news filler. To convince publishers reluctant to commit this breach of ethics, Wetherald reminded them that attacks on patent medicines had "depressed the trade" to the extent that many patent medicine manufacturers had quit advertising entirely. He concluded, "Instead of asking you to insert these small readers complimentary [*sic*], as many advertisers would, we have made them a part of the regular schedule, and authorize you to charge them *pro rata*."[61]

The reading notices ran under the headlines "The Value of

Proprietary Medicines," "Physicians Are Naturally Prejudiced," "Pure Foods and Pure Medicines," "Alcohol Is A Preservative," and others. Wetherald, misrepresenting the Pure Food and Drugs Act, led readers to believe that it abolished dangerous drugs and left only safe and harmless preparations on the market. Describing the Pinkham Vegetable Compound as "An Honest Proprietary Medicine," he emphasized its herbal ingredients. His only mention of alcohol came in the charge that doctors' prescriptions contained a good deal more than the Compound. Repeatedly he emphasized that proprietary medicines were cheaper and more effective than medical treatment. Doctors, he alleged, prescribed patent medicines "under Latin names" so that they could charge more for their prescriptions. At the same time that he attacked the medical profession, he sought to give legitimacy to the Vegetable Compound by asserting that "honest doctors" urged their patients to take the Pinkham medicine. Readers who mistook the Pinkham copy for news came away either with the impression that the Vegetable Compound had the approval of the Bureau of Chemistry and the medical profession, or that the law had been perpetrated by jealous and inept doctors intent on swelling their own practices. Either way the company profited from the publicity.[62]

As Wetherald's advertising campaign became bolder, Pinkham sales pulled out of a five-year slump and began a slow but steady recovery. To credit Wetherald for the resurgence in sales, however, would be to give him credit for the shortcomings of the muckrakers, the limitations of the law, and the sorry state of medical practice. Taken together, those factors contributed to a climate which allowed the Pinkham company, through Wetherald's vigorous advertising policies, to recoup its losses.

Men like Bok, Sullivan, and Adams had pitched their patent medicine exposés to an audience hungry for sensation. Their articles aimed to shock as much as they hoped to educate the public. The sensational tone more than the facts and figures produced the effect. Bok, particularly, displayed in his writing the combination of sensationalism and prudery Wetherald used so successfully in Pinkham advertising. The editor of *The Ladies' Home Jour-*

nal approached his audience with a genteel condescension. The posture he adopted in much of his writing was not unlike that of a parent toward a willful and slow-witted child. He lectured, he scolded, he cajoled in an attempt to shame his female readers into acting as he thought proper. His impatience was everywhere apparent, as when he editorially scored the temperance movement: "Let the officers of the WCTU look into the advertising columns of the religious papers of the country, and see how their columns fairly reek with the advertisements of these dangerous concoctions. Yet in these very same so-called religious papers there are official WCTU columns setting forth the 'official' news of the organization and its branches."[63] He coupled his indignation with an exaggerated, sentimental regard for womanhood, which led him rhetorically to invoke the sacredness of mother's name or woman's honor in passages liberally dotted with exclamation points and fairly seething with manly indignation.

Behind it all one senses Bok's dissatisfaction with his role as a ladies' editor in a man's world. He seemed to recoil from too close an association with the female sex. In his autobiography, Bok hinted at his discomfiture. "It is a curious fact," he wrote, referring to himself in the third person, "that Edward Bok's instinctive attitude toward woman was that of avoidance. He did not dislike women, but it could not be said that he liked them. They had never interested him. Of women, therefore he knew little; of their needs less. Nor had he the slightest desire, even as an editor, to know them better, or to seek to understand them."[64]

Bok's callousness, real or feigned, colored his attack on patent medicines in *The Ladies' Home Journal*. Perhaps he shamed a temperance leader into renouncing her patent liquor, or scared into silence—with his stories of the ribald jokes of the correspondence room—women who had written for advice to the mythical Lydia Pinkham. He did not, however, educate his audience in any real or lasting sense. He played to women's emotions, not to their intellect. And, as he confessed, he steadfastly refused to understand their needs or sympathize with their desires.

Adams and Sullivan, who wrote for an audience of men as well as women, adopted a less patronizing tone. First and foremost, they were reporters out to get a story. The patent medicine business provided enough unsavory details to satisfy even the most jaded audience of exposé. The story to be told was both shocking and sensational by its very nature. But true to their calling, they could not resist wringing it dry. Adams consciously refused to draw distinctions between "good" and "bad" patent medicines. Consequently he lumped together medicines like Mrs. Winslow's Soothing Syrup, an opiated nostrum which could and did drug children to death, and medicines like Lydia Pinkham's Vegetable Compound, which, at worst, produced an alcoholic haze in women suffering from female complaints. To his uncompromising eyes, a fraud was a fraud, pure and simple. His lack of discrimination produced the exaggerated sense of danger and deception which made his articles so powerful. In the heat of his withering criticism, the patent medicine business seemed to dry up. For a time.

Muckraking journalism, by its very intensity, risked losing its effectiveness. The public could withstand only so much shock and sensation before it became inured to the techniques of the muckrakers. In the short run, muckraking provided a stimulus to reform. In the long run it was not capable of the sustained effort and the systematic criticism necessary to produce lasting social change.

Bok, Sullivan, and Adams deserved credit for their role in the passage of the Pure Food and Drugs Act. Yet as Sullivan observed, it was ironic that the public reacted most dramatically to a piece of fiction and not to the facts and figures documented by the muckraking reporters. Upton Sinclair's *The Jungle,* however realistic, was, after all, a novel intended as a socialist critique of the wage system and not a call for food and drug legislation. As Sinclair himself admitted, "I aimed at the public's heart, and by accident I hit it in the stomach."[65]

The law that emerged as a result of the public's outrage at what went into sausage and potted beef, insofar as it dealt with patent medicines, owed as much to the Proprietary Association as it did to Wiley and the muckrakers. In public the proprietors adamantly opposed regulation; behind the scenes the Proprietary Association worked to insure a law the patent medicine manufacturers could live with. The *National Druggist* boasted, "[L]et it not be supposed that the law would have been enacted in its present rather innocuous form but for hard, intelligent and most tactful work on the part of the representatives of the interests it is intended to regulate."[66] Progressive legislation—and the food and drugs law was no exception—did as much to rationalize as to regulate industry. It was clearly in the interests of the large proprietors to eliminate the most noxious frauds in the business—those who gave patent medicines a bad name. Enforcement of the law by the Bureau of Chemistry worked to drive the worst quacks out of business and, as well, to squeeze out the small "fly-by-night" operators. The end result was to give the big proprietors more control of the market.

The Pure Food and Drugs Act was weak not only because it left patent medicine advertising untouched, but also because it created in its language ambiguity as to whether or not misbranding provisions applied to curative claims made on the label. In 1911 the Supreme Court cleared up the ambiguity to the satisfaction of the proprietors by ruling that the misbranding provision applied only to the ingredients listed on the label. "We are of the opinion," wrote Associate Justice Oliver Wendell Holmes, Jr., "that the phrase ["false or misleading in any particular"] is aimed not at all possible false statements, but only at such as determine the identity of the article, possibly including its strength, quality and purity. . . ." Holmes concluded his majority opinion with the remark that Congress surely had not intended to enter into a therapeutic controversy by proposing to judge what could cure and what could not. Justice Charles Evans Hughes dissented. Congress, he insisted, had intended precisely to prohibit false and misleading statements with regard to curative properties. "[G]ranting the widest domain of opinion, and allowing the broadest range to the conflict of medical views, there still remains a field in which statements as to curative properties are downright falsehoods and in no sense expressions of judgment. This field I believe this statute covers."[67]

Congress evidently agreed with Hughes. In 1912 it passed the

Sherley Amendment which explicitly declared misbranded those labels containing "false and fraudulent" curative or therapeutic claims. But in the interim between the Court's decision and Congressional action, proprietors had resumed "sure cure" claims with impunity.

The Pure Food and Drugs Act drove from the market the most egregious of the patent medicine fakers, those who chose to go out of business rather than reveal their dangerous ingredients. And it did lead some of the worst offenders, like Mrs. Winslow's Soothing Syrup, to change their formulas to lessen or eliminate dangerous drugs. But because of the inadequacies of its provisions and the problems raised in its enforcement, the law left patent medicines free to flourish. Sales, instead of dropping, soared.

Consumers, for the most part, naively assumed that the law insured the safety of the medicines they bought over the counter at the local drugstore. Reassured, they forgot the warnings of the muckrakers and returned to their favorite remedies for the same reasons they had taken them to begin with. Nothing had changed. The medical profession could offer no miraculous cures to end disease or delay death. Surgery continued to be a risky endeavor at best. The relationship between the psychological and physiological remained an area into which most practitioners preferred not to venture. A doctor writing in *The Ladies' Home Journal* in 1907 discouraged women from confiding in their family physicians with a warning that doctors were, after all, only human and endowed with "perfect, active virility" which precluded intimate confessions.[68] Meanwhile patent medicine advertising appeared in the daily press with a regularity no muckraker could match, promising sure cures and offering free advice. No disease baffled the patent medicine proprietors' skills. No intimacy shocked their sensibilities.

The American consumer, then as now, was slow to change habits. The muckrakers briefly roused consumer consciousness, but when the prodding ceased, men and women resumed their old patterns. Women who took Lydia Pinkham's Vegetable Compound because they found the doctor too expensive, or because they feared surgery, or because a mild alcoholic tonic helped them to relax, required something more than a sermon or a set of statistics to wean them from the medicine. Their needs were real and immediate. Pinkham advertising promised, persistently and persuasively, to meet those needs, often when doctors could not or would not.

The Teeth of the Law

Passage of the Pure Food and Drugs Act ushered in an era of prosperity for the Lydia E. Pinkham Medicine Company. Sales increased not quite two and one-half million dollars between 1910 and the company's peak year in 1925. Regulation brought its share of problems for the business, but on the whole the government preferred conciliation to coercion and wielded its limited power with a light hand. Until 1925 the Pinkham enterprise had every reason to concur with journalist George Creel, who described the Pure Food and Drugs Act as having "about as much bite as a canton flannel dog."[1] By the time it showed its teeth, the company was too demoralized by internal disputes to fight back effectively.

Encouraging signs in 1912 indicated that the Pinkham business had weathered the sales slump which had persisted intermittently since 1899. Wetherald's aggressive advertising campaign, begun in 1910, helped push sales back up over the million dollar mark in 1912 for the first time since the food and drugs law had taken effect over five years earlier. In 1913 sales climbed even higher, to $1,185,847—an annual increase of more than $132,000. At the same time, Wetherald managed to hold the proportion of advertising spending to gross sales revenue at a reasonable 44 per cent ($525,000), down from the 58 per cent expended in the previous decade. Certain that sales were on the upswing, J. T. regained his old equanimity.[2]

The Pinkham company's new prosperity reflected that of the patent medicine industry as a whole. In the decade between 1902 and 1912, the total production of patent and proprietary medicines in the United States increased by 60 per cent, from $100 million to $160 million. Clearly the industry had not been materially damaged to any significant extent by the passage of the food and drugs law.[3]

Reformers soon began to grumble that the law had been fatally flawed from the first. It had failed to include provisions aimed at curbing patent medicine advertising and thereby left the medicine maker's most effective avenue to profit wide open. The law, weak as it was, had been hamstrung by the Supreme Court's 1911 decision which stated that the misbranding provision did not apply to curative or therapeutic claims made on the label. The Court's ruling effectually quashed over 150 cases against patent medicine interests then pending in the courts. Although the Sherley Amendment of 1912 attempted to plug the loophole that led to the Court's decision, it, too, contained an ambiguity convenient for patent medicine makers. Because the amendment read "false *and* fraudulent," the governemnt had to prove not only that a medicine was falsely labeled, but that its sale involved bad faith and dishonest intention on the part of the manufacturer. To make matters worse, bureaucratic wrangling, inadequate appropriations, and an administrative procedure both clumsy and dilatory, acted together to hamper the enforcement of the law. By 1915 George Creel was not alone when he growled that the food and drugs law was little more than "a joke."[4]

Among the growing chorus deploring the deficiencies of the Pure Food and Drugs Act, the American Medical Association soon emerged as the strongest voice against the patent medicine interests. The AMA, strengthened and united after a decade of internal reorganization and reform, proved eager to lead the fight against the "nostrum evil." The Association quickly moved to fill the vacuum created by the demise of the muckrakers.[5]

The task of alerting the public to medical quackery and drug frauds fell to Arthur J. Cramp, head of the AMA's Department of Propaganda. A shy, quiet man with a passion for ornithology, Cramp carried out the attack on medical quackery with a zeal born of personal hatred. As a young man he had watched helplessly as his daughter died at the hands of a spurious "doctor." He obtained a medical degree and in 1905 joined the staff of the *Journal of the American Medical Association* with the single-minded desire to expose the fake and the fraud.[6]

Cramp kept the tradition of the muckrakers alive by reissuing Samuel Hopkins Adams' "Great American Fraud" series. The AMA printed 150,000 copies, which it distributed throughout the nation at a low cost. Dissatisfied with the hit-and-miss approach of the earlier writers, Cramp soon tried a little muckraking of his own. In 1911 he published a five-hundred-page exposé entitled *Nostrums and Quackery,* which featured articles he had authored in the AMA *Journal.* His rhetoric revealed him a true disciple of Adams: "When the veil of mystery is torn from the medical faker," he promised, "the naked sordidness and inherent worthlessness that remains suffices [*sic*] to make quackery its own greatest condemnation. This is the mission on which 'Nostrums and Quackery' goes forth." A promotional blurb described the book, which went through several subsequent editions, as "a veritable 'Who's Who in Quackdom.'"[7]

Lydia Pinkham held a prominent place in Cramp's rogues' gallery. His treatment of the Vegetable Compound in *Nostrums and Quackery,* however, added little to the charges Adams and Sullivan had made earlier. Once again readers were told that Lydia Pinkham had been dead for over two decades. The letters sent to "Mrs. Pinkham," Cramp pointed out, were in fact answered by a paid secretarial staff. The company's claim that Mrs. Jennie Pinkham handled the correspondence, Cramp dismissed as an intentional deception. He concluded that the medicine was no more than a worthless fraud whose popularity depended entirely upon the high percentage of alchohol it contained.[8]

Unfortunately for the Pinkham company, Cramp did not confine his attack on the Vegetable Compound to the pages of *Nostrums and Quackery*. In 1913 an analysis of the Vegetable Compound published in the *British Medical Journal* came to Cramp's attention. The British chemists reported that the Compound contained 19.3 per cent alcohol by volume and only 0.6 per cent solid substances. They could find no evidence of any active ingredients, "except a trace of a bitter substance." The 0.3 per cent or 0.4 per cent of vegetable extractives, they concluded, "possessed no distinctive characters." Armed with these facts, Cramp wrote the Commissioner of Internal Revenue in September of 1913 to suggest that the Vegetable Compound belonged on the Treasury Department's tax list. The government had for some time taxed as beverages patent medicines with a high alcoholic content. Peruna's business had been hurt badly in 1906 when its proprietor was forced to take out alcohol and add laxatives in order to evade the excise tax. Cramp intended a similar fate for Lydia Pinkham's medicine.[9]

Less than a month after Cramp wrote his letter, the Commissioner of Internal Revenue informed the Pinkham company's president, Will Gove, that in the opinion of the Treasury Department, the Vegetable Compound did not contain sufficient medicinal ingredients to prevent its use as a beverage. Unless the company revised its formula, the IRS would tax the Pinkham Compound as a "medicated liquor." Fortunately for the company, the Commissioner proved accommodating. The government did not seem eager to tax the Pinkham concern. Instead Commissioner W. H. Osborn agreed to let Gove continue to market the Vegetable Compound until a new formula could be perfected. In consultation with chemists at the Treasury Department, Gove moved to comply.[10]

The company slowly fortified its formula. In January, 1914, a batch of the medicine purporting to be 50 per cent stronger, failed to meet government standards. Impatient, Osborn warned Gove that the company had ninety days to file a satisfactory formula or else the Vegetable Compound would go on the tax list. Four days later Gove submitted a revised formula which contained, in addition to significantly larger quantities of Lydia Pinkham's original ingredients, substantial amounts of Dandelion, Chamomile, and Licorice root, as well as Gentian, another new ingredient. The alcoholic content remained at 18 per cent. According to the company, the new medicine contained seven times the solid content of the Compound as it had been originally prepared.[11]

On May 5, 1914, the Treasury Department approved the new formula. Commissioner Osborn notified Gove, "In the opinion of the Chief Chemist of this office, a preparation compounded in accordance with the [new] formula would be sufficiently medicated to be unsuitable for use as a beverage."[12]

In the meantime Cramp had grown impatient. Early in June he wrote to the Internal Revenue Service asking what had been done in the Pinkham matter. Osborn replied that the medicine, "as it is now compounded and placed on the market, measures up to the standard adopted."[13] Shortly thereafter Cramp noticed that Pinkham bottles carried a small sticker with the words, "New Form, Adopted June 12, 1914." Cramp surmised that "a hint from the Internal Revenue Department caused the Pinkham concern to add more drugs to its alcoholic nostrum." He noted with some satisfaction that the formula change had not been entirely successful: "The proprietor of a large pharmaceutical jobbing house in Chicago reports that since the formula has been changed a number of complaints have come in from retail druggists to the effect that the nostrum does not 'keep' but is 'blowing up' on their shelves."[14]

Manufacturing the new fortified formula caused the company considerable difficulty. The amount of alcohol no longer was sufficient to hold the increased quantity of vegetable matter in solution. Thick sediment formed at the bottom of the bottle. The Compound fermented, causing the explosions the Chicago jobber reported, and turning the medicine sour. Consumers wrote to complain and drug wholesalers returned shipment after shipment of the Compound.[15]

Nevertheless, the company tried to put a good face on the formula change. Vegetable Compound labels cautioned that the medicine might have "a different taste and appearance from the Compound as formerly prepared." The change resulted from "certain additions" which "improved" the medicine. The new formula, the label promised, "contains precisely the same medicinal ingredients as formerly and in the same proportions, and consequently retains all its old virtues."[16]

Consumers were not convinced. Sales fell over $95,000 in the span of two years. The manufacturing process, as much as the new formula, was to blame. The spoilage problem persisted until the company replaced its old wooden storage tanks with glass-lined vats and began sterilizing its bottles and pasteurizing the Compound. Once these changes were made, the Compound kept as well as before, though consumers complained that it never tasted quite the same.[17]

Cramp's intervention, although it did not permanently damage the company, indicated the strength and the strategy of the AMA. Even more effective than the Propaganda Department's muckraking campaign was the close relationship the AMA cultivated with the government. The extent of the collaboration between the two was remarkable. In 1905 when the AMA established its Council on Pharmacy and Chemistry to investigate new and non-official remedies, the AMA House of Delegates formally requested the aid of the Bureau of Chemistry. Secretary of Agriculture James Wilson, who controlled the Bureau, responded enthusiastically, "It seems to me that the collaboration with the great body of American physicians who form the American Medical Association affords a splendid opportunity to carry out the work which Congress intended to be done." Accordingly, Wilson instructed the Bureau to make its facilities available to the AMA Council. In its early years, the Council of Pharmacy and Chemistry used both the staff and facilities of the Bureau's laboratory to carry out chemical examination of the products submitted for AMA approval. To further cement its ties with the government, the AMA made sure to include as members on the Council, medical doctors like Harvey Washington Wiley, his assistant, Lyman F. Kebler, and his successor as Chief Chemist, Carl Alsberg. Much of the AMA's effectiveness in combating patent medicines can be attributed to the spirit of cooperation existing between the Association and the Bureau of Chemistry.[18]

Patent medicine manufacturers soon recognized the AMA as a

powerful adversary. *Standard Remedies,* the publication of the Proprietary Association, denounced the AMA for using "Hun methods" and labeled its anti-proprietary campaign "journalistic prostitution." "Is this a free country, or are we to be Russianized?" the editors asked rhetorically. Despite its bluster, the Proprietary Association was clearly on the defensive.[19]

Not until 1915 did a patent medicine manufacturer attack the AMA directly by seeking damages through the courts. John C. Patten, proprietor of Wine of Cardui (a female weakness cure that competed with the Vegetable Compound) became incensed after the AMA *Journal* denounced the remedy as a "vicious fraud" and scolded the Methodist Episcopal church for allowing the manufacturer of a highly alcoholic nostrum to hold an influential position in its laymen's organization. As a result of the publicity, the Methodists moved to strip Patten of his offices. Patten promptly sued the AMA for $200,000 in personal damages. His brother and partner followed with a $100,000 libel suit in the name of the Chattanooga Medicine Company, the producer of Wine of Cardui. Although Patten's death in April of 1916 stopped the progress of the personal suit, the company, seeing Patten as a martyr, determined to press its case. After thirteen weeks of testimony which pitted one set of experts against another, the jury reluctantly rendered a verdict in favor of the Chattanooga Medicine Company. But to indicate where its true sympathy lay, it awarded the company only one cent in damages.

The AMA gloated, "To the Association a moral triumph; to the 'patent medicine' interests a Pyrrhic victory." The Cardui suit had, however, hurt the AMA. Legal expenses totalling $125,000 left the organization with an annual operating deficit for the first time in twenty-five years. Had the proprietors been willing to risk equally high legal fees, it is possible that they might have done some harm to the AMA. But the insignificant damages awarded the Cardui people served to discourage further suits. The AMA continued its fight against patent medicines unimpeded.[20]

In the midst of the Cardui case, the Pinkham company again had reason to suspect that the AMA had been working behind the scenes to cause trouble. Scarcely a month after the Treasury Department approved the Pinkham's new formula, the Department of Agriculture issued a citation against the company which declared the Vegetable Compound misbranded under the Sherley Amendment. During the summer of 1914, the company met with representatives of the Bureau of Chemistry in an attempt to iron out differences. The Bureau objected to label claims which recommended the medicine in cases of prolapsed uterus, painful menstruation, inflammation and ulceration of the womb, and for other types of female weakness. Even more damaging, in the eyes of the Bureau officials, was the Bottle Book included in the Pinkham carton which contained claims more sweeping than those on the label. The company promised to tone down its language to meet the government's objections. Repeatedly Will Gove submitted copy which the Bureau scrutinized and sent back for further modifications. The process dragged on for five months.[21]

In February of 1915, Lyman Kebler, Chief of the Bureau's Drug Division, grew exasperated and decided to take the Pinkham company to court. In a letter to Carl L. Alsberg, who had succeeded Wiley as Bureau Chief, Kebler recommended prosecution. Alsberg promptly approved the recommendation and notified the Solicitor to begin criminal action in the courts against the Lydia E. Pinkham Medicine Company.[22]

The United States Attorney filed in the District Court of Massachusetts in September of 1915 a complaint against the Pinkham company which alleged that the Vegetable Compound was "falsely and fraudulently" claimed by its manufacturers to be effective as a remedy for falling of the womb; as a treatment for leucorrhea, inflammation and ulceration of the womb; as a cure for all female ailments and affections, as well as diseases of the bladder; as an effective cure for dysmenorrhea, uterine tumors, and diseases of the ovaries; and as a preventive for miscarriage, "when in truth and in fact, it was not." The government supported its case with affidavits from Dr. Francis P. Morgan and Clarence D. Wright of the Bureau of Chemistry. Morgan, a medical doctor and chemical analyst, testified that he found no ingredients in the Compound which justified the company's claims. Wright concurred.[23]

Pinkham attorneys protested that the complaint made against the company was based on analysis of medicine seized in March of 1913, more than two and a half years earlier. They argued that the medicine had been manufactured prior to the company's change in formula and that the analysis used as a basis for prosecution was therefore invalid. Similarly, they pointed out that the Pinkham literature and labels cited by the U.S. Attorney had been revised following hearings with the Bureau of Chemistry in the summer and fall of 1914. The complaint, they argued, was out of date; the prosecution unnecessary and unwarranted.

In a letter to George Anderson, the U.S. Attorney, Pinkham's lawyers asked that the case be dropped. "[T]his is the first case in which after having satisfactorily adjusted matters with the Bureau of Chemistry, the Government has begun prosecution based upon labels and literature which has [*sic*] been discontinued," they argued. The intent of the Pure Food and Drugs Act, as they saw it, was not to punish manufacturers who willingly complied with government standards, but to go after those who refused to heed the Bureau of Chemistry's warnings.[24]

The Pinkham lawyers had a point. The notion that the food and drug law had been designed to perform an educational rather than a punitive function gained currency even before the law went into effect.[25] The enforcement procedure set up by the Department of Agriculture—first seizure, then citation, then hearings, and then and only then, a formal complaint and court case—reinforced the idea that manufacturers could avoid prosecution by negotiating with the Bureau of Chemistry. From the first, the Bureau encouraged voluntary compliance; it was more expeditious and less expensive than legal action.

The Pinkham letter sounded convincing to the U.S. Attorney. He wrote his superiors for advice. As it turned out, the Pinkham company had not, as its lawyers indicated, "worked things out satisfactorily" with the Bureau of Chemistry. The Bureau's assistant chief, W. P. Jones, remarked sarcastically that "It is possible that the defendant company may have been justified in believing that their half-hearted revisions removed all offense. . . ." Nevertheless, he insisted, "[T]he shipment of this article in interstate commerce was an offense against the Food and Drugs Act, and [the

Bureau] cannot allow that any subsequent revision of labels, *etc.*, can lessen or remove an offense already committed." "Nor," he added, "has [the Bureau] ever stated that the revision is satisfactory."[26] The Solicitor advised Anderson to continue his case.

The Pinkham company avoided a courtroom showdown with its attendant publicity by entering a plea of no contest (*nolo contendere*). The government objected to the plea, which allowed patent medicine manufactures to escape with light fines. But the judge overrode the objection by stating that inasmuch as he was satisfied that the defendant had discontinued the use of the offending labels and literature before the government initiated court action, he would accept the *nolo* plea. On October 16, 1916, the Court imposed a fine of fifty dollars which the Pinkham company promptly paid.[27]

More than three and a half years had elapsed between the government's initial seizure of the Vegetable Compound and the close of the case. In the interim the Compound went through yet another formula change which reduced the amount of alcohol to 15 per cent. To meet the charge of false labeling, the company had in 1915 abandoned claims dealing with conditions the medical profession and the Bureau of Chemistry insisted could be treated only by surgery. A new label, revised to omit reference to prolapse, read:

Recommended for the Treatment of
Non-Surgical Cases of Weakness and Disorders
of the Female Generative Organs,
Catarrhal Leucorrhea and Irritations.[28]

A later version, in use throughout the early 1920's, dropped the mention of leucorrhea and irritations and substituted "Pleasant to the taste and strongly recommended as a good help in pregnancy and for relieving pain during labor."[29] The company's shift was ingenuous. No one could argue that normal pregnancy constituted a surgical problem; and whether or not customers found the medicine pleasant, remained, after all, a matter of taste.

The Compound's new claims did not entirely satisfy the government. "The submitted label could not be successfully attacked today," an official in the Sherley amendment office lamented. "Perhaps someday we can force in this and other labelings (for the evasion is being adopted by other manufacturers) the better definition of so-called 'non-surgical diseases.' The phrase carries no information to the purchaser, and is, in essence a fraudulent device to 'get across' something."[30]

The Pinkham company's skirmish with the government dramatized the difficulties inherent in the enforcement of the Pure Food and Drugs Act. The Bureau of Chemistry, which initiated federal action against misbranded foods as well as medicines, had neither the staff nor the resources to act as an effective watchdog. Under Wiley, whose chief concern had been food adulteration, the Bureau mounted few cases against drug-makers. Of the first 1,000 judgments rendered under the law, only 135 concerned proprietary medicines. Each court case cost the government an estimated $30,000–$50,000. Yet proprietors rarely went to jail and fines were never high enough to act as deterrents. In the first thirty years of enforcement, judges levied fines averaging sixty-seven dollars apiece and sentenced only two patent medicine proprietors to jail. To make matters worse, proprietors forced to change their labels frequently replaced one claim with another equally objectionable. The government could do nothing but begin the procedure all over again. George Creel summed up the difficulties of enforcement in 1915 when he wrote, "The Bureau [of Chemistry] is in the position of one who tries to mop up water on the floor while the spigot is still turned on."[31]

Government regulation caused the Pinkham company only minor setbacks. The formula change in 1914 led to a temporary sales slump. Once the company overcame its manufacturing difficulties, sales surpassed all previous levels. The curtailed claims on Pinkham labels that came about as a result of the misbranding charge did little to deter customers. Between 1917 and 1925, gross sales revenue increased over two million dollars, an average increase of over $230,000 a year. The headaches caused by federal regulation were more than offset by the high profits the company enjoyed—profits which reached over a half million dollars annually by the middle of the 1920's.[32]

The Pinkham company's success, as always, rested on its newspaper advertising. Wetherald, as architect of Pinkham ad policy, soon devised a foolproof system. In a quandary as to what claims the company could legally make for its medicine, Wetherald decided to let Pinkham users speak for themselves. By 1910 ads for the Vegetable Compound consisted of little more than testimonials under eye-catching headlines. A typical ad featured a photograph of an attractive middle-aged woman. The accompanying headline read, "NEARLY INSANE AT TIMES." In the letter that followed, the woman described how Lydia Pinkham's Vegetable Compound helped her through the "Change of Life," after doctors had failed.[33]

The company followed the same strategy in its booklets. Pinkham copy virtually disappeared. In its place appeared testimonials interspersed among household hints, recipes, and stories. Titles like "Recreation," "Bedtime Stories," "Home Dressmaking," and "The War Time Cook and Health Book," cleverly camouflaged the advertiser's intent. Between the covers, testimonials vied for space with instructions on embroidery, how to bake a fudge cake, and other helpful items. Sometimes the juxtaposition proved jarring—in one recipe book "Leucorrhea" was sandwiched between "Banana Cantaloupe" and "Date Whip."

To convey its medical message the company put out a special eighty-page booklet entitled "Lydia E. Pinkham's Private Textbook on the Ailments Peculiar to Women." Still smarting from charges that the pamphlets were obscene, the company made the book available only upon written request. The first page cautioned the reader, "This little book treats of delicate subjects. . . . It is not intended for indiscriminate reading, but for your own private information." Inside, the copy had been watered down considerably since Wetherald's first efforts in the 1890's. By 1907 Wetherald had given up playing doctor and hired Dr. Finley Ellingwood to revise the "Textbook." The revisions, not surprisingly, evidenced a more charitable attitude toward the medical profession. Women with kidney trouble or cancer were counseled to seek medical advice immediately.[34]

Elsewhere, however, Pinkham copy continued to emphasize the

high costs and dubious results of surgery. "A hospital experience is painful as well as costly and frequently dangerous," breathed one ad. "There is something about the word [operation] that brings a feeling of faintness to the heart and a fear of death to the mind. . . . That is the time for women to remember that many women avoid operations by taking Lydia E. Pinkham's Vegetable Compound."[35]

Such fear tactics incensed patent medicine critics. George Creel began his 1915 series in *Harper's Weekly* with the charge, "Six hundred thousand people die each year in the United States whose lives might have been saved by prompt or proper treatment." Blame for this carnage he placed on "the criminal activity of the patent medicine industry."[36] Creel made no attempt to document his assertion or indicate how he had arrived at his figure. His method, not unlike Wetherald's, was to shock and frighten his readers. The new wave of muckraking, in that respect, resembled the old. But its tactics differed significantly. The worst of the "killer" drugs—the opiated soothing syrups and the heart-depressing headache powders—were, by and large, things of the past. Writers in the 1910's and 1920's shifted their line of attack to argue that patent medicines were harmful not because of what they contained, but because of what they did *not* contain; not because of what they did, but because of what they did *not* do. *Hygeia,* a glossy AMA magazine aimed at laymen, repeatedly emphasized that men and women who relied on worthless nostrums wasted valuable time. Instead of seeking medical help, they dosed themselves with patent remedies until it was "too late." Implicit in the argument was the idea that the doctor, who in the past had been called only when all else failed, should be consulted routinely.

Drug manufacturers and pharmacists countered hotly that the AMA's advice was clearly self-serving. Its attack on patent medicines masked a strategy to end the venerable American tradition of self-medication. In rhetoric typical of the Progressive era, they accused the AMA of trying to establish a "doctors' trust." "If any member of my family wants to take a laxative," cried J. H. Rehfuss of the New York Pharmaceutical Association, "why should I have to send to some doctor for a prescription?" Especially if that prescription was for a medicine that could be purchased over the counter. Peter Diamond, a New York retail druggist, testified in 1915 that half the doctors' prescriptions he filled were for proprietary medicines.[37]

The AMA cleverly side-stepped charges that it acted from pecuniary motives. Arthur Cramp claimed that the AMA's muckraking actually hurt doctors "from a dollars and cents viewpoint." "Every piece of advertising devised to convince the public that a pain in the lower part of the back means kidney disease," he wrote in 1936, "will send, probably, as many people to the family physician as it will send to the drug counter."[38]

Perhaps. But one intention of the new muckrakers, undeniably, was to keep Americans away from the drug counter. In this crusade, as in the earlier attack on patent medicines waged by Bok and Sullivan, women's magazines played a significant role. In 1912 Dr. Harvey Washington Wiley quit the Bureau of Chemistry and joined the staff of *Good Housekeeping.* His contract with the Hearst publication carried the stipulation that no product could be advertised in the magazine without his approval, an arrangement that led to an institution in American advertising—The Good Housekeeping Seal of Approval. Although food still interested Wiley more than drugs, he fired occasional volleys at what he termed "The 'Inherent No-Accountness' of Patent Medicines." In "The Question Box," a monthly feature, Wiley responded to selected letters from women readers. Many asked about patent medicines. Wiley invariably told women to avoid self-dosing. His free advice actively competed with that of the patent medicine proprietors.[39]

The Ladies' Home Journal, not to be outdone, hired Arthur Cramp. The magazine advertised that Cramp would personally answer every letter addressed by women who wished to know about patent medicines. When a high school girl wrote that Lydia Pinkham's Vegetable Compound had "helped considerably" and asked if it could harm her if she took it regularly, Cramp responded, "We believe it is highly unwise for drugs of this type to be taken except under medical supervision, if, indeed, there is ever any justification in young girls being given products containing this amount of alcohol." Lydia Pinkham's granddaughter, Mary Gove, playfully wrote to ask about the Vegetable Compound and received from Cramp a free copy of his exposé, "Female Weakness Cures." Cramp repeatedly cautioned that women who took the Vegetable Compound as directed consumed the equivalent of "more than a pint of whiskey each month." On the eve of Prohibition, his warning must have sounded ominous indeed.[40]

Prohibition and the passage of the Volstead Act in 1919 led to even shriller attacks on alcoholic nostrums. The Pinkham company began to worry that further attempts to classify the medicine as an alcoholic beverage might put them out of business completely. In 1919 and again in 1922, the company sought to buttress its claim that the medicine could not be abused as a liquor. Two local doctors were hired to test the effects of the Pinkham Compound on "habitual drinkers." The doctors rounded up town drunks and invited them to sample the medicine. The "subjects" reportedly experienced "no stimulating or exhilarating symptoms." Instead they complained of nausea, vomiting, headaches, dizziness, and loss of appetite—symptoms the company greeted warmly as indications of the potency of the herbal ingredients in the Compound. Lydia Pinkham's Vegetable Compound, it turned out, was actually a cure for alcoholism, or so one test case indicated:

When nearly through with the bottle, [the subject] began vomiting which persisted all night, could not stand up without falling over; he was more than dizzy, thought his head was whirling around. He had been sick from drink a number of times, but not anywhere near as bad as this. Thought he was going to die, no more of the stuff for him, he was going to cut out all kinds of boozy drinks.[41]

In spite of this evidence, the company did consider cutting the alcohol in the Compound from 15 to 9 per cent—a move which would save an estimated $100,000 a year, in addition to placing the medicine absolutely on the safe side of the law. The Pinkham company never implemented the formula change, although shipping damages recorded during Prohibition suggested that not all those who tried the Vegetable Compound swore off liquor. Railroad workers told stories of gangs breaking into Pinkham shipping crates to drink the Vegetable Compound. Freight damages ran as high as $1,021 a month in the summer of 1922.[42]

To counteract adverse criticism, Wetherald defended the Compound in ads headed "Are Medicines Liquors?" "A certain class of prejudiced and jealous doctors call patent medicines only alcoholic beverages," the ad began, with Cramp obviously in mind. "They will tell you that such and such a medicine contains as much alcohol as a glass of beer or a certain quantity of whiskey." Their motive, the ad continued, was to frighten and deceive. "What they do not mention [is] that the beer or whiskey is swallowed in one draught, while only a small quantity of medicine is taken at one dose." The ad concluded, "Take Lydia E. Pinkham's Vegetable Compound, which complies with all requirements of the Pure Food and Drugs law."[43]

In the 1920's the company's compliance with the law came about partially at the prompting of the Proprietary Association. To stave off new legislation which might strike at patent medicine advertising, the Association adopted a policy of self-regulation. In 1915 the national convention approved a set of minimum requirements for patent medicines "in order to render them safe for Direct sale to the General Public." Among the requirements was the stipulation that statements on the package and label regarding therapeutic claims should be neither unreasonable nor demonstrably false. As for advertising, the Proprietary Association stated, "The preparation must not be advertised or recommended as a cure for diseases or conditions which are generally recognized as incurable by the simple administration of drugs." To enforce its rulings, the organization established a Requirements Committee which scrutinized label claims and suggested changes. Failure to comply led to expulsion from the Proprietary Association.[44]

The Requirements Committee, according to *Standard Remedies,* filled a gap created by an obstinate bureaucracy. In the early days of enforcement, "Government bureaus could not—or would not—instruct. They could only prosecute and correct." Accordingly the Committee set out to inform proprietors how best to stay within the law. Citations against patent medicines diminished and fewer cases of misbranding resulted. The Association also cultivated contacts in government bureaus which proved useful to patient medicine makers who came under investigation. The Proprietary Association boasted that "if it had no other claim upon its members, [it] would more than justify itself by its bureau contacts." In return for its services, the Association assessed each member company one-fifth of 1 per cent of its annual sales revenue. In the case of the Pinkham company, membership in the organization cost an average of $6,000 a year in the 1920's.[45]

At the urging of the Requirements Committee, the Pinkham company in 1920 dropped from its wrapper the words, "For female complaints." The Proprietary Association pointed out that the Bureau of Chemistry found no ingredients in the Compound which justified its claim to act as a "specific" for women's ailments. With representatives from the Proprietary Association acting as liaison, the company negotiated with Bureau officials and in 1921 received permission to recommend the Vegetable Compound for the treatment of "non-surgical cases of weakness and disorders of the female generative system." With the tacit approval of the government and the trade, the company continued to claim in its advertisements that the Vegetable Compound effectively treated menstrual disorders and menopausal symptoms.[46]

The incident demonstrated the power of the Proprietary Association as a pressure group capable of influencing both proprietors and bureaucrats. Frank Blair, the organization's president, liked to credit the Association for improved relations between patent medicine manufacturers and the government. But the mood of the Harding, Coolidge, and Hoover years, as much as Blair's efforts, brought about the era of good feelings between government and business. Increasingly the regulators worked side by side with the regulated. In informal meetings with Bureau of Chemistry officials, proprietors learned just how far they could go without running the risk of prosecution. Instead of printing the label and waiting in fear of seizure, the proprietor could be reasonably assured of immunity from prosecution before he put his bottle on the market. The Bureau of Chemistry often took the initiative by notifying drug manufacturers of label violations so that they could voluntarily make the necessary changes. Paul Dunbar, chief of the regulatory division of the Bureau, wrote in 1926, "It is the bureau's theory that more is to be accomplished by acting in an advisory capacity . . . than by accumulating a record of successful prosecutions. . . ."[47]

Officials from the Bureau of Chemistry became regular speakers at Proprietary Association conventions, where they reassured drug-makers that the Bureau saw its function as informative rather than punitive. John S. Jamieson in one such speech declared that the Bureau of Chemistry was "ready and willing to be of what assistance it can" and urged proprietors uncertain about their label claims to consult his staff, which, he promised, would be "pleased to offer such appropriate suggestions as may seem indicated."[48] In an atmosphere of polite concern, proprietors and bureaucrats did business together.

The spirit of negotiation and compromise that grew up between the enforcers and the enforced disturbed Harvey Washington Wiley, who saw in it an attempt to undermine the provisions of the food and drugs law. Lamenting what he termed "the sleeping sickness of educational procrastination," he called for more rigorous law enforcement. "There is no warrant in the law, nor any suggestion of a warrant," he protested, "that offenders should be called before the Bureau of Chemistry for the purpose of receiving instructions in ethics, nor that the Bureau of Chemistry should waste its energies and appropriations in trying in a kind of ethical, Sunday-school fashion, to persuade manufacturers to be good."[49]

Wiley's vigorous and often bitter criticism had little impact on administrators. Self-regulation of business had become the slogan of the day. It was cheaper, quicker, and brought better results than criminal action against proprietors, or so government officials argued.

Late in 1925 the Pinkham company experienced the government's new enforcement strategy first hand. In November the Bureau of Chemistry filed a citation of misbranding against the Vegetable Compound. This time, instead of initiating court action as it had done in 1915, the Bureau pressed for voluntary compliance. In hearings with Pinkham representatives, officials warned that the company must drastically revise its labels, circulars, and textbook. Chemical analysis indicated that the Compound acted only as a bitter tonic, equally suited to men and women. The government was no longer willing to wink at Pinkham claims that the Compound could treat menstrual cramps or menopausal symptoms. To avoid prosecution the company would have to stop selling the Vegetable Compound as a women's medicine.[50]

The government's ruling caught the company flushed with success after a banner year in which sales had reached an unprecedented three and a half million dollars. Unable to draw on scientific research to support its claim that the medicine treated female complaints, the company chose to comply with the government. Before the end of 1925, less than a month after the hearings ended, the Pinkham company changed all its labels, wrappers, inserts, and booklets to conform to the new ruling. Pinkham employees worked overtime during the Christmas holidays to relabel shipments of the Vegetable Compound. All mention of female weakness and disorder disappeared. Instead the new label stated that the Compound was "Recommended as a Vegetable Tonic in conditions for which this preparation is Adapted"—a statement so meaningless that Arthur Cramp joked it might as well read, "For Those Who Like This Sort of Thing, This Is The Sort of Thing That Those People Like."[51]

The government ruling dealt the Pinkham company a stunning blow. For fifty years the Pinkhams had marketed the Vegetable Compound as a cure for "female weakness." Now they could only hint at "conditions for which this preparation is adapted." Regular customers, of course, would continue to buy the medicine. But how would the company attract new users with claims so vague? In the past Wetherald had relied on newspaper advertising to expand upon claims made on the label. This time the Bureau of Chemistry threatened to scrutinize Pinkham ads. Their warning was clear: Unless and until the company could muster scientific evidence to prove the Vegetable Compound contained ingredients capable of treating specific women's problems, Pinkham advertising could do no more than offer the medicine as a tonic.

The tough, new policy demonstrated the increasing resourcefulness of the Bureau of Chemistry. During the 1920's, the Bureau managed informally to get around the greatest weakness of the Pure Food and Drugs Act—its failure to deal with advertising. Gradually the Bureau instituted the policy of examining "collateral advertising." When a medicine carried vague and unspecific claims on its label, Bureau officials insisted that they had the right to examine advertising in newspapers and magazines to determine the manufacturer's intent. If the therapeutic claims in the collateral advertising exceeded those allowed on the label, the Bureau initiated action against the proprietor. At the same time, the Bureau put an end to the testimonial dodge by ruling that manufacturers were responsible for the accuracy of therapeutic claims made by their customers in print. To enforce its new dictates without resorting to the courts, the Bureau adopted the strategy of multiple seizures. Entire shipments of misbranded medicine were waylaid at a dozen sites at a time and confiscated by the government. Although the Proprietary Association protested that such strong-arm tactics unduly stretched the law, the Bureau of Chemistry continued to interpret its powers broadly in an effort to put some teeth into the food and drugs law and make of it something more than the "canton flannel dog" George Creel had disparaged a decade earlier.[52]

To some extent a failure of nerve on the part of proprietors, as well as increasing vigilance on the part of the government, gave the food and drugs law its new bite. Increasingly, as in the Pinkham case, proprietors gave in to government demands without a fight. The spirit of cooperation between government and business, which Wiley had predicted would make the regulators lackeys of the industries they regulated, turned out in the Pinkham case to have a very different impact. The Pinkham company's voluntary compliance saved the government time and money; it is difficult to see precisely what the company gained in return. Possibly the Pinkham company feared multiple seizures if it failed to comply. Yet the government rarely used that weapon unless there was a clear threat to public health. Had the company chosen to resist the government's citation, the case would have gone to the courts, where, as history demonstrated, the patent medicine maker had little to fear. Why, then, did the company capitulate?

In retrospect, the answer seems to lie in the Proprietary Association's campaign to make patent medicines "respectable." In 1916, Will Gove, as vice-president of the Association, congratulated his fellow members on their new image. No longer were they viewed as "snake-oil salesmen"; instead they could pride themselves on heading substantial, firmly established businesses.[53] The new respectability Gove greeted so warmly came about partially from the Proprietary Association's efforts at policing its own industry and partially from the spirit of cooperation urged upon proprietors by the government and the Proprietary Association alike. In order to be respectable, patent medicine makers were encouraged to avoid open confrontation with the government. The rhetoric of cooperation and compliance ultimately led patent medicine manufacturers to confuse image with economic reality.

The Pinkham company paid a high price for a dubious gain in 1925 when it agreed to quit selling the Vegetable Compound as a women's medicine. In return for its compliance, it gained no more than the slender hope that by earning a reputation as a cooperative, respectable concern, it might avoid future government scrutiny. And yet as long as the AMA kept hammering at patent medicines, it remained unlikely that patent medicine makers would achieve the legitimacy or the freedom from government interference they desired.

The government citation caught the Pinkham company at a time when its capacity to respond decisively and imaginatively was badly undermined by power struggles within the family. The Pinkham-Gove feud had not ended in 1901 when the Goves reluctantly allowed Arthur Pinkham and his mother a voice in the business. A reservoir of bad feeling remained which soon spread to the second generation. The six Pinkham children and the four children of Will and Aroline Gove were hardly kissing cousins. When Lydia Pinkham Gove arrived at Smith College in 1903 only to discover that the dean had unwittingly assigned her a room with cousin Lucy Pinkham, the fireworks that followed made a lasting impression on the girls' classmates. Lydia stormed into the dean's office and threatened to leave school rather than room with the hapless Lucy. Under fire, the college quickly remedied the blunder.[54]

Rivalry between Arthur Pinkham and William Pinkham Gove, four years his junior, was more subtle and more serious. Arthur, as vice-president of the company, supervised foreign trade. Between 1901 and 1920 he opened up Pinkham plants in Canada, England, and Mexico, as well as directing Pinkham sales strategy in Europe, South America, and Asia. Arthur also served as president of the Lynn National City Bank, a position he had held since 1909, when, at the age of twenty-nine, he enjoyed the distinction of being the youngest bank president in the country. His cousin, Bill Gove, joined the company in 1908 shortly after graduating from Harvard's law school. Gove handled the company's general advertising department, a job which involved the printing and distribution of Pinkham pamphlets and booklets. Each man hoped to become the next president of the Pinkham company.[55]

When Will Gove died of cancer in 1920, his death brought the rivalry out into the open and touched off a power struggle between the two families. Gove's death left his wife, Aroline, and Jennie Pinkham the only surviving members of the company's Board of Directors. Each woman was determined that her son would be the next company president. At first the Goves appeared to have the edge. In 1900, at the time Will and Aroline Gove seized control of the company, they had called a directors' meeting and voted that in the event of Will's death, Aroline would succeed him as head of the company. Acting on that vote, Aroline sought to push Arthur Pinkham aside. The Pinkhams argued that the change in by-laws that Arthur had successfully forced on the

Goves in 1901 abrogated the earlier vote by giving the vice-president control of the company in the president's absence.

The showdown dragged out over a year, threatening to disrupt business completely. Aroline insisted on her authority to run the company; Arthur refused to yield his prerogative as vice-president. Nothing could be decided until the Board of Directors met to elect a successor to Will Gove. Jennie Pinkham repeatedly called for a meeting, but Aroline blocked attempts to elect a new president by refusing to attend, thus making a quorum impossible. Exasperated, the Pinkhams took the company to court to demand an election.[56]

In an effort at compromise, attorneys for the Pinkhams and the Goves drafted a new set of by-laws allowing for six directors, three representing the Pinkham interests and three the Goves'. Under the terms of the arrangement, the Pinkham side of the family controlled the management of the business; the Gove side handled the company's finances. Arthur Pinkham became president of the company; his brother Daniel, recently graduated from Brown in business, was named first vice-president; and Charles H. Pinkham, Jr., then a Brown undergraduate, became the corporation's secretary. Jennie Pinkham resigned from the Board in order to let her sons hold the three Pinkham directorships. The Gove directors were Aroline, who remained treasurer; Bill Pinkham, who was named second vice-president; and Lydia Pinkham Gove, who later received the title of assistant treasurer.[57]

Inadvertently the arrangement established in 1921 operated as an invitation to deadlock. With half the family running the company and the other half holding the purse strings, the meticulous equality created between the Pinkhams and the Goves demanded cooperation in order for the business to operate at all. Neither side saw the problem until it was too late. Arthur Pinkham greeted the reorganization optimistically. In 1922 he remarked to the president of the Proprietary Association, "Everything seems to be running along very nicely. I believe the members of both families are trying to have things continue."[58]

Conservative and thoughtful, Arthur Pinkham managed the company much as his father had. Wetherald continued to map out the advertising strategies which sold the Vegetable Compound. Pinkham knew the importance of newspaper advertising and budgeted accordingly. By 1922 the company spent more than a million dollars a year to place advertising in the papers.

Bill Gove, as second vice-president, continued to run the company's general advertising department. Gove converted one floor of the factory into a printing plant to cut costs. By 1920 the company put out eleven million copies of its booklets annually, often printing as many as three titles a year. Ten million books in each lot were sent to druggists, who then arranged for local distribution. The remaining million the company mailed to rural areas, where house-to-house distribution was impractical. To check on his distributors, Gove inserted a questionnaire in the back of each booklet that asked women where they had found their copy and what they had noticed about the distributor's methods. In return for their response, the company offered free novelty items. Women by the hundreds of thousands answered in order to get the sewing kits, sachets, bookmarks, perfume, and other free gifts.

The questionnaire worked so well that Gove decided to ask about the medicine itself. "Did this medicine help you?" he queried. "Kindly tell us for just what trouble you took this medicine." Results indicated the impact of changes in labeling and advertising. Of the women who responded to the questionnaire in the early twenties, 55 per cent said they took the Compound for menstrual troubles; 21 per cent for nerves; 9 per cent for pregnancy; 7 per cent for menopause. Only 2 per cent mentioned kidney troubles; 2 per cent leucorrhea; and 1 per cent prolapse—conditions no longer mentioned in Pinkham ads. The remaining 3 per cent named stomach troubles. Gove tabulated the responses and concluded that ninety-eight out of every one hundred women had been helped. He accepted the overwhelmingly favorable response without questioning the effect the free gift had on women's estimate of the Compound. Ignoring the women who did not respond, he saw to it that Pinkham booklets carried on the inside front cover the headline, "98 out of 100 Women Benefited."[59]

Although Arthur Pinkham and Bill Gove worked hard to make the business successful, the harmony which greeted the company's reorganization in 1921 proved short-lived. By 1925 the Pinkhams and the Goves were again at sword's point, largely due to the personality of Lydia Pinkham Gove. After her graduation from Smith in 1907, Lydia returned home determined to take an active role in the family business. Like her namesake, Lydia cut an impressive figure. She stood over six feet tall, a big-boned, handsome woman with the look of a person used to having her own way. After Will Gove's death, Aroline increasingly deferred to her daughter and allowed her to take over more and more of the treasurer's duties. Bill Gove resented his sister's imperious ways and her hold over their mother, whom he described as "a pawn in her hands."

Tempers flared in 1924 when Aroline asked Bill to return to her a part of his company stock. She feared that she had given Bill more than a fair share and that her two younger daughters might be slighted. Bill refused to relinquish the stock. As he saw it, his mother and sisters did little for the company while he worked full time. In retaliation for his insubordination, Lydia and her mother threatened to vote a reduction in his salary. Gove grew so angry that he severed relations with his mother and sister and made overtures to the Pinkhams. His interests, he confided to Dan Pinkham, were now practically identical with theirs. Bill's threatened defection would have upset the balance of power so carefully built into the company's by-laws in 1921. At one point Gove told Dan Pinkham he would join the Pinkham stockholders in the next general election, vote to do away with the two classes of stock, and elect a Board of Directors "WITHOUT ANY WOMEN ON IT."[60]

Bill Gove died of bleeding ulcers at the age of forty-two, before he had a chance to make good his threat. His death in September of 1925 precipitated a head-on collision between the Pinkham men and the Gove women. The day after Bill Gove's funeral, Lydia arrived at the factory and announced that she intended to take over her brother's general advertising department. She had "inherited" the job, she told her stunned audience. The next day Lydia moved into Bill's office and proceeded to make radical changes in the company's advertising. Using her power over company finances as a lever to gain her ends, she took control of newspaper advertising as well as the distribution of booklets.[61]

Lydia Pinkham Gove's advertising policy differed markedly from that of Wetherald. No bill of fare or institutional copy announced her ad's intent. So oblique were references to the Vegetable Compound that the reader might miss them entirely. "Do You Know As Much As Your Cat?" one ad began. The copy read in part:

What does your cat do when she is not well? She eats catnip, if she can find it. She eats grass and certain green plants to which her instinct leads her.

The ad concluded by urging women to be as smart as cats and turn to an herbal remedy, the Vegetable Compound.[62]

Arthur Pinkham and Wetherald were appalled, but they could do little. Lydia refused to appropriate funds to pay for any but her own ads. During the first two months of 1926, the company ran not one line of newspaper advertising because the Pinkham and Gove directors could not agree on copy. Worried that a protracted halt in advertising might irreparably harm the business, the Pinkhams reluctantly agreed to let Lydia manage the advertising campaign that year. She spent nearly two million dollars in less than ten months. Sales fell more than a half million dollars.[63]

Blame for the decline in advertising effectiveness could not be laid entirely upon Lydia Pinkham Gove. The government's belated but effective curtailment of Pinkham labeling and collateral advertising played a significant role in the sales slump. But Lydia's determination to wrest control of the company from the Pinkhams paralyzed the business. As long as she controlled the finances, Arthur Pinkham had little choice but to accept her dictates. Lydia was headstrong and ruthless, and she used every method at her disposal to drive out her cousins. She had neither the skill nor the experience to formulate an advertising strategy to combat increased government intervention. Yet she refused to yield to wiser heads. Her recalcitrance again and again led to stalemate where vigorous action alone was needed to save the company.

The New Woman...
The Same Old Medicine

In the summer of 1926 Lydia Pinkham Gove took time away from her self-imposed duties as Pinkham advertising agent to spend six weeks with friends and relatives in California. There she discovered, as she put it, a "new and fascinating sport—riding in aeroplanes." Flying appealed to Lydia's taste for the daring and the dramatic. So much so that she determined to leave to the rest of her party the heat and dust of train travel. She would fly back to Boston. When her friends objected that the venture was foolhardy, and besides, no proper young woman would fly cross-country with an unknown pilot, she persuaded the Rev. James Luther Adams to desert the group and accompany her. The next day the two went to the Los Angeles airport where they inquired of an incredulous pilot the price of a transcontinental flight. Lydia's characteristic strong will (coupled with her fat checkbook) carried the day. Within twenty-four hours she commandeered a plane and pilot and took off for the East Coast.

The cross-country trip was a leisurely affair with frequent stops for meals and gasoline. The pilot did not attempt to fly at night, so Lydia and Adams combined the excitement of daytime flying with the amenities of the finest hotels en route. Yet the seven day cross-

country flight in an open plane made history of a sort. Lydia
Pinkham Gove became the first commercial passenger to fly
across the United States.[1] Lydia received a celebrity's welcome at
the East Boston airport where she was met by a group of photog-
raphers and reporters on hand to record the event. As she
climbed out of the cockpit in her leather aviator's helmet and
goggles, Lydia, smiling into the cameras, epitomized the distance
traveled in the half-century since her grandmother and namesake
had posed for another, more famous picture. The genteel female,
that paradigm of the nineteenth century, had disappeared utterly
and in her place appeared, in bold capital letters, the New
Woman, followed shortly by her kid sister, the infamous Flapper.

The demise of the genteel female began quietly in the last decades of the nineteenth century. Gradually women began to shed
the Victorian languor that had turned American middle-class society, in the words of William Dean Howells, into a hospital for
female invalids. In ever increasing numbers, women deserted the
stuffy parlor, with its claw-footed sofas and bric-a-brac, for the
open road and the out-of-doors. Bicycling became a national
craze in the nineties. Almost immediately the popularity of the
bicycle led to dress reforms that the feminist Bloomers of the
1850's had despaired of achieving: Women cyclists abandoned the
whaleboned corset and took to wearing shorter skirts with modest
pantalettes. The typical cycling costume of the late nineties consisted of boots, spats, pantalettes, a skirt (properly loaded with lead
weights in the hem to resist air curents and ensure modesty in
mounting and dismounting), a shirt or waist, gloves, and a hat.
Nevertheless, doughty moralists complained that female cyclists
were immodest, indecent, and mannish. Critics predicted ruinous
social and moral consequences from bike-riding. More than one
physician hinted darkly that bicycling would "beget and foster the
habit of masturbation among women." In spite of the prediction
that the "wheel" was the "advance agent of the devil," nothing
curbed the bicycle's popularity. Most Americans seemed to agree
with the words of the popular song, "You'll look sweet upon the
seat of a bicycle built for two."[2]

The advent of exercise, or "physical culture" for women, coupled with Americans' growing enthusiasm for "sports," led to a new ideal in feminine beauty. The New Woman, much talked about at the turn of the century, radiated health, vigor, and a certain something later writers called sex appeal. She played tennis instead of croquet, took up golf at that new American upper-middle-class institution, the country club, and swam in an abbreviated bathing dress that for the first time allowed some freedom of movement. Illustrator Charles Dana Gibson captured her in his drawings and gave American its first pin-up—the Gibson Girl.

Gibson's famous drawings, featured in *Life* magazine for over two decades, owed much to their handsome bachelor illustrator's frank appreciation of the subtle eroticism of the femme fatale. Gibson's girls were restless, confident, and sexually powerful in a way the genteel female had never been. They carried their pompadoured heads held high and looked down their noses through heavy-lidded eyes at the men who vied for their attention. The Gibson Girl at first glance represented the antithesis of the passivity and submissiveness associated with the womanly woman of the ninetenth century. Gibson portrayed her in one illustration which he captioned "Dangerous," arming herself for the battle of the sexes by adjusting her modish hat with wicked-looking hatpins. Regal, haughty, and of Amazonian proportions, the Gibson Girl was both worthy adversary and coveted prize.[3]

Yet Gibson's femme fatale, dangerous and powerfully attractive though she was, was strangely vulnerable in her own right. While she might for a season dominate and manipulate her suitors, Gibson made it clear that she herself was in thrall to a higher force—a force he illustrated in the form of Cupid. Gibson's cupids can best be understood as symbols for what George Bernard Shaw in *Man and Superman* christened the Life Force—a blind, impersonal drive to creation and procreation. Woman's erotic power as Gibson portrayed it was beyond her control and ultimately as dangerous to herself as to her suitors. In one revealing sketch he pictured a woman, her head thrown back, her eyes half shut in indeterminate agony or ecstasy. Below, three of Cupid's arrows painfully pierce the flesh above her deep décolletage. While artists like Gibson and Shaw broke Victorian restraints by avowing women's sexual power, they perceived that power in classically Victorian terms, as the result of biological function, not individual force of will. For this reason the women in many of Gibson's drawings have an almost somnambulant quality, as though they are being drawn through life unconscious, pulled by invisible strings in the hands of a master puppeteer.

For all her haughty, sexual power, the Gibson Girl as an ideal type did not seriously undermine those virtues of piety, purity, domesticity, and submissiveness associated with the nineteenth-century cult of true womanhood.[4] Her power was limited and circumscribed. She ruled her father's life as the daughter he must marry well, ruled her suitors through her alluring sexual power, but was herself ruled by her passions—passions which inevitably led her to marriage and motherhood. Once she married, Gibson was no longer interested in her (unless she married for money or title, in which case he mercilessly satirized her as a neurasthenic victim of her unfulfilled desires). By implication Gibson seemed to say that her erotic power was extinguished in its very fulfillment.

The New Woman of the 1890's, like her counterpart the Gibson Girl, almost invariably settled down to marriage and a family. Over 90 per cent of the female population married in the nineteenth century and, although the birth rate declined steadily during the century, by 1910 married women still produced an average of three children. The ideal American woman remained religious, if not pious; virginally pure before marriage, if flirtatious; and if in her heyday she was a sportswoman pictured out-of-doors, in marriage she became as domestic as her mother had been. Only 5 percent of married women worked in 1900.[5]

Yet change there was, if only in perception. And the changes that were to topple the edifice of Victorian culture and lead to the birth of modernity continued apace in the period before World War I. Although the full impact of change was not felt until the 1920's, when critics blamed it on the dislocating effect of the Great War, the groundwork was laid in the Progressive period and the New Woman played an impressive role in the groundbreaking.

The New Woman was many women. She was the college graduate, determined to be more than an ornament, who sought outlets
for her energy and education; she was the sportswoman who
posed for pictures clutching her tennis racquet or golf clubs; she
was the middle-aged clubwoman who met monthly or weekly for
lectures and discussions on topics ranging from Egyptian art to
city lighting; she was the reformer out to purify society and politics; she was the much maligned suffragist; she was the new professional in medicine, law, or social work; she was these and many
more.

Between the 1890's, when she first caught America's attention,
and 1920, when she was superseded by the Flapper, the New
Woman made news. Cultural commentators inspected her cri-
tically in the pages of newspapers and magazines to determine her
impact on traditional values and morés. Often they did not look
too closely or too seriously, but few failed to notice that the New
Woman looked and acted in ways that set her apart from her
mother and grandmother.

Superficial changes can be easily cataloged. The simplication of
women's clothing begun in the 1890's continued, until by 1912
the president of the New York Cotton Exchange lamented that
women had shed "at least twelve yards of finished goods for each
adult female inhabitant." The tailored shirtwaist popularized by
the Gibson Girl, with its narrow skirt and middy blouse, made way
for the ankle-length sheath dress, cut with straight up-and-down
lines and a dropped waist. The corset and the hourglass figure
were relegated to antiquity, but the girdle held its own. The trim
lines of the new fashions made women increasingly weight conscious and those who could not achieve the proper silhouette by
diet gratefully accepted elastic bondage. Shorter shirts exposed
women's legs and flesh colored silk or rayon stockings added to
the new sense of bareness. In 1913 the dancer Irene Castle popularized the Panjola bob and thereafter bobbed hair became a
badge of the New Woman. Those who cringed before the shears
wore their long hair pulled back and up on their necks to give the
illusion of short hair. By 1916 not only the sophisticated *Smart Set*
but the conservative *Ladies' Home Journal* featured cover girls with

short hair. As women's costume became less elaborate, their toilet became more so. Cosmetics and so-called beauty aids, once associated with "women of the night," became acceptable, almost essential.[6]

Critics of this transformation in women's fashion agreed that the new styles were odious, but they were strangely confused as to why. Some attacked the new fashions as unfeminine and mannish. Others declared them indecently provocative. The confusion marked an anomaly: As women bared more and more of their figure in shorter, sleeveless dresses they seemed at the same time, in the eyes of their critics, less womanly than their predecessors. It can be argued that the new styles paradoxically diminished sexual provocativeness precisely because they exposed more of the body and in so doing blunted the sexual curiosity, bordering on prurience, characteristic of the days when the sight of a woman's ankle raised a man's blood pressure. Certainly the straight lines of the sheath dress did less to emphasize women's hips and bust than the wasp-waists and bustles of the 1880's. Some muting of sexuality seemed called for when women began to leave home and work in business alongside men.

More and more often the New Woman was a working-woman. The first decade of the twentieth century witnessed a significant movement of women into the work force. The proportion of all women holding jobs jumped from 20.4 per cent in 1900 to 25.2 percent in 1910—an increase that would not be matched until the 1940's. Even more striking was the shift in the type of work women performed. Domestic servants, agricultural workers, and unskilled factory operatives drawn from the lower socio-economic strata constituted the bulk of women workers at the turn of the century. Middle- and upper-middle-class women who desired work, whether from inclination or necessity, found few suitable jobs available to them. One young woman who grew up in the 1880's described the dearth of opportunities open to women of her class. "In our town few women earned money except as teachers, dressmakers, milliners or domestics," she recalled. "A few girls gave music lessons, a few taught a curious thing called china-painting, and on the fringes of society there were girls, usually with dissipated fathers, who had taken up stenography and typewriting."[7] By 1910 the pattern began to change perceptibly. Women in increasing numbers entered the work force in clerical or sales positions deemed appropriate for daughters of the middle class. Between 1910 and 1920 over one million women joined the clerical force—an increase of nearly 300 per cent over the previous decade. Thus the most significant changes in the relative size and composition of the female labor force occurred before either World War I or the enactment of woman suffrage.[8]

Rheta Child Dorr, a journalist and social statistician, was among the first to note the change. "I began to see them as never before," she wrote, "hundreds and thousands of women, every evening crowding the subways, the elevated, the surface-cars, the streets; hundreds and thousands going home from work." In 1905 at the instigation of the Women's Trade Union League and the Association of Social Settlements, Dorr gathered a volume of *Statistics of Women at Work* and had the satisfaction of telling the American people "for the first time, that one woman in five in the United States was a wage-earner."[9]

No longer able to ignore the growing number of women workers, Americans struggled to come to terms with the discrepancy between traditional assumptions about woman's place and irrefutable evidence of her new economic activity. The fear that women might willfully abandon their place in the home to seek satisfaction as wage-earners led many writers to harsh criticism of the new working-woman. John Martin, writing in *Survey* magazine in 1916, warned that women who worked violated nature's law and abrogated their responsibility to the race. Ignoring the economic necessity that drove many women into the workplace, he castigated them for their selfishness. The working mother particularly outraged his sensibilities. "Her example is pernicious," he wrote, "her ethics immoral, her selfishness destructive to the nation." And to dampen the enthusiasm of single women who coveted a career, he reminded them "even one baby is a creative work that absorbs more vital force and utilizes more executive skill than a third-rate novel or a pettifogging law practice."[10]

Martin's hysterical prose highlighted the extent to which women's economic activity was perceived as a direct threat to home and family. Throughout the nineteenth century, woman's place in the home had been justified on the theory that only there could she avoid the contaminating influence of the male world and nurture those domestic and spiritual virtues which allowed her to play the useful role of guardian of morality. Faced with a generation of New Women who actively sought work outside of the home, many critics forecast the decline of civilization. For if women would no longer guard morality, who would?

The notion of women as moral guardians, however, cut with a double blade. Women were quick to point out that their moral superiority was badly needed in the work-a-day world. Many feminists appropriated the rhetoric of their critics to argue that women should play a more active role in the world. It was woman's duty, they argued, to purify society. The suffragists were to use the argument to good effect in their struggle for the vote.

The desire to cleanse society of moral evil led many women into the social hygiene movement in the early decades of the twentieth century. Social hygiene, a euphemism for the campaign against prostitution and venereal disease, became a popular cause which brought together in unlikely alliance advocates of moral purity, Greenwich Village bohemians, and not-so-disinterested academics, social workers, and physicians. Together these diverse groups fought for an end to the conspiracy of silence that shrouded sexual matters. Social hygienists argued that innocence could not be equated with ignorance when it came to sex. Education alone could alert youth to the dangers of prostitution and venereal disease. With the help of the medical profession, advocates of social hygiene launched a campaign to educate young people to the dangers of immorality.

After a good deal of soul-searching, Edward Bok at *The Ladies' Home Journal* joined the social hygiene crusade. In 1906 Bok published a full-page editorial declaring that seventy of every one hundred special operations on women resulted directly or indirectly from venereal disease and that sixty of every one hundred children born blind were blinded by the effects of gonorrhea.

Thousands of indignant readers cancelled their subscriptions. Bok later wrote in his autobiography that he had the "grim experience of seeing his magazine, hitherto proclaimed all over the land as a model advocate of the virtues, refused admittance into thousands of homes. . . ." In spite of the opposition, Bok continued his articles and supplemented them with twenty-five-cent pamphlets called "The Edward Bok Books" which contained information on venereal disease. In the pages of *The Ladies' Home Journal,* Bok concentrated his efforts against venereal disease by calling for the prohibition of the public drinking cup, supposedly a carrier of venereal contagion. Within six months his readers organized a legislative campaign leading to state statutes outlawing the "germ-laden common drinking cup." The fact that articles on sex education and venereal disease appeared in the pages of *The Ladies' Home Journal* was itself an indication of the new frankness in sexual matters inspired by the social hygiene movement.[11]

Social hygiene reformers turned to the stage, as well as the printed page, to publicize their campaign against venereal disease. Eugene Brieux, a French playwright, wrote *Les Avaries* to dramatize the horrible consequences that ensue when a man with venereal disease marries a pure woman. Translated into English and performed under the title *Damaged Goods,* the play was promoted in the United States by advocates of social hygiene, including John D. Rockefeller, Jr., who provided financial backing for the American production. In 1913 the play achieved a notable commercial success on Broadway.[12]

The more conservative among the ranks of the social hygiene movement argued, with some basis, that the breakdown of the conspiracy of silence led as much to sensationalism and titillation as to education. America in the 1910's witnessed a "repeal of reticence."[13] Once the restraints fell away, topics never before discussed in public became commonplace. An eyewitness to the changes taking place before World War I outlined the impact of the social hygiene movement:

Subjects formerly tabooed are now thrust before the public. The plain-spoken publications of the social hygiene societies are distributed by

hundreds of thousands. Public exhibits, setting forth the horrors of venereal diseases, are sent from place to place. Motion-picture films portray
white slavers, prostitutes, and restricted districts, and show exactly how
an innocent girl may be seduced, betrayed, and sold. The stage finds it
profitable to offer problem plays concerned with illicit love, with prostitution, and even with the results of venereal contagion.[14]

Distressed by the new freedom in language and literature, *Current Opinion* proclaimed in 1913 that it had struck "Sex O'Clock
in America." "Is this over-emphasis of sex a symptom of a new
moral awakening," the magazine queried, "or is it a sign that the
morbidity of the Old World is overtaking the New?"[15]

Americans who prided themselves on the wholesome moral superiority of the United States over decadent Europe had good
reason to question the effects of the social hygiene movement. For
however unwittingly, the movement served to popularize the radical views of Europeans like Havelock Ellis, Ellen Key, Auguste
Forel, Edward Carpenter, and Sigmund Freud. Ellis in particular
attracted a wide American audience. In the eclectic bibliographies
put together by advocates of sex education, Ellis' work appeared
next to tracts by Sylvannus Stall and other purity writers. Yet
readers who perused the six volumes of *Studies in the Psychology of
Sex* found a radically different message. Ellis was openly and unabashedly a "sexual enthusiast." In opposition to the prevailing
view of sexuality as a moral threat and a potentially destructive
force, Ellis preached the beneficence of the sex instinct and the
importance of sexual fulfillment. Although he by no means advocated sexual abandon, he strongly believed that his contemporaries suffered more from the effects of restraint than from the
damages of excess. Readers who had grown up on the purity literature of the nineteenth century were suddenly told that absti-
nence, not indulgence, threatened their physical and mental
well-being. To many it appeared that Ellis, along with other sexual theorists, had turned Victorian morality topsy-turvy.[16]

Certainly Ellis called into question one of the tenets of the Victorian moral order—the belief that women were naturally pure
and without strong sexual passion. In "The Sexual Impulse in

Women," published in 1905, he attacked the stereotype of the
genteel female head-on. Arguing from his own case studies that
women were as capable of sexual feeling as men, he blamed male
ineptness and ignorance of "the arts of love" for creating the mistaken stereotype of the passionless woman. "When once duly
aroused," he wrote, "there cannot usually be any doubt concerning the strength of the sexual impulse in normal and healthy
women." Ellis also exploded the myth that in women the maternal
instinct substituted for sexual instinct. Woman's sexual nature was
to Ellis more than the blind working of the Life Force. Although
he enthusiastically endorsed motherhood as woman's supreme
function, he insisted that women, like men, had sexual desires
quite apart from the desire to have children. Those who defined
sex euphemistically as "the reproductive instinct," he dismissed as
"unconsciously dominated by superstitious repugnance to sex."[17]

Ellis' belief in the importance of sexual fulfillment implied a
necessary loosening of old restraints, which brought him into conflict with accepted standards of morality. In place of the old morality, with its emphasis on self-denial and duty, Ellis and others
posited a new morality based on greater freedom and self-expres-
sion. Nowhere was the debate between old and new more fiercely
waged than over the issue of marriage. To cultural conservatives
like Theodore Roosevelt, marriage signified an indissoluable
bond. Two years after the death of his first wife, on the eve of his
second marriage, Roosevelt is said to have paced the room of a
friend's house, pounding his fist into his palm and expostulating,
"I have no constancy! I have no constancy!"[18] No wonder Roosevelt and others who had been raised to place duty and order
before personal happiness viewed mounting divorce statistics as
symptoms of social decay. In contrast, Ellis maintained that true
marriage rested on fact and not on contract. Society, Ellis insisted,
had no right to shackle together two people who no longer found
physical or psychological fulfillment in one another.[19]

Far from encouraging hedonistic license, the new morality posited its own rules and restraints. Though Ellis repudiated "artificial marriage," he clung to monogamy. For all his supposed
radicalism, he remained at heart a romantic. The ideal sexual

relationship, as he conceived of it, involved far more than casual or promiscuous sex. Instead it rested on a complex emotional relationship between one man and one woman bound together by sexual love in what he termed "natural monogamy." Likening legal marriage to a corset, Ellis argued that it enfeebled and cramped natural development. "It is only by the process of loosening the artificial restraints [of marriage] that the natural restraints can exert their full control."[20]

In practice, Ellis advocated a form of trial marriage in which lovers formed informal, extra-legal relationships that could be legally countenanced when and if the couple decided to have children. A necessary corollary to the arrangement was, of course, the availability of effective means of contraception, and Ellis, for this reason, played an active role in the fight for birth control. Ellis and other sexual modernists sought to reform marriage, not to abolish it. Advocates of the new morality optimistically proposed that relaxing the bonds of marriage would transform it from a sullen bondage into a fulfilling union.

To credit Ellis and the European sex theorists with inventing the new morality would be to overlook the extent to which they simply provided a rationale for changes already taking place. The years before World War I witnessed a change in manners and morals so marked that some have called it a revolution. The acceptance of female sexuality, the breakdown in the double standard, the movement for birth control, the increased incidence of divorce, and the new atmosphere of sexual experimentation that caused so much controversy in the 1910's indicate a watershed between the Victorian period and the modern. In the ferment of change the New Woman became a symbol and a symptom of the new morality.

"Restless! Restless!" cried novelist Margaret Deland, searching for the word to describe women in 1910. Everywhere she encountered "a prevailing discontent among women," a "restlessness infinitely removed from the old content of a generation ago." Assessing the change in the feminine ideal epitomized in the shift from the genteel female to the New Woman, Deland found much that troubled her. "The young woman of today," she observed, "is supplementing a certain old-fashioned word, *duty,* by two other words, 'to myself.' "[21] Not only the young woman, but older women, too, restlessly sought fulfillment outside of traditional roles and restraints. "Most men don't know that a woman has a life of her own—apart from her children, from her husband, from all," complains Margaret Pole, one of a gallery of new women in Robert Herrick's best-selling novel, *Together.* "I have a soul—a life to be satisfied," asserts the anguished Margaret as she embarks upon an adulterous affair. "A woman's life is not closed at thirty-two!"[22] Herrick, who heartily disapproved of the New Woman, presented her so vividly that his audience frequently missed his heavy-handed criticism and took her on her own, and not the author's terms. That readers could mistake Herrick's profoundly conservative novel for a manifesto of sexual freedom indicated the confusion that surrounded the whole question of the new morality.

To writers more sympathetic to the New Woman, her increasing sexual freedom came as no surprise. Beatrice Hinkle, a physician, psychoanalyst, and something of a new woman herself, stated flatly that women who had broken away from their economic dependence on men could not be expected to personify the morality which men demanded of women but never practiced themselves.[23] With a rather naïve economic determinism, writers like Hinkle perhaps overemphasized women's role as economic free agents. Yet they correctly perceived that women who worked before marriage, especially those who escaped the social confines and parental restraints of the small town for the greater anonymity of city life, developed different expectations and experimented with different behaviors than had their mothers.

The New Woman in the period before World War I earned her own money, carried her own latchkey, smoked cigarettes, drank cocktails, and danced to the new rhythms of the tango and the turkey trot. In short, she began to adopt patterns of behavior previously the prerogative of men. Obviously some women had provided Victorian gentlemen with company when they sowed their wild oats, but rarely had they come from the same social ranks as the women they married. What distinguished the prewar revolution in morals and manners was the behavior of women one observer described as "nice girls, good girls, girls in good positions in society."[24] In the absence of hard data on the actual behavior of a geographical and economic cross-section of American women, it is impossible to say how extensive (or indeed how accurate) were the changes in manners and morals described at the time. But the perceptions gleaned from contemporary literature are themselves indicative of a change in the popular conception of women.

"Is 'the old-fashioned girl,' with all that she stands for in sweetness, modesty, and innocence, in danger of becoming extinct?" asked *Literary Digest.* A chorus of voices responded in the affirmative. According to advice columnist Dorothy Dix, the "type of girl that the modern young man falls for" was in 1915 a "husky young woman who can play golf all day and dance all night, and drive a motor car, and give first aid to the injured if anybody gets hurt, and who is in no more danger of swooning than he is."[25]

Just as the Gibson Girl provided a prototype of the New Woman of the 1890's, the Flapper became her symbol by the 1920's. H. L. Mencken called her to America's attention in 1915. Noting that the American language had no word for her, he borrowed the English word "Flapper."

Observe, then, this nameless one, this American Flapper. Her skirts have just reached her very trim and pretty ankles; her hair, newly coiled upon her skull, has just exposed the ravishing whiteness of her neck. A charming creature! . . . Youth is hers, and hope, and romance, and—

Well, well, let us be exact: let us not say innocence. This Flapper, to tell the truth, is far, far from a simpleton. . . .

This Flapper has forgotten how to simper; she seldom blushes; it is impossible to shock her. She saw *Damaged Goods* without batting an eye, and went away wondering what the row over it was all about. . . . She plans to read Havelock Ellis during the coming summer. . . .

As I have said, a charming young creature. There is something trim and trig and confident about her. She is easy in her manners. She bears herself with dignity in all societies. . . . There is music in her laugh. She is youth, she is hope, she is romance—she is wisdom![26]

To observers less sympathetic than Mencken, she was nothing but trouble.

The most striking characteristic of the Flapper was her youth. Where the New Woman had ranged in age from sixteen to sixty, the Flapper, according to F. Scott Fitzgerald, her contemporary and her chronicler, was "lovely and expensive and about nineteen."[27] A middle-aged Flapper was a contradiction in terms, although the cult of youth she inspired led many mothers and older sisters to emulate her style. By definition the Flapper was an ephemeral creature: As even her fiercest detractors agreed, the hoydenish Flapper of today grew up to become the wife and mother of tomorrow. As a cultural prototype, then, the Flapper subtly acknowledged the extent to which the so-called revolution in manners and morals was turning out to be no more than an adolescent rebellion.

By the 1920's, debates on the new morality focused more and more on what came to be called the "Revolt of Modern Youth." In many ways the key word in the description was "modern." What set the youth of the 1920's apart from their parents and older brothers and sisters was the growing conviction that they lived in a world so changed that the old rules no longer applied. Contemporary writers, both old and young, cataloged a sweeping set of social changes. One of the more whimsical of the lists included along with the automobile, the telephone, the motion picture, the radio, electric appliances, bathrooms, steam heat, and electric lights such modern phenomena as "the jazz dance, jazz music, jazz booze, jazz journalism, 'crime wave,' the permanent wave, the permanent passing of the chaperone, [and] the parking of the corset. . . ." The author concluded somewhat breathlessly that "the boy who can grind the valves or adjust the carburetor of an automobile . . . has learned a way of thought and scientific respect for facts to which his father at his age was a stranger." Similarly, the Flapper, "who makes her own living, votes, holds her own in competition with men, refuses to let the corset-maker put stays on her, and snaps her fingers at 'styles' dictated by the makers of clothes, is capable of doing things her mother couldn't come within sight of."[28]

Parents who had grown up in a horse-and-buggy era suddenly found that the wisdom of their years counted for little in an automobile age. Advice columnist Dorothy Dix insisted that social conditions had changed so drastically in twenty years that "the parent of today is absolutely unfitted to decide the problems of life for the young man and woman of today."[29] Such counsel only increased the sense of parental impotence. Helen and Robert Lynd in *Middletown*, their study of Muncie, Indiana, in the mid-twenties, observed that parents seemed confused and uncertain. Not only were they finding it difficult to hold their children to established rules of conduct, they were having a hard time determining the rules in the first place. "When I was a girl," remarked one young mother, "a girl who painted was a bad girl—but now look at the daughters of our best families!" "My daughter of fourteen thinks I am 'cruel' if I don't let her stay at a dance until after eleven," confessed another mother. "I tell her that when I was her age I had to be in at nine, and she says, 'Yes, Mother, but that was fifty years ago.'" Everywhere the Lynds encountered the same confusion. "You see other people being more lenient and you think perhaps that is the best way," confided one woman. "But you are afraid to do anything very different from what your mother did for fear you may leave out something essential or do something wrong." She concluded plaintively, "I would give anything to know what is wisest, but I don't know what to do."[30]

Concern over "what to do" soon spawned a literature of advice and alarm written by a group of experts who made it their business to interpret, explain, and intercede for the young. Dorothy Dix and Beatrix Fairfax, with their syndicated advice columns, provided only the most obvious examples. Perhaps the best known of the new youth experts was a fifty-five-year-old judge. In 1925 Judge Ben Lindsey of the Denver Juvenile Court published *The Revolt of Modern Youth*, which went through seven printings in less than a year. Lindsey's message was at once shocking and reassuring. Modern youth, he stated unequivocally, were in fact in revolt against conventional moral standards. Lindsey estimated that over 90 per cent of Denver's high school population "indulge in hugging and kissing." Of that number over half experimented with what Lindsey delicately referred to as "other sexual liberties." For some 15–20 per cent, sexual experimentation culminated in intercourse. Lindsey concluded that "sex delinquency," as he labeled such behavior, had become widespread.[31] Yet Lindsey viewed youth's break with accepted patterns of behavior as a salutary restructuring of outmoded and often hypocritical standards of conduct. Like so many of the youth experts, Lindsey had a low opinion of American parents. Behind the Judge's sympathy for the young lay his disdain for the old—a disdain he did not hesitate to express.

> Your own children, Sir and Madame, are intelligent, right-minded, and full of fine aspirations and quick sympathies, . . . Believe this of them, and rejoice in your hearts, on comparing them with yourselves, that they in the days of their youth, at least, are an improvement on the ragtag and bobtail of adult Puritanism that begot them.[32]

Convinced of the mental and moral superiority of the young, Lindsey predicted confidently that the revolt of modern youth signalled a better future.

Not all of the so-called youth experts took so sanguine a view. A host of doctors, teachers, social workers, and anyone else who could claim inside knowledge of the ways of the young rushed into print with exposés of the new morality. Much of what passed for expert opinion remained little more than sensationalism not far removed from the muckraking of the previous generation. Precisely how close were the ties between the two genres is best revealed in *Flaming Youth*, a best-selling novel published in 1923 and later made into a motion picture. The author, writing under the pseudonym Warner Fabian, purported to be a family physician acquainted first-hand with the habits and vices of youth. He chose fiction, he explained, because professional ethics forbade him to reveal either his own or his patients' true identities. In fact the novel was written not by a doctor, but by muckraker Samuel Hopkins Adams. After making his name with the patent medicine exposés in *Collier's* "Great American Fraud" series in 1905, Adams turned to didactic fiction, much of it dealing with medicine and doctors. In *Flaming Youth,* written when he was fifty-four, Adams experimented with a new kind of muckraking.

Advertisements for *Flaming Youth* promised "the truth, bold, naked, sensational."[33] But an audience expecting the "neckers, petters, white kisses, red kisses, pleasure-mad daughters, sensation-craving mothers" featured in the blurbs found instead a moral tale with a strange twist. The novel's flapper heroine, Pat Fentriss, is an earnest but flighty eighteen-year-old who loses her virginity not to some reckless young man, but to a close family friend, Cary Scott, a married man of forty. Oddly enough it is Scott, not the girl, whom Adams portrays as the victim of seduction. Scott is "ensnared" by the "innocent" but "dangerously inflammable" Pat. When the love-sick Scott vows to leave his wife and marry Pat, the capricious flapper refuses to be tied down. She sends him away and determines to live an independent life. In the end all is righted. Scott divorces his wife and Pat, by now a sensible twenty-year-old, agrees to give up her freedom and marry him. "But, oh, Cary darling!" she laughs. "As a husband you'll have to be a terribly on-the-job lover. There are so many men in the world!"[34]

Adams' novel is at once sensational and conventional. The novelist seems as bewildered by the young as his middle-aged hero and, as a result, his exposé has an unsatisfactory, second-hand quality. Like Judge Lindsey, Adams vacillates between attacks on the hypocrisy of the old morality and fulminations against the excesses of the new. *Flaming Youth* at first glance appears modern in that it spurns the melodramatic formula of seduction and betrayal. Adams allows his heroine to commit adultery without remorse or the punishment of pregnancy. But marry she must, and she comes to Scott in the end chaste but for their brief affair. Adams' conventional happy ending resolves all conflict. Pat may taunt her lover, but the taunt merely masks her surrender. Youth submits to age; woman submits to man. The Flapper, underneath her jaunty exterior, turns out to be at heart monogamous and domestic.

By the end of the twenties, the shrewder cultural analysts began to question the reality of the "revolution" in morals and manners.

How much, after all, had changed? Anthropologist Elsie Clews Parsons spoke of a "release from verbal taboo," which gave "a sense of change in general greater perhaps than the facts themselves warrant."[35] Writer Florence Guy Seabury agreed. "Old adages are put in more racy vernacular," she observed, "but when the broth of their engaging frankness disappears, hoary old ideas remain thick in the tumbler." Attitudes toward women, Seabury insisted, had changed little.

Whatever she actually is or does, in the stereotype she is a creature specialized to function. The girl on the magazine cover is her symbol. She holds a mirror, a fan, a flower and—at Christmas—a baby. Without variety, activity, or individuality her sugary smile pictures satisfying feminity.[36]

So long as women were regarded "not as people but as functions," so long as they were defined "merely in relationship to men," Seabury argued, "nothing new or strange or interesting is likely to happen. The old order is safe."[37]

And safe it was if the experience of the Pinkham company may be taken as evidence. Busts and bustles went out, rolled hose and cloche hats came in. Pinkham ads dutifully mirrored the changes. Booklets on diet and exercise, sports and marital advice replaced earlier issues devoted to recipes and health hints. Advertising copy applauded women's new freedom. "The days of the 'clinging vine' are a memory," ran one ad. The new woman, "is strong, self-reliant, self-supporting, healthy, happy, round, and rosy." Unblushingly Pinkham ads claimed credit for women's transformation. Without Lydia Pinkham and her Vegetable Compound, one ad insisted, women would still be languishing on the couch.[38]

As more and more women entered the work force, Wetherald revamped his copy to include more mention of the benefits working women could derive from the Vegetable Compound. "My work is to run a power-machine," began one testimonial, which credited the medicine with curing ovarian pain and weakness. In other letters, women claimed they held onto their jobs only with the help of the Compound. Ad copy urged women to be "100% efficient" at work by taking the medicine. Occasionally Wetherald's copy called into question women's new economic roles. "Women are too ambitious," complained one advertisement. "Excessive ambition leads women to exert themselves beyond their strength . . . then come nervous troubles, backaches, headaches, and frequently organic troubles." The solution, however, was not less ambition but more of Lydia Pinkham's medicine.[39]

The coming of modernity did little to hurt sales of the Vegetable Compound. In 1925, sales reached an all-time high of over three million dollars. The new woman, it appeared, still suffered from female complaints and still turned to the same old medicine.

At first glance it would seem that women who bought the Vegetable Compound in 1925 should have known better. Why, in the face of advances in medical science, tighter governmental regulation of patent medicines, and an assumed greater sophistication on the part of American consumers, did women continue to take the same medicine their grandmothers had relied upon?

In fact medical practitioners had little more to offer in the way of effective treatments for women's diseases in 1925 than they had at the close of the nineteenth century. Although the rise of bacteriology in the 1870's and 1880's brought with it a momentous breakthrough in the diagnosis of disease, its contribution to therapeutics proved disappointing. It was one thing to identify the bacteria that caused tuberculosis, gonorrhea, or syphilis; another to develop cures for these and other diseases. The celebrated "microbe hunters" Robert Koch, Louis Pasteur, Albert Neisser, and others who painstakingly isolated pathogenic microorganisms gave to the world, at long last, validation of the germ theory of disease. Flushed by their triumphs, enthusiastic bacteriologists predicted that medicine was on the threshold of conquering disease. Artificial antitoxins, poetically described as "magic bullets," would enable doctors to kill disease-causing microbes without killing the patient in the process. Success appeared certain when in 1909 the brilliant Silesian scientist Paul Erlich developed salvarsan, an arsenical drug which attacked and destroyed the spirochetes that caused syphilis. Erlich's great contribution to chemotherapy was hailed as the beginning of a new era in therapeutics. But in fact Erlich's discovery stood alone for over two decades. Not until the 1930's, with the development of the sulfa drugs, did the promise of medical weapons against bacterial infection become a reality. Penicillin and the other antibiotics came even later, during and after World War II.[40]

However disappointing its initial results in medicine, bacteriology did have a significant impact on the practice of surgery in the early twentieth century. Since the 1860's the British physician Joseph Lister had insisted that antiseptic procedures could cut down the risk of mysterious and deadly postoperative infections. With the advent of bacteriology, Lister's work was confirmed and expanded by a group of physicians who sought not simply to kill germs (antisepsis) but to operate in a germ-free environment (asepsis). The acceptance of aseptical surgical techniques in America came slowly, however. A twentieth-century obstetrician and gynecologist recalled that when he entered medical school in 1904, his instructor "always wore a frock coat while operating and delicately held the knife between his lips when it wasn't in use." By the time the student became an intern, hospitals had inaugurated a new regime. Surgeons donned "hoods and masks resembling the Ku Klux Klan," rubber gloves, and short-sleeved sterile gowns before they entered the operating room.[41]

Gynecological surgery itself underwent changes as a result of new medical technology. After the development of X rays and radium therapy in the late 1890's, doctors relied less on radical hysterectomy and more on radiotherapy to treat conditions such as cervical cancer. The "cooking process," according to gynecological authority Franklin H. Martin, marked an advancement over the "cold knife." Only later, when doctors became alarmed at the side effects produced by reckless irradiation, did many return to hysterectomy.[42]

In obstetrics the trend in surgery was the reverse. The early twentieth century witnessed an alarming increase in surgical intervention. Caesarian section, once a perilous last resort in cases where pelvic bone structure did not allow for normal delivery, became a remarkably common recourse. Anxious to depose female midwives, who in 1914 still presided over some 40 per cent of deliveries, obstetricians attempted to convince American women that childbirth was a dangerous process which required the direction of a skilled physician. To buttress their claim to special expertise, they relied more and more on instruments and surgery. The result was at once tragic and ironic. Maternal mortality grew in direct response to the growth of obstetrical practice. Between 1915 and 1928, America's maternal mortality rate compared unfavorably to that of nearly every major European country and was over twice that of Japan. The fact that the mortality rates appeared as high among urban, middle-class populations as among the rural poor, highlighted the extent to which doctors and not ignorant midwives were responsible for the alarming death tolls.

"Belly-ripping has become a mania," complained one writer, who went on to lambast the arrogance of obstetrical surgeons.

I have sometimes suspected that the surgeon is either unaware of the existence of a birth canal or that he labors under the impression that the delivery of a child through natural passages is a provision for those who do not have a competent surgeon at hand. . . .[43]

Even when physicians did not resort to surgery, they all to often attempted to improve on nature by using instruments or inducing labor. Obstetrics in the automobile age took on a frighteningly literal meaning in one story recounted by a physician in his autobiography. In his early practice he accompanied a colleague called upon to help with a difficult delivery. Unable to extract the baby with forceps, the senior obstetrician tied a rope to the forceps' handles, threw the line out the window, attached it to his car, and hauled the baby out.[44]

Obstetrics and gynecology were not the only two medical specialties which attempted to treat female complaints in the 1920's. The impact of Freudian psychology placed psychiatry in the vanguard of American medical practice by the mid-twenties. Most

American practitioners ignored the complexity, the pessimism, and the full radicalism of Freud's work. Their often erroneous interpretations of Freud's theories were further bowdlerized by a horde of popularizers who reduced Freudianism to a series of catchwords and clichés. Soon sophisticated men and women spoke knowingly of "complexes," "neuroses," and "sublimation" with a naive facility which would have astonished Sigmund Freud.[45]

For women, Freud's ideas proved as confining as they were liberating. While Freudianism, as it was popularly interpreted, belied the notion that women were asexual, it encouraged women to find fulfillment through the traditional avenues of marriage and motherhood and to seek in sexual expression some ultimate meaning for their lives. Women who desired a wider range of activity ran the risk of being labeled neurotic or maladjusted. Just as nineteenth-century doctors had argued that such nontraditional female activities as education, suffrage, or work in the professions would lead to womb diseases, many twentieth-century psychiatrists and psychologists claimed that feminist aspirations either resulted from or led to neurosis.

The antifeminist potential of psychotherapy became obvious in the 1920's with the publication of a spate of books and articles which demonstrated how concepts borrowed from psychiatry could be used to curb women's demands for greater freedom. In 1927 Abraham Myerson, professor of neurology at Tufts Medical College, published a book entitled *The Nervous Housewife*. Her numbers were legion, he insisted, and her presence threatened to disrupt not only her own family, but the American home itself. "The neurosis of the housewife has a large part of its origin in the increasing desires of women," Myerson stated, "in their demands for a more varied life than that afforded them by the lot of housewife." For Myerson the housewife's dissatisfaction marked the symptom of a "disease" which could be cured only through "the painstaking adjustment of [the] individual woman." Through therapy he sought to "establish an ideal of fortitude, of patience, and of fidelity to duty." Those were, he admitted, "old-fashioned words," but he insisted "serenity of spirit is in their meaning."[46]

Once again women took to the couch—not the fainting couch of the nineteenth century, but the psychiatrist's couch. Of course only a privileged few could afford the time or the money to become analysands. The vast majority of American women worried about their nervousness were more likely to respond to ads like those of the Pinkham company which promised women could calm their jangled nerves with the Vegetable Compound.

Certainly American medicine experienced significant changes in the half-century between 1875 and 1925, both in terms of advances in medical science and in the professionalization of medical practice. Yet it was not until after 1910, according to a recent medical historian, that "a random patient, with a random disease consulting a doctor chosen at random stood better than a 50–50 chance of benefiting from the encounter."[47]

The prognosis for women suffering from female complaints was surely no better. In spite of the high hopes of doctors and scientists, no new wonder drugs had been developed to treat women's diseases. And although many viewed psychoanalysis as something of a miracle cure, its benefits for women were limited and ambiguous. Endocrinology was in its infancy, more a fad than a science. In the 1920's, Austrian doctor Eugen Steinach piqued America's interest when he claimed to be able to restore lost youth through hormone injections. Gertrude Atherton, the popular novelist, treated the theme in *Black Oxen,* the story of a rejuvenated sextuagenarian who falls in love with a man half her age.[48] The discrepancy between the miracles promised in fiction and the therapies employed in fact only highlighted the extent to which doctors themselves, not simply the women who bought Lydia Pinkham's Vegetable Compound, still relied on the same old medicine.

Rule or Ruin?

"How the dickens are we going to do business in the future with any degree of comfort and success?" Pinkham advertising manager J. T. Wetherald queried early in 1926 after Lydia Pinkham Gove had strong-armed control of advertising strategy. "I should think you would be [going] crazy," Wetherald commiserated with company president Arthur Pinkham. "Can't you kill the 'duck' some way? Looks like she is going to rule or ruin."[1]

Wetherald's words proved prophetic. After her cross-country flight, Lydia Pinkham Gove returned to work determined to drive out her Pinkham cousins and take over the company, no matter what the cost. Lydia, something of a New Woman, sought an arena for her ambitions and energies larger than the circumscribed round of social engagements common to women of her class and time. Had she been more like her namesake, her story might have been that of a successful businesswoman. Instead her domineering personality and her flat refusal to learn from others more experienced than herself spelled disaster for the company. In the next fifteen years, as the family feud reached its climax, it appeared that Lydia would wreck the business in her struggle to control it.

Lydia's stranglehold on the company came about largely as the result of the 1921 bylaws. By giving the Pinkhams control of the executive branch of the company and the Goves control of the purse strings, the stockholders had sought to establish a scrupulous balance of power. Instead they engineered a deadlock. Aroline Gove increasingly deferred to her strong-minded daughter, who, as her mother's assistant treasurer, took over more and more control of the company's finances. Lydia used her power over the treasury to veto Pinkham advertising policy. If she did not like Wetherald's copy schedules, she simply refused to pay for Pinkham advertising.

The Pinkham stockholders feared that capitulating to Lydia's whims would ruin the business. Desperate, they filed for receivership in Maine. In a bill in equity filed in 1927, the Pinkhams claimed the company was entangled in "a complete and hopeless deadlock," which warranted the appointment of a receiver and the dissolution of the corporation.[2] The Pinkhams' drastic action sobered the Goves. Together the two sides worked out an elaborate compromise designed to save the business and enable the company to function. The bylaws were amended to allow for the selection of a neutral director who would act as a balance wheel and break the corporate stalemate. Robert H. Gross, a corporation president and director of one of Boston's banks, agreed to undertake the delicate task of mediating between the two factions.

Gross quickly alienated the Gove women, however, and soon found his position so untenable that he resigned from the Board. But not before he had joined with the Pinkham directors in voting to grant Arthur Pinkham, as president of the company, the power "to exercise general supervision and control over the various departments of the company's business, to hire and discharge all employees therein and to issue such directions as in his judgment are proper from time to time to carry out the votes of the Board of Directors."[3] The resolution carried over the Goves' objection, thanks to Gross's deciding vote. Arthur Pinkham appeared confident that at last he could run the company without interference from Lydia or her mother. Writing to thank Gross for his aid, Arthur optimistically observed, "I feel that after several years of grief, the business is back on a normal basis."[4]

Arthur's high spirits did not last long. Before the year ended,

Wetherald died. For almost forty years, he had masterminded the company's advertising, both under the Pinkhams and the Goves. He knew the business, knew the families, and knew his craft. When he died the company lost its strongest ally. With Wetherald out of the way, Lydia Pinkham Gove saw nothing to thwart her ambition to take over Pinkham advertising. Swiftly she moved to consolidate her power. At her prompting, the company agreed to set up its own advertising agency to handle the Pinkham account. In this way, she argued persuasively, the stockholders could save the 15 per cent commission otherwise paid to an outside agency.

The Northeastern Advertising Agency, Lydia's brainchild, took over Pinkham advertising in 1929. Ironically, its organization duplicated the division of power that caused the medicine company so much trouble. Stock in the new corporation was split equally between Pinkhams and Goves, as was management. Charlie Pinkham, Arthur's youngest brother, headed the agency. Charlie had a passion for advertising and a firm belief it could be reduced to a science. After graduating from Brown, he had gone to work for Wetherald to learn the advertising business from the ground up. Lydia Pinkham Gove, who had never agreed with Wetherald's policies, wanted little to do with her upstart cousin Charlie or his fancy ideas on plotting advertising effectiveness. Soon the two were at loggerheads. Unable to agree on how, when, or where Pinkham advertising should be placed, they split the advertising budget and wrote their own copy. Under this clumsy system, sales declined for the fifth straight year, and for the first time in almost four decades the Lydia E. Pinkham company operated in the red.[5]

By 1931 Charlie Pinkham had had enough. He hired J. Sterling Getchell, an energetic young copywriter from New York, to prepare Pinkham advertising. Charlie tested Getchell's copy for effectiveness and discovered the lesson Wetherald had learned in the 1890's—that the pain-and-agony pitch worked best to sell the Vegetable Compound, particularly in Depression years. The ads which scored highest in Charlie's inquiry tests featured headlines reading "These Hysterical Women" and "Keep Your Husband's Love." Ads with healthy, happy women and headlines like "The

Thrill of Motherhood" proved less effective. But tests or no tests, Lydia Pinkham Gove had her own ideas about what constituted effective advertising. Getchell's ads, she complained, were "distasteful."[6] She preferred testimonial advertisements, although Charlie repeatedly warned her that the Food and Drug Administration would no longer allow testimonials which made claims the company could not substantiate. In keeping with the government's 1925 dictum forbidding the company to make claims regarding female problems, Getchell's copy steered away from mention of menstrual pain or menopause and focused instead on the tonic qualities of the Vegetable Compound. His ads urged women to calm jittery nerves and restore pep and vitality by taking Lydia Pinkham's medicine.

It soon became clear that in order to advertise effectively, Charlie would have to find some way to circumvent Lydia. When Edythe Bradford, one of the Gove stockholders, showed signs of disaffection, Charlie quickly enlisted her aid by promising to make her joint advertising manager of the Northeastern agency. Convinced that Lydia was "a crazy lunatic," Bradford joined the Pinkhams to pass a vote giving herself and Charlie Pinkham full power to place company ads. The new directorate bypassed Lydia in matters of policy, took charge of her books, and even had her name removed from the office door. Lydia retaliated by refusing to sign checks. She also sent letters to editors and publishers across the country, warning that Pinkham advertising had not been authorized by the company treasurer and threatening to withhold payment if the ads appeared in print.[7]

Once again the company found itself deadlocked. With the Northeastern agency unable to get its ads printed, the medicine company suffered. In 1932 the Pinkham stockholders went to court to force Lydia Pinkham Gove to sign checks and authorize contracts for the Northeastern agency. Recounting the intricate history of the family feud to the judge, one lawyer joked, "A Kentucky feud was only differentiated from the feud between the Goves and the Pinkhams [by] the fact that they used guns in Kentucky and here they used bylaws."[8] His joke turned out to be extremely apt. The Pinkhams dropped the suit and decided to settle their differences with the Goves by amending the bylaws to do away with the neutral director. The agreement placated Lydia and Aroline, who had feared the position might fall to the treacherous Mrs. Bradford. With the elimination of the neutral director, the business reverted to a fifty-fifty basis. The Pinkhams and the Goves might well have heeded the judge, who, after hearing the history of the company, observed, "I have always been in doubt as to how any corporation that is organized on a fifty-fifty basis can ever get anywhere except in[to] court."[9]

For the next three years the Pinkhams avoided a major showdown, but at a high cost. "If you let me run the business," Lydia told Arthur, "I'd make a lot of money, but if you keep interfering you won't get any of it." Arthur gave Lydia her way. He did not have much choice. The Goves boycotted directors' meetings and refused to allocate money for any but their own advertising. When Arthur protested Lydia's actions, she retorted, "You are no businessman, and neither you nor your brothers knows anything about business."[10] Left to her own devices, Lydia authorized advertising which amounted to over 80 per cent of the company's gross sales. In 1933 she spent over a million and a half dollars. In spite of her massive spending, the company continued to lose money.

Lydia Pinkham Gove was no fool, although on the surface her advertising policy argued to the contrary. Her strategy was to drive down profits in order to buy out the Pinkham stock. As she told the company's vice-president, the Goves had "plenty of money," whereas the Pinkhams did not. Knowing that they were dependent for their livelihood on their salaries and on company dividends, she could afford to wipe out profits in the short run in order to force the Pinkhams out of the business. To further her scheme, she and her mother loaned the company, without authorization, over $250,000 at 5 per cent interest and then, as treasurers, refused to pay off the loans, even though the company had more than enough money in its surplus to cover the debt. In this fashion, Lydia contrived to retain an excellent investment, as well as to make herself the company's largest creditor, a position she hoped to use to bring about a receivership as a means of acquiring the Pinkhams' share of the business.[11]

To Lydia Pinkham Gove the medicine company her grandmother had founded was a handsome toy, one she did not care to share with her Pinkham cousins. Lydia collected many expensive toys. One was the Lydia E. Pinkham Memorial, a free baby clinic in Salem that the Goves set up in 1922. Another was the Howard Johnson restaurant chain. Lydia financed Howard Johnson's move into New York state in the late thirties and built him a string of elaborate restaurants. The most splendid of the establishments, located on Queens Boulevard in Elmhurst, was decorated by Lydia herself, with crystal chandeliers imported from Italy. Her triumph was "Carcassonne," a Norman style mansion she and her mother built on the ocean side of Marblehead Neck. The house, as pretentious as its name, cost an estimated $250,000 upon its completion in the midst of the Depression. Try as she might, Lydia could never get the townsfolk to call the place "Carcassonne." To the hundreds and thousands who came to gawk, it was then and remains today, simply "The Castle."[12]

Lydia's strategy to drive out the Pinkhams did not escape Arthur's notice. In the spring of 1935, he moved quickly to stop the drain on the company's finances. With the year not yet half over, Lydia had already spent more than $800,000 on advertising, largely for posters and booklets which Charlie Pinkham felt were ineffective and which contained copy that had already prompted the Food and Drug Administration to take action against the company.[13] When Lydia demanded another $500,000 to complete her campaign, the Pinkhams stunned her by responding with a flat "no." Lydia threatened that unless she got her own way, there would be no Pinkham advertising. The Pinkhams stood pat. They preferred to stop advertising entirely rather than let Lydia drive down profits. For the next six months not a single Pinkham advertisement appeared in print.

Arthur Pinkham, who had developed bleeding ulcers in the course of his daily battles with Lydia, was by now thoroughly fed up with the Goves and the Northeastern agency. Determined to test his powers as president, he abandoned the house agency and signed a contract with Erwin, Wasey of New York. No sooner had the new agency's ads begun to appear than Lydia fired off telegrams to the papers, warning that she would not pay for the advertising. Once again the Pinkhams and the Goves had reached an impasse. There was no place to turn but to the courts.

For the next five years the Pinkham men battled the Gove women in court. At stake was Arthur Pinkham's power to run the company—power he claimed he had won when the directors voted in 1927 to grant him executive prerogatives. The Pinkhams initiated legal action early in 1936 by going to court in Massachusetts to demand an injunction against the Gove women, preventing them from "interfering in any manner with the conduct of the business."[14] The Goves retaliated by filing a petition for receivership in Maine, claiming the resources of the business were in danger of being wasted and lost due to protracted deadlock and "gross mismanagement" on the part of the Pinkhams.[15]

The fact that the Pinkham medicine company held its corporate charter in Maine but did business in Massachusetts caused an initial jurisdictional dispute. When the Massachusetts Supreme Court ruled that the Goves must refrain from mounting their suit in Maine until after the Massachusetts case had been decided, the Pinkhams won a significant advantage.

Lydia and Aroline Gove, confident that they would win in Maine, chose to ignore the Massachusetts proceedings. Leaving their lawyers in charge, they sailed for Europe. In their absence, the Massachusetts court appointed a Master, Owen Lovejoy, a businessman who acted as a neutral party. Lovejoy held hearings to determine the facts in the case. On the stand the Pinkham brothers told their story eloquently. Arthur detailed how the Gove treasurers had loaned unnecessary funds to the company and then refused to follow his instructions and repay the loans. Charlie Pinkham, armed with charts and graphs, documented how Lydia's advertising strategy seemed calculated to lose the company money and financially embarrass the Pinkhams. And vice-president, Daniel Pinkham II, recounted a conversation in which Lydia had threatened to withhold dividends as a means of pressuring the Pinkhams to sell their stock.

The Goves' European trip proved a costly mistake. In the absence of testimony from the defendants, Lovejoy geared his findings to the Pinkhams' evidence. The Master's report characterized

Lydia Gove as an "energetic and dominating" woman, who completely controlled her eighty-year-old mother, a woman suffering from hardening of the arteries. The Goves, the Master concluded, "were not acting for what they believed to be the welfare of the corporation as such, but were acting for their own individual benefit at the expense of the corporation."[16]

The case then went before the full bench of the Massachusetts Supreme Court, which, after studying the Master's report, found that the defendants Gove "have violated their fiduciary obligations," "acted in excess of their authority," and "used their official positions in the corporation in detriment of its interests from motives of personal advantage. . . ."[17] In July of 1937, the Court granted the Pinkhams an injunction against the Goves to prevent them from interfering in the business. The judge recommended that the company be awarded damages for the losses incurred as a result of Lydia's double-dealing. The Pinkhams had won round one.

In a fit of pique, Lydia Pinkham Gove dismissed her lawyers without pay and refused to sign company checks made out to the Pinkham company's counsel. Her action forced another suit. Once again the Court found in favor of the company. The judge admonished Lydia, "The Treasurer is not given veto power over the acts of other officers."[18]

The Pinkhams did not fare as well in their attempt to collect a million dollars in damages from the Goves. The Court ruled that they were entitled to claim money that Lydia and Aroline had collected as interest on their "loans" and money expended in excess of authorized advertising budgets. However, the judge concluded that the Pinkham company could not reclaim the salaries paid to the Gove women or losses incurred as a result of the company's inability to advertise between 1936 and 1937.[19] The Goves, it appeared, had won round two.

Ironically, the Internal Revenue Service proved the largest beneficiary. In their attempt to prove that the Goves had not earned the $27,000 a year paid to them as salary, Pinkham lawyers presented evidence which indicated that Gove salaries bore no relationship to compensation for services rendered. The IRS spotted the testimony and took the company to court to reclaim deductions the corporation had taken on moneys paid to Lydia and her mother.[20]

The final chapter of the Pinkham–Gove feud was recorded in Maine, before the Supreme Judicial Court, where the Gove stockholders had filed for receivership. In the interim between their first petition, filed in 1936, and the Maine trial in 1940, Aroline Gove had died at the age of eighty-two. Lydia saw the Maine suit as the last chance to vindicate herself and her mother. The Pinkhams, she insisted, had won the Massachusetts case, "because of their perjured testimony."[21] She looked forward to the opportunity to take the stand in Maine and set things straight.

Lydia soon had her day in court. The new Gove lawyers, more sophisticated than their predecessors, mounted an interesting case. With the Pinkham company holding assets of over a million dollars and business on the upswing since the court awarded Arthur Pinkham power to run the company, the Gove lawyers found it difficult to claim that the corporation was "in danger of being wasted and lost." Instead they argued that the Massachusetts decision to give power to the Pinkham president thwarted the equality on which the company had been founded. The corporation, they claimed, should rightly be regarded as a corporate *partnership*. To support their case they cited the scrupulously equal division of stock, officers, directors, salaries, and profits. The lawyers contended that the Goves had been wrongfully deprived of an equal voice in the running of the corporation and therefore its dissolution was warranted.

Their case looked promising when Lydia Pinkham Gove took the stand on the last day of the trial. Under questioning from her lawyer, she testified that absolute equality between the two families had always been intended and upheld by both sides until Arthur Pinkham sought to usurp control of the business. "Arthur always had his own ideas," she stated. "After my brother died he had his ideas more." When asked if her intent had been to "rule or ruin," Lydia responded: "Certainly not." All she wanted was the equal control to which the Goves were entitled.[22]

The Pinkham counsel's cross-examination was at first puzzling.

He produced a note written two years earlier by Lydia thanking several company employees for sending flowers on her mother's eightieth birthday. Had Lydia written the note? She had. Would she read it to the Court? Unsure of its import, Lydia began to read:

> My mother's mother, Lydia E. Pinkham, arranged that the Gove interests should control the management of the Lydia E. Pinkham Medicine Company for as long a time as possible and her choice has been amply justified by the splendid record of success which has been obtained until the present time.[23]

As the significance of the words dawned upon Lydia and her lawyers, their faces fell. No matter that the note contained a patent lie. Here, in Lydia's own words, was proof that the equal division the Goves had built their case upon had never been recognized or accepted by Lydia or her mother. They had wanted to rule, not to share equally in the management of the company. An alert observer in the courtroom noted that Lydia's lawyer "cast at her as eloquent a glance as I have ever seen, and seemed to long to cast at her something far more tangible."[24] In one stroke, the promising case the Goves' lawyers had constructed caved in. Judge Sidney St. F. Thaxter dismissed the case in February of 1941 with the observation that Arthur Pinkham "seems to me to have acted with restraint under great provocation," whereas Lydia Gove had carried on her fight to rule or ruin "with unparalleled venom, and with an utter disregard of the welfare of the company." "We are reminded," he concluded, "that there is no war like a civil war and no feud like a family feud."[25]

In the long run the Pinkham company and not Lydia Pinkham Gove proved the biggest loser in the Pinkham–Gove feud. The lengthy wrangling between the families badly crippled the business. During the early years of the court fight, advertising virtually ceased, and sales declined precipitously. In 1937, after the Massachusetts Court awarded Arthur Pinkham authority to run company advertising, sales began to pick up. Arthur approved judicious spending for newspaper and magazine advertising and experimented with radio commercials. But passage in 1938 of

New Deal legislation aimed at patent medicines spelled trouble for the Pinkham company.

Since the early days of the New Deal, advocates of a stronger food and drug law had been at work in Congress. Although the Federal Food, Drug, and Cosmetic Act which passed in 1938 showed the marks of repeated compromises and concessions to the drug industry, it nevertheless broadened the powers of the Food and Drug Administration and placed new restrictions on drug makers. For the first time, patent medicines were required to carry a list of their ingredients on their labels. The most disappointing aspect of the new law was its failure to place patent medicine advertising under the jurisdiction of the FDA. The Federal Trade Commission, an agency with a reputation for leniency, continued to control the surveillance of advertising under the terms of the 1938 Wheeler-Lea Act.[26]

Early in 1938, F. J. Adams of the FTC alerted Arthur Pinkham that the company's advertising had come under scrutiny. The Pinkhams quickly moved to fortify the Compound liquid with vitamin B_1 and to add iron to the tablets in order to support advertising claims. Pinkham advertisements since 1937 had urged women to go "Smiling Through." Precisely what situations they were to smile through were indicated in the boxed copy accompanying each ad:

For three generations one woman has told another how to go "smiling through" with Lydia E. Pinkham's Vegetable Compound. It helps Nature tone up the system, thus lessening the discomforts which must be endured, especially during

THE THREE ORDEALS OF WOMAN

1. Passing from girlhood into womanhood.
2. Preparing for Motherhood.
3. Approaching "Middle Age."[27]

The FTC, at the prompting of the AMA, issued a citation against the Pinkham company in August, 1938, banning further use of the "smiling through" copy. Citing scientific opinion compiled by the Food and Drug Administration, the FTC stated:

> The advertising representations made by these products [the Vegetable Compound liquid and the tablets] are objectionable in their entirety. Neither of these products, taken singly or together, constitutes a competent or adequate treatment for any female condition, disorder or disease. References thereto, direct or implied, are grossly false.[28]

The FTC citation hit the company at a time when it was unprepared to argue the merits of the Vegetable Compound. Research and development had suffered throughout the 1930's as a result of Lydia Pinkham Gove's flat refusal to fund clinical studies or laboratory work. Not until 1937 had the company taken steps to support its claims through clinical or pharmacological testing. During the thirties other, shrewder proprietors hired scientists and physicians willing to vouch for the effectiveness of their medicines. As long as one set of experts disagreed with another, their medicines were safe. In 1938, when the FTC issued its citation against the company, the Pinkhams had only just begun testing and could not yet show results to substantiate their claims. Hurriedly they put together a case for the merits of the medicine, which they based for the most part on the improved formulas containing the vitamins and minerals. The FTC remained unconvinced.

As a last resort the company hired Dr. Charles W. Green. "Doc" Green had worked for years as a liaison between drug companies and the FTC. When the Pinkhams asked him if he could help the company establish tonic claims for the Compound, he responded, "Tonic, hell! You boys ought to be ashamed to let down your grandmother this way. That Vegetable Compound helps female ailments. It always has. It always will. We won't be satisfied with anything less than uterine sedative claims!"[29] For the next two years Green ignored company research on the medicine's tonic properties and combed medical literature for evidence that the

Vegetable Compound's ingredients acted on the uterus. In addition, he engaged in astute lobbying, and as a result the company obtained what it regarded as an extremely favorable stipulation from the FTC in 1941. Reversing the FDA's 1925 ruling, the FTC signed an agreement with the Pinkham company which forbade tonic claims, but allowed the Compound to be advertised as a uterine sedative capable of relieving symptoms associated with menstrual aberrations and menopause.[30] Patent medicine critics at the AMA and FDA must have marveled at the way in which Green convinced the FTC to allow expanded claims based on medical literature largely outdated and with little or no clinical or pharmacological evidence to support such claims.

The Pinkham company emerged from its bout with the FTC in a stronger position than it had enjoyed for years. Not since 1925 had the company been able to make such strong copy claims for its medicine. Beginning in 1941, Pinkham ads promised relief from menstrual pain and menopausal symptoms. Once again ads claimed that the Vegetable Compound would "Help Relieve Distress of Female Periodic Complaints" and promised relief for "Women Who Suffer From Hot Flashes." When several Pinkham relatives became sensitive to criticism from their friends regarding the blatant headlines, the company replaced the offensive ads with more subtle copy. "Are You Just a Plaything of Nature?" queried one ad. And in spot commercials, radio announcers described "What Suffering a Society Girl and a Scrub Woman Have in Common." The forties saw an increase in sales which reached $2,636,000 in 1945.[31]

Late in the forties, the Food and Drug Administration, unhappy with the action of the FTC, began to wage what one Pinkham associate described as a "cold war" against the company.[32] The FDA demanded to know what medical proof the company could muster to support its advertising claims. Significant medical developments in hormone therapy during the 1940's led the Pinkhams to hope that they, too, could cash in on the hormone craze. Extensive research was conducted to establish what, if any, hormone action the Vegetable Compound could claim. When a Pinkham researcher uncovered vegetable estrogens in licorice root, a flavoring used in the Compound, the company was elated.

Perhaps the thousands of women who wrote testimonials to the medicine had been right all along. Perhaps the Compound contained a potent hormonal ingredient that accounted for its success in treating female complaints.

Laboratory tests indicated that if such were the case, Lydia Pinkham could take little credit. Licorice had not been one of her original ingredients. It was added in 1914, when the company fortified its formula to avoid having the Vegetable Compound taxed as a beverage. Although traces of estrogenic materials were later found in several of the Compound's original ingredients, researchers were unable to isolate or identify these estrogenic properties. Nevertheless, the company rushed into print claiming that scientific research vindicated Lydia Pinkham and proved her medical perspicacity.[33]

The FDA and the AMA were not impressed with the Pinkham claims, despite the fact that the company hired several prominent medical doctors to test the Compound. Although the government chose not to mount a case against the company, FDA officials remained highly skeptical that the Vegetable Compound contained significant amounts of estrogenic substances. They continued to keep a sharp eye on Pinkham advertising.

As if to mock claims of the Vegetable Compound's efficacy, Lydia Pinkham Gove died in 1948 of ovarian cancer.[34] After her defeat in her struggle to run the company, she had retreated to "Carcassonne," where she lived out her last years as a virtual recluse. After Lydia's death, the surviving Gove relatives entered into an uneasy alliance with the Pinkhams. Three new Gove directors were named, all of whom indicated their willingness to support Arthur Pinkham and his brothers as long as company sales and profits continued to rise.

Sales rose in the 1940's, but not as fast as taxes, manufacturing costs, and overhead. And as profits fell, some of the company's directors expressed the opinion that the Pinkham company was a "dead duck." In 1950, when sales fell off more than 10 per cent, slipping below the two-million-dollar mark for the first time in a decade, the directors began to grumble openly that it was time for the family to get out of the business.[35]

Lydia Pinkham had become a liability. To the young consumer

of the 1950's she was merely an old woman dressed in old-fashioned clothes, whose face appeared on a decidedly old-fashioned medicine. A company survey in 1951 indicated that non-users ridiculed the medicine as an outdated "cure-all." The liquid Vegetable Compound, which still outsold the tablets at a ratio of two to one, had a solid consumer following among older women. The tablets, designed for the convenience of modern women, who would not think of toting a pint-sized bottle in their handbags, had gained little following among the younger set. They relied on analgesics like aspirin or Midol for the relief of periodic pain.

To modernize its image, the company hired the Harry B. Cohen agency in 1951. In a desperate attempt to appeal to a younger audience, Cohen replaced Lydia Pinkham in company copy with a new advertising personality named "Ann Pinkham." Lydia had to go, said Cohen. "Her picture did not create confidence among the younger generation." The Cohen agency designed Ann "to look as though she might be a nurse . . . old enough to speak with authority, but young enough to understand the problems of teen-agers and girls in their early twenties."[36] To introduce Ann to the public, Cohen issued an update of the old Pinkham pamphlets. "A Woman's Guide to Health," which appeared in 1952, could never be mistaken for its predecessors. Its cover featured an alluring woman in a diaphanous negligé, shielded from the waist down by the title insert. On the inside flap, the traditional portrait of Lydia Pinkham seemed to glower disapproval. The juxtaposition, jarring to say the least, spoke to the paradox implicit in the company's new image.

Cosmetic attempts at modernization did little to stimulate the market. A study submitted by a marketing research group in 1957 underscored the problem. Druggists described the typical Pinkham customer as a mature woman, usually well over thirty, less educated than her contemporaries. In the South and in urban areas of the Northeast and Midwest, she was often black. The Vegetable Compound, the researchers concluded, was outmoded. Not only was it "distinguished by one of the most noxious tastes among contemporary proprietaries," its very name evoked a derisive laugh. The market analysts advised the company to revamp

and sold out to Cooper Laboratories, a large and diversified pharmaceutical company. Cooper Labs could afford to pay over a million dollars for the business to trade off its dying market. The new management cut costs by eliminating advertising entirely and by moving the plant from Massachusetts to Puerto Rico, closer to its source of raw materials. Cooper Labs, drawing on a residual demand created by past advertising, manages to gross over $700,000 annually on sales of the Vegetable Compound.[38]

In its hundred-year history, Lydia E. Pinkham's Vegetable Compound survived the repeated attacks of the medical profession and the muckrakers, weathered government regulation, and outlived the Pinkhams and the Goves who feuded for control of the company. Arthur Pinkham died in 1960. When the Lydia E. Pinkham Medicine Company itself died out, it was not so much a victim of government regulation or increased consumer consciousness as a casualty of internal dissension and a marketing and advertising policy which had failed to keep pace with the times.

Conclusion:
The Business of
Women's Medicine

It would be convenient to record that Lydia E. Pinkham's Vegetable Compound is dying out today because of advances in medical science which rendered the medicine hopelessly obsolete. But that would exaggerate the case as baldly as a Pinkham ad. The eclipse of the Vegetable Compound, like its spectacular success a century earlier, is part of the larger story of the business of medicine in general, and women's medicine in particular.

Women have always had a special interest in medicine, perhaps because menstruation and parturition influence a woman's life so directly; more likely because women are entrusted with the health of infants and children. In the nineteenth century the laywoman, more often than her male counterpart, played the role of healer, apothecary, midwife, and nurse. Medical historian Joseph Kett uncovered records for the state of New Jersey which indicate that in 1818 medical practice, except for extraordinary cases, was mainly in the hands of women.[1] Because women's practice was occasional and because they did not generally receive pay, women did not think of themselves as "doctors." But they practiced medicine nevertheless. Their therapies, which did not rest on the spurious monistic pathology systems put forth by the medical elite, often proved more beneficial to the patient. While they could not always save lives, at least they did not employ the heroic measures that so frequently resulted in iatrogenic, or doctor-induced, diseases such as the mercury poisoning brought on by heroic dosing with calomel. Their treatments were the result of empiricism, experience, a special knack, or the accumulated wisdom of mothers and grandmothers. In the stable environment of the rural village, a woman's ability to brew medicine, break a fever, set bones, or help in childbirth earned her the respect of her neighbors, who called on her in their time of trouble. In such an informal fashion, some women developed a medical practice of sorts. It is these women who are listed in town records as domestic practitioners.

The popular health movements of the 1830's provided an opportunity and an impetus for women to develop their medical skills. Women like Lydia Pinkham followed the principles of Sylvester Graham, subscribed to the botanical sect of Thomsonianism, or attended the lectures on anatomy and physiology sponsored by the Ladies' Physiological Societies in order to gain, as best they could, information on health and medicine. Samuel Thomson, who believed each man should become his own family physician, might well have changed his slogan to read "each woman." For it was women who swelled the ranks of his Friendly Botanical Societies in search of knowledge that would enable them to minister more effectively to their families. With the channels for orthodox medical training closed to them on account of their sex, many women embraced popular medicine for the opportunity it provided to add to their store of medical knowledge.

Yet by the Civil War, the days of the domestic practitioner were numbered. Increasingly, Americans accepted the idea that some formal schooling, and not simply natural skill, was required in order to practice medicine effectively. Where in 1790 there had been no more than one doctor for every ten domestic practitioners, by 1860 states that listed medical practitioners had ceased counting any but those who claimed to be doctors. Medicine had become an occupation which demanded training and a business which promised monetary reward.

The change came about largely as a result of a burgeoning business in proprietary medical schools during the Jacksonian era. In 1800 there had been only four medical schools in the country, elite institutions modeled along European lines. By 1900 over four hundred schools had been founded, most of them proprietary institutions which offered a course of lectures for a specified fee.[2] Any doctor enterprising enough to hire a hall, buy a skeleton or some sort of medical apparatus, and lecture for four to six weeks on anatomy and the practice of physic could advertise as the proprietor of a medical school entitled to grant degrees. Of course not all physicians trained in schools. Many students attended the lecture courses merely to supplement apprenticeship training with a regular physician. But the rise of the proprietary schools had a significant impact on medical practice. By offering an alternative to apprenticeship training or education at the elite medical colleges in the United States and abroad, the proprietary schools helped to break down class barriers and throw the profession of medicine open to all comers—all, that is, but women. Prejudice against women made it difficult for any but the most determined and undaunted to receive formal medical schooling in America.

The professionalization of medicine, which occurred belatedly in the late nineteenth century with the enactment of licensing laws and the establishment of standards for training and practice, cannot be held responsible for driving women from the medical profession. There had never been many women among the ragtag and bobtail of medical practitioners turned out by the proprietary schools.[3] But professionalization did deal a death blow to domestic practice and in so doing undermined women's role in healing. The new medicine, which rather prematurely claimed the status of a science, brought with it the mystification of medical knowledge. Pseudo-science, whether phrenology or the mind cure, furthered the mystification by embracing obfuscatory terminology and medical mumbo-jumbo in an effort to gain scientific stature. In the process, confidence in the plain-speaking domestic practitioner declined. Science and pseudo-science united in ridiculing the knowledge of the domestic practitioner as no more than superstition or "old wives' tales."

In spite of the growing number of doctors churned out by the proprietary schools, the majority of Americans continued to get their medical treatment for minor ailments from sources outside the medical profession. By the 1870's, patent medicines and popular health manuals of the *Family Guide to Health* variety served many of the functions domestic practitioners had performed earlier in the century. Not surprisingly, women constituted the largest consumer audience for both the medicines and the health books. The rhetoric of perfectionism, which insisted that disease was no longer God's retribution for moral sins, but rather the result of violating "Nature's laws," instilled in women the idea that poor health was their own fault. In their zeal for patent medicines and health manuals, women showed their eagerness to take responsibility for their health and to seek cures for conditions once accepted simply as a woman's lot.

When Lydia Pinkham began marketing her Vegetable Compound in 1875, it represented what might be described as domestic practice turned commercial. Her own history epitomized the transition from female domestic practitioner to dispenser of patent medicine. To what extent the patent medicine boom in the years following the Civil War was the result of a similar development is unclear; certainly not every patent medicine proprietor had been a domestic practitioner. Yet the Pinkham experience is informative in that it underlines the way in which both the proprietor and the customer saw in patent medicine a replacement for domestic practice. Surely many of the women who wrote to Lydia Pinkham for advice at the close of the nineteenth century viewed her as not unlike the wise woman of the village who had ministered to her neighbors in an earlier era. But patent medicines like the Vegetable Compound did not simply appeal to nostalgia for the old; they drew on the power of the new. The Pinkhams claimed scientific potency for their product, and in so doing promised the best of both worlds. Women who bought the Vegetable Compound could be reassured that it was an herbal remedy not unlike the ones their mothers or grandmothers had brewed, and at the same time gain confidence from the catchwords of the new science spelled out in company advertising.

The business of women's medicine by the late nineteenth century included not only patent medicines and health manuals, but the growing medical specialties of gynecology and obstetrics. For medicine, whatever its claims to disinterested science, was clearly a business. Doctors repeatedly complained of the unfair competition from homeopaths and other sectarians and sought to devise ways to increase their own financial stability at the expense of their rivals. Specialization, at first feared as a threat to the financial health of the general practitioner, soon gained adherents who recognized the prestige and the profits that accrued to its successful practitioners.

Middle- and upper-middle-class women who could afford the treatment of the new specialists fared little better in their hands than they had under the heroic ministrations of the old-time general practitioner. Nineteenth-century gynecologists tended either to exaggerate women's problems and resort to radical surgery, or to minimize their physical suffering and prescribe lengthy and expensive rest cures. Women went to doctors, it would seem, almost in spite of the treatment they received and not because of its benefits. Where medicine did have boons to offer, as in the case of anesthesia for childbirth, the profession proved remarkably slow to pass those benefits on to patients. Citing the Biblical injunction that women should bring forth children in suffering, many physicians refused to use chloroform or ether to ease the pains of childbirth. As late as 1908, hospital deliveries, generally the recourse of only the poorest patients, were performed without anesthesia on the theory that lower-class women did not need the coddling reserved for private patients. The ghastly history of puerperal fever, which increased in incidence as women abandoned midwives for male obstetricians, offers further testimony to the dubious benefits of early medical specialization.

Early in the twentieth century, American medicine moved to enhance the prestige and professional standing of the physician by undertaking a series of educational reforms. Here, as elsewhere in the history of medical professionalization, doctors acted on the theory that their private interest coincided with the public good. Closing down the worst of the proprietary schools, they reasoned, would improve the quality of medical care by ensuring more rigorous scientific training and, at the same time, would benefit physicians financially by cutting down on the number of doctors. "Fewer and better doctors" became the slogan of the reformers.

To achieve its goals, medicine entered into a fruitful alliance with philanthropy. It was the Flexner Report, published by the Carnegie Foundation in 1910, which rated the nation's medical schools and ultimately dictated which were worthy to receive Carnegie and Rockefeller money. Instead of upgrading the poorer institutions, the Flexner Report worked to funnel foundation money to the richer and more prestigious schools like Johns Hopkins, Yale, and Harvard. In the process, medicine became less democratic. The doctor of the twentieth century was more likely than ever to be urban, white, middle- or upper-middle-class, and male.[4]

In the 1920's, the medical profession, strengthened and united after a decade of reorganization and reform, launched a calculated campaign against patent medicines and quackery. The American Medical Association, acting in close association with federal regulatory agencies such as the Bureau of Chemistry and later the Food and Drug Administration, sought to discredit patent medicines in the eyes of consumers and force the companies out of business. Although physicians criticized the mercenary instincts of the patent medicine makers, their own motives were less disinterested and scientific than they claimed. Patent medicines operated in direct competition with doctors' services. A study of the costs of medical care conducted by the government in the late twenties and early thirties indicated that many Americans saw over-the-counter drugs as satisfactory substitutes for doctors' care. Of the money spent on medicines in 1929, patent medicines accounted for more than twice the amount spent for prescription drugs—$149 million as comparted to $56 million.[5]

Like the muckrakers of the early twentieth century, the AMA persistently refused to distinguish between harmless proprietary medicines and dangerous quack preparations. Yet according to the Committee on the Costs of Medical Care, the "fraudulent fringe" of the patent medicine industry was small and growing smaller, thanks to the self-regulatory efforts of the Proprietary Association. The Committee chastised the AMA for "the purely negative manner" in which it dealt with patent medicines, noting that the AMA's lack of discrimination only reinforced the suspicion that the doctors' attack on patent medicines was prompted by the desire to increase their own share of the medical dollar.[6]

For their part, the patent medicine proprietors, as in the case of the Pinkham company, made the mistake of thinking they could blunt the attack on their businesses by cooperating with governmental agencies and courting the favor of the medical profession in ads that urged consumers to "consult your doctor." When their conciliatory efforts failed, they went on the offensive. Stressing the greed of the doctors, medicine makers insisted that expert medical attention was priced beyond the means of the poor and that patent medicines provided a cheap means for effective self-medication.

The Committee on the Costs of Medical Care lent some support to the notion that patent medicines were the poor man's friend when it published its final report in 1932. The report dramatically documented the high cost of medical care and pointed out the unequal provisions for the delivery of health care in America. During the Depression more and more Americans began to question whether, in fact, expensive laboratory equipment and extensive scientific training—the hallmarks of modern medicine—spelled better health for the nation. Medical care was certainly better than it had been fifty years earlier, but it was becoming so expensive that it was increasingly out of the reach of the average wage earner. To further aggravate matters, the trend toward specialization and the growing emphasis placed on hospital practice drew physicians into towns and cities, leaving rural areas without adequate medical care. Thus, in spite of dramatic scientific and technological advances, the net gain in public health proved disappointing.

The rising cost of medical care seemed to lead logically to the enactment of some system of national health insurance. During the Progressive period, the AMA tentatively supported a national health scheme. But during the twenties, opposition to compulsory medical insurance grew within the profession. By the time of the New Deal, the organization reversed its stand and blocked efforts to include health coverage in the Social Security Act. The AMA's increasingly adamant stand against compulsory insurance resulted in the prolonged failure of the United States to enact a system of national health insurance long after it had become commonplace in western Europe. To critics of the medical profession, the AMA's conservatism was taken as a symptom that the profession had become a self-serving elite, callous to the needs of the people.

Progress in chemotherapy and pharmacology did much to soften criticism of medicine in the period following World War II. The "wonder drugs"—penicillin, followed by other antibiotics, anti-malarials, synthetic vitamins, new vaccines, steroids, antihistamines, tranquilizers, and other new drugs—placed in the doctor's hands powerful and truly effective therapeutic agents. As the death rate from infectious diseases dropped dramatically, doctors experienced a corresponding rise in status and public esteem.

The new drugs revolutionized the pharmaceutical industry. Medical authorites revised the *Pharmacopeia,* dismissing thousands of old botanical standbys as obsolete. Drug companies curtailed their production of botanicals to concentrate on the potent new chemical agents. Federal controls on the new substances, which mandated that many be administered only through doctors' prescriptions, led to a boom in prescription drugs. By 1949 ethical drugs (drugs requiring a doctor's prescription) easily outsold proprietary remedies.

Patent medicines like Lydia Pinkham's Vegetable Compound, which relied heavily on botanical ingredients judged worthless by pharmacologists, faced the growing threat of action by the Food and Drug Administration to limit their therapeutic claims at a time when they were already losing sales. In addition to the competition from the prescription market, effective over-the-counter medicines like the analgesic and antihistamine preparations pushed aside the old-time "patent medicines"—a term that had become increasingly pejorative and served to brand a medicine as "old fashioned." As the Pinkham company discovered in its 1957 marketing survey, consumers did not regard Bufferin and Midol in the same negative manner as they did the Vegetable Compound, even though technically all three were proprietary medicines. "Lydia E. Pinkham's Vegetable Compound" sounded as quaint and outmoded to modern women as "female complaints."

Doctors who practiced women's medicine in the 1950's and 1960's enthusiastically endorsed the new drug therapy. They prescribed Darvon to quell menstrual cramps, administered hormone therapy for hot flashes and menopausal symptoms, recommended tranquilizers like Miltown and later Librium and Valium to calm jittery nerves, gave out amphetamines like Dexadrine to women who needed more pep or who wanted to lose weight, and after 1960 urged women to trade in their diaphragms for "the Pill," a synthetic hormonal anovulent. Doctors prescribed—often overprescribed—with little thought of dangerous side effects.

The large pharmaceutical companies, which marketed the brand-name ethical drugs, spent an estimated $4,000 per physician per year to push their products.[7] Overwhelmed by the sheer volume of new drugs, physicians trusted to FDA regulations and to the drug companies' research to keep harmful preparations off the market. Only later did doctors learn that the hormones they prescribed so freely produced fatal tumors, that birth control pills posed serious health problems, and that a generation of women had become hooked, psychologically if not physically, on "mother's little helpers."

In at least one respect, contemporary gynecology can be said to resemble nineteenth-century practice. Doctors continue to resort to radical surgery with troubling frequency. Hysterectomy has become so prevalent that, according to a recent estimate, over half the women in the country who reach the age of sixty-five will have had their uteruses removed. In a 1977 hearing before the Congressional Commerce Oversight Committee investigating unnecessary surgery, critics within the medical profession testified that perhaps as many as 40 per cent of the hysterectomies performed were "questionable." Among the questionable operations were cases cited where doctors removed the uterus as a treatment of "hysterical" symptoms—obsessive fear of pregnancy and "acute cancerphobia." Of the 725,000 hysterectomies performed in 1975, only 20 per cent could be justified as treatment for cancer and other life-threatening disorders.[8]

The feminist movement of the 1960's and 1970's, alarmed at the high incidence of radical hysterectomy and mastectomy and convinced that doctors over-treated and maltreated women patients, mounted an open attack on the medical profession. Feminists urged women to learn about their own bodies, to become less passive as patients, and, in some cases, to treat themselves rather than trust to male medical practice.

The feminists were not alone in their harsh criticism of the medical profession. In increasing numbers, Americans were becoming disillusioned with medical practice. The thalidomide tragedy of 1961 triggered a re-evaluation of "wonder drugs." By the 1970's, it had become obvious that the strong new drugs were as potent for harm as for good. America witnessed an alarming increase in iatrogenic disease. One medical authority estimated that perhaps one in every five patients contracted a disease caused by the treatment itself.[9] Because doctors prescribed so many different drugs, it was often impossible to ascertain which of the medicaments had done the damage.

Currently we speak of a "crisis in American medicine," a term that takes in a variety of complaints—the high cost of medical care, the grossly inadequate system of health care delivery, and the mounting incidence of malpractice—along with larger questions of what constitutes sickness (particularly mental illness) and who shall have the power to distinguish the sick from the well and order treatment. Increasing criticism of medicine has led to a number of conflicting calls for medical reform. Some argue that we need more medical care, or at least that medicine should be placed within the reach of all. Others claim that the care itself is insidious—that doctors are too preoccupied with disease and fail to practice preventive medicine. And still others insist that we should abjure medicine—whether preventive or otherwise—as it is practiced by doctors. Instead, they call for individual autonomy and with it personal responsibility for health care and healing—a philosophy which evokes the days of the domestic practitioner.[10]

Americans in the 1970's, disillusioned with medicine and confused by a plethora of popular medical cults, resemble their predecessors of the previous century. The growing vogue of health foods and natural vitamins, herbal remedies, and so-called natural wonder drugs like laetrile, testifies to a growing dissatisfaction with the therapies of the medical profession in much the same way that Thomsonianism and the health movements of the nineteenth century spoke to the desire of earlier Americans to find alternatives to heroic practice.

While it is unlikely that Lydia Pinkham's Vegetable Compound will share in the new popularity of natural medicines, it would not be surprising to see some new product appear on the market, claiming to relieve menstrual cramps or menopausal symptoms through some combination of "natural ingredients."

Today, a little over a half century since the Lydia E. Pinkham Medicine Company marked its best sales year, it is easier to find a Vegetable Compound bottle in an antique store than on a druggist's shelf. A generation of Americans enamored of health foods, herbal cosmetics, and natural vitamins has never heard of Lydia Pinkham or her medicine. If you ask a druggist, he may produce a bottle from the back room, after fixing you with a quizzical stare. More likely, he will say he hasn't carried the stuff for years. The demise of the Vegetable Compound is almost—but not quite—complete.

Notes

I. THE WOMAN BEHIND THE TRADEMARK

1. Charles E. Estes, *Estes Genealogies 1097–1893* (Salem, Mass.: Eben Putnam, Publisher, 1894), pp. 1–28.

2. Paul Gustaf Faler, "Workingmen, Mechanics and Social Change: Lynn, Massachusetts 1800–1860" (unpublished Ph.D. dissertation, University of Wisconsin, 1971), p. 51; Alan Dawley, *Class and Community: The Industrial Revolution in Lynn* (Cambridge: Harvard University Press, 1976), pp. 51–56.

3. Ralph Waldo Emerson, quoted in Joseph H. Kett, *The Formation of the American Medical Profession: The Role of Institutions 1780–1860* (New Haven: Yale University Press, 1968), pp. 149–150.

4. Emanuel Swedenborg, *Heaven and Its Wonders and Hell* (New York: Swedenborg Foundation 1974), p. 341.

5. Marguerite Beck Block, *The New Church in the New World: A Study of Swedenborgianism in America* (New York: Octagon Books, Inc., 1968, originally published by Holt, Rinehart and Winston, Inc., 1932), p. 130.

6. Ralph Waldo Emerson to Thomas Carlyle, October 30, 1840, in *The Correspondence of Emerson and Carlyle*, ed. John Slater (New York: Columbia University Press, 1964), p. 283.

7. Faler, "Workingmen, Mechanics and Social Change," pp. 76 and 215; Nathaniel P. Rogers, letter from Lynn in *Herald of Freedom*, May 27, 1842.

8. Alonzo Lewis and James R. Newhall, *History of Lynn, Essex County Massachusetts, Including Lynnfield, Saugus, Swampscot, and Nahant* (Boston: John L. Shorey, Publisher, 1865), pp. 401–402.

9. "Clerical Impudence—The Climax," from the *Liberator,* quoted in the *Herald of Freedom,* September 2, 1842; "Resolution of the Essex County Anti-Slavery Society," quoted in the *Herald of Freedom,* October 14, 1842.

10. "Album of Lydia E. Pinkham," Vol. 538, papers of the Lydia E. Pinkham Medicine Company, Arthur and Elizabeth Schlesinger Library on the History of Women in America, Radcliffe College, Cambridge, Massachusetts [hereafter cited as LEP SL].

11. Frederick Douglass, *Life and Times of Frederick Douglass* (Boston: De Wolfe, Fiske and Company, 1895), pp. 277–279.

12. Letter from William Bassett, quoted in the *Herald of Freedom,* March 11, 1842.

13. "Journal of Lydia E. Pinkham," Box 180 (Folder 3365), LEP SL.

14. *Herald of Freedom,* May 23, 1840.

15. *Ibid.,* June 13, 1840, and September 18, 1840.

16. Nathaniel P. Rogers, *Collection from the Miscellaneous Writings of Nathaniel P. Rogers* (Manchester, New Hampshire: William H. Fisk, 1849), p. xxi; *Herald of Freedom,* March 21, 1840, and April 4, 1840.

17. John Pierpont, "Introduction," in *Collection from the Miscellaneous Writings of Nathaniel P. Rogers,* pp. xiii–xxiii.

18. "Picture of Lydia E. Pinkham at the age of 25," Box 119 (Folder 2379), LEP SL.

19. "Journal of Lydia E. Pinkham," Box 180 (Folder 3365), LEP SL.

20. "Medical Directions for Ailments," Vol. 537, LEP SL.

21. Arthur W. Pinkham, *Reminiscences* (Lynn, Mass.: published by the author, 1954), pp. 34–35, listed as Vol. 531, LEP SL.

22. "Journal of Lydia E. Pinkham," Box 180 (Folder 3365), LEP SL.

23. "Obituary, Daniel Rogers Pinkham," *Lynn Transcript,* October 15, 1881, in "Lydia Pinkham's Scrapbook," Vol. 556, LEP SL.

24. "Photographs," Series IV, Oversize 5, LEP SL.

25. Arthur W. Pinkham, *Reminiscences,* p. 28, Vol. 531, LEP SL.

26. Robert Collyer Washburn, *The Life and Times of Lydia E. Pinkham* (New York: G. P. Putnam's Sons, 1931), p. 91.

27. Daniel Rogers Pinkham, quoted in *Lynn Daily Item,* January 23, 1893.

28. "History and Development of the Company's Methods of Manufacture," (Typescript, n.d.), Box 132 (Folder 2635), LEP SL.

29. "Medical Directions for Ailments," Vol. 537, LEP SL.

30. "Cashbook," Vol. 74, and "Cashbook," Vol. 69, LEP SL.

31. Daniel Pinkham's letters often lack a full date. For convenience I refer the reader not to individual letters, but to the entire collection and will therefore refrain from noting the letters separately. *See* "Letters: Thirty-eight Original Letters from Daniel Rogers Pinkham to William H. Pinkham, 1876–1879," Box 167 (Folder 3117), LEP SL.

32. Lydia Pinkham, quoted in Harlan Page Hubbard, "The True Story of Lydia Pinkham," *Fame* I (November 1892), in Box 164 (Folder 3035), LEP SL.

33. *Ibid.*

34. The quotations that follow are from Daniel Pinkham's letters, see Box 167 (Folder 3117), LEP SL.

35. Charles N. Crittenton, *The Brother of Girls, The Life Story of Charles N. Crittenton as Told by Himself* (Chicago: World's Events Company, 1910), pp. 195–205.

36. Daniel Pinkham's letters, Box 167 (Folder 3117), LEP SL.

37. Newsclipping in "Lydia Pinkham's Scrapbook," Vol. 556, LEP SL.

38. *Ibid.*

39. Handbill in "Lydia Pinkham's Scrapbook," Vol. 556, LEP SL.

40. Daniel Pinkham's letters, Box 167 (Folder 3117), LEP SL.

41. Hubbard, "True Story," *Fame,* Box 164 (Folder 3035), LEP SL.

42. Newsclipping in "Lydia Pinkham's Scrapbook," Vol. 556, LEP SL.

43. *Ibid.*

44. "Medical Directions for Ailments," Vol. 537, LEP SL.

45. Lydia E. Pinkham to Daniel R. Pinkham, n.d., illustration in Eleanor Early, "The True Life of Lydia E. Pinkham," clipping in Box 164 (Folder 3028), LEP SL.

46. "Obituary, Daniel Rogers Pinkham," clipping in "Lydia Pinkham's Scrapbook," Vol. 556, LEP SL.

47. William H. Gove, "In Memoriam," obituary of William H. Pinkham, clipping in "Lydia Pinkham's Scrapbook," Vol. 556, LEP SL.

48. Washburn, *Life and Times,* p. 166.

49. John Wallace Hutchinson, *Story of the Hutchinsons: Tribe of Jesse,* (Boston: Lee and Shepard, Publishers, 1896), II, p. 110.

II. THE POISONING CENTURY

1. Johann Peter Frank, quoted in Erwin H. Ackerknecht, M.D., *Therapeutics From the Primitives to the 20th Century* (New York: Hafner Press, 1973), p. 81.

2. "Medical Directions for Ailments," Vol. 537, LEP SL.

3. The late George Rosen of the Department of History of Science and Medicine, Yale University, suggested that a vitamin deficiency might have produced the symptoms described in the letter to Lydia Pinkham.

4. "Medical Directions for Ailments," Vol. 537, LEP SL.

5. *Ibid.*

6. Jacob Bigelow, M.D., "On Self Limited Diseases," a paper presented before the Massachusetts Medical Society, May 27, 1835, reprinted in *Medical America in the Nineteenth Century: Readings from the Literature,* ed. Gert H. Brieger (Baltimore: The Johns Hopkins Press, 1972), p. 99.

7. Benjamin Rush, M.D., *Six Introductory Lectures to Courses of Lectures upon the Institutes and Practices of Medicine Delivered in the University of Pennsylvania* (Philadelphia: M. J. Conrad and Company, 1801), p. 69.

8. Rush, quoted in Martin Kaufman, *Homeopathy in America* (Baltimore: The Johns Hopkins Press, 1971), p. 2.

9. *Ibid.*, p. 3.

10. Daniel Drake, M.D., quoted in Madge E. Pickard and R. Carlyle Buley, *The Midwest Pioneer: His Ills, Cures, and Doctors* (Crawfordsville, Indiana: R. E. Banta, 1945), p. 29.

11. Rush, quoted in *Ibid.*, pp. 108–109.

12. A. Hunn, "Essay on Bilious Fever and the Use of Calomel," *Thomsonian Recorder*, I (1832), pp. 53–54.

13. Benjamin Silliman, M.D., quoted in J. A. Brown, *The Family Guide to Health* (Providence: B. T. Albro, 1837), p. 111.

14. *The Hutchinson Family's Book of Words* (New York: Baker, Goodwin and Company, 1852), pp. 41–42.

15. *See* William G. Rothstein, *American Physicians in the Nineteenth Century* (Baltimore: The Johns Hopkins Press, 1972), p. 53; and George Rosen, M.D., Ph.D., "Sir William Temple and the Therapeutic Use of the Moxa for Gout in England," *Bulletin of the History of Medicine*. XLIV (January–February 1970), pp. 31–39.

16. Quoted in Pickard and Buley, *Midwest Pioneer*, pp. 102–103.

17. Austin Flint, M.D., quoted in Brieger, ed., *Medical America*, p. 87.

18. Brown, *The Family Guide to Health*, introductory quotation, n. pag.

19. Samuel Thomson, *New Guide to Health or Botanic Family Physician to which is prefixed a Narrative of the Life and Medical Discoveries of the Author,* 2nd ed. (Boston: E. G. House, 1825), pp. 121 and 106.

20. *Ibid.*, p. 24.

21. *Ibid.*, p. 27.

22. Samuel Thomson, *New Guide to Health or Botanic Family Physician* (Boston: E. G. House, 1822; p. 18.

23. Brown, *Family Guide to Health,* pp. 39–40.

24. Samuel Thomson, *Report of the Trial of Dr. Samuel Thomson* (Boston: printed by the author, 1839), *passim;* and John Thomson, *A Vindication of the Thomsonian System* (Albany: Webster and Wood, 1825), pp. 24–52.

25. Thomson, *New Guide to Health*, 1st ed., 1822. Introduction, n. pag. Thomson's twenty dollar fee for a family right was expensive by contemporary standards. But it was intended more as a guideline than as a price tag. For comparison *see* George Rosen, *Fees and Fee Bills: Some Economic Aspects of Medical Practice in Nineteenth Century America* (Baltimore: The Johns Hopkins Press, 1946). Thomson had a good deal of trouble collecting his fees from his itinerant agents, who branched out on their own, marketed his system, and pocketed the proceeds. *See* Thomson, *Narrative*, pp. 117–122 and pp. 162–172.

26. For a full discussion of the pharmaceutical end of the business *see* Alex Berman, "The Thomsonian Movement and Its Relation to American Pharmacy and Medicine," *Bulletin of the History of Medicine*, XXV (September–October 1951), pp. 405–428; continued in XXV (November–December 1951), pp. 519–538.

27. Thomson, *Report of the Trial,* p. 51.

28. *See* Joseph F. Kett, *The Formation of the American Medical Profession* (New Haven: Yale University Press, 1968), pp. 117–121.

29. Bigelow, "On Self Limited Diseases," in Brieger, ed., *Medical America*, p. 104.

30. Robert Grant, *Unleavened Bread* (New York: Charles Scribner's Sons, 1900), pp. 261–262.

31. Samuel Hahnemann, *Organon of Homeopathic Medicine*, 1st American ed. (Philadelphia: North American Academy of the Homeopathic Healing Art, 1836), p. 200.

32. *See* Oliver Wendell Holmes, *Homeopathy and Its Kindred Delusions* (Boston: W. D. Ticknor, 1843).

33. Quoted in Brieger, ed., *Medical America*, p. 82.

34. Dan King, *Quackery Unmasked* (Boston: David Clapp, 1858), p. 110.

35. *See* Kaufman, *Homeopathy*, pp. 61–62.

36. Daniel Webster Cathell, *The Physician Himself*, 2nd revised ed. (Baltimore: Cushings and Bailey, 1882), p. 65.

37. *Ibid.*, p. 142.

38. Quoted in Kaufman, *Homeopathy in America*, p. 30.

39. Graham insisted that man was a "frugivorous animal." "His *natural* food appears to consist of fruits, roots, and other esulent parts of vegetables." *See* Sylvester Graham, *Lectures on the Science of Human Life* (New York: Fowler and Wells Publishers, 1883), p. 345.

40. *Ibid.*, pp. 304, 425, and 557.

41. *Ibid.*, p. 438.

42. For the following discussion of the new therapy I am indebted to Rothstein, *American Physicians*, pp. 177–97.

43. Austin Flint, M.D., "Conservative Medicine," in Brieger, ed., *Medical America*, p. 141.

44. Quoted in Pickard and Buley, *Midwest Pioneers*, pp. 242–43.

45. Richard Harrison Shryock, *The Development of Modern Medicine* (New York: Alfred A. Knopf, 1947), p. 270.

III. THE AGE OF THE WOMB

1. Jules Michelet, *L'Amour*, trans. from 4th Paris ed. by J. W. Palmer, M.D. (New York: Carleton, Publisher, 1868), p. 1*.

2. Alexis de Tocqueville, *Democracy in America* (New York: Vintage Books, 1959), II, p. 212; first published in 1840.

3. Lydia Kingsmill Commander, *The American Idea* (New York: A. S. Barnes and Company, 1907), p. 192.

4. *See* Nancy F. Cott, *The Bonds of Womanhood: "Woman's Sphere" in New England, 1780–1835* (New Haven: Yale University Press, 1977), pp. 48–50; Patricia Branca, *Silent Sisterhood, Middle Class Woman in the Victorian Home* (Pittsburgh: Carnegie-Mellon University Press, 1975), pp. 1–19.

5.   Thorstein Veblen, *The Theory of the Leisure Class* (New York: The Macmillan Company, 1908), p. 81.

6.   Albert Hayes, M.D., *Physiology of Woman and Her Diseases* (Boston: Peabody Medical Institute, 1869), p. 56.

7.   Veblen, *Theory of the Leisure Class,* p. 83.

8.   Feminists Olive Schreiner and Charlotte Perkins Gilman, emphasizing the economic relationship between men and women, spoke disapprovingly of "female parasitism." The term ignores the socio-psychological dynamics between men and women in which patterns of dependency were less one-sided. As psychologist Havelock Ellis observed, men were "domestically parasitic" in that they required women to provide domestic services and comfort. The term "forced symbiosis" would seem to indicate more accurately than "parasitism" the interdependencies between men and women in nineteenth-century society. The symbiosis was forced by a society which roundly condemned the middle-class woman who attempted to escape her economic dependency on men by seeking a wider sphere of activity than the domestic world of the genteel female. For discussion of "female parasitism" *see* Olive Schriener, *Women and Labor* (New York: Frederick A. Stokes Company, 1911), chapters 1–3; and Charlotte Perkins Gilman, *Women and Economics* (Boston: Small, Maynard and Company, 1898), sections 1 and 2. For men's "domestic parasitism" *see* H. Havelock Ellis, *Little Essays of Love and Virtue* (New York: George H. Doran Company, 1922), p. 95.

9.   Albert Hayes, a doctor of dubious professional standing, plagiarized repeatedly from William Acton's well-known *Functions and Disorders of the Reproductive Organs* (1857) in his own *Physiology of Woman.*

10.   Henry Maudsley, M.D., *Body and Mind* (London: Macmillan and Company, 1870), p. 32.

11.   Frederick Hollick, M.D., *The Origin of Life and the Process of Reproduction* (New York: The American News Company, 1878), p. 683. Hollick, a licensed M.D., was nevertheless considered a quack by many in the medical profession who argued his books were designed to promote a line of patent medicines and services. Hollick's books enjoyed a large popular audience. Lydia Pinkham was among his readers.

12.   I am indebted for this quotation to Carroll Smith-Rosenberg and Charles Rosenberg's "The Female Animal: Medical and Biological Views of Woman and her Role in 19th Century America," *Journal of American History,* LX (September 1973), p. 335. The quotation is from M. L. Holbrook's *Parturition Without Pain* (1882).

13.   Edward H. Clarke, M.D., *Sex in Education, or A Fair Chance for Girls* (Boston: Robert Brothers, 1873), p. 33.

14.   Quoted in Mary Putnam Jacobi, *The Question of Rest for Women During Menstruation* (New York: G. P. Putnam's Sons, 1877), p. 8.

15.   Michelet, *L'Amour,* p. 48.

16.   Sylvester Graham, *Lecture to Young Men on Chastity* (Boston: George W. light, 1839), pp. 51–52. Graham draws heavily on Samuel Tissot, a Swiss writer whose *Onanisme* (1758) marked one of the earliest anti-masturbation tracts.

17. Frank Harris, *My Life and Loves* (New York: Grove Press, 1963), p. 26; originally published 1925.

18. *Ibid.,* p. 46.

19. Graham, *Lecture to Young Men,* p. 78.

20. G[eorge] L. Austin, M.D., *Perils of American Women, or a Doctor's Talk with Maiden, Wife, and Mother* (Boston: Lee and Shepard, Publishers, 1883), pp. 54, 105, and 88.

21. Augustus K. Gardner, M.D., *Conjugal Sins Against the Laws of Life and Health and Their Effects Upon the Father, Mother and Child* (New York: J. S. Redfield, Publisher, 1870), p. 82.

22. Compare William Acton, M.R.C.S., *Functions and Disorders of the Reproductive Organs in Childhood, Youth, Adult Age, and Advanced Life,* 4th American ed. (Philadelphia: Lindsay and Blakiston, 1875), p. 162 to the 4th ed. (London: John Churchill and Sons, 1865), p. 112.

23. Clarke, *Sex in Education,* pp. 26–27.

24. Horatio Robinson Storer, M.D., *The Causation, Course, and Treatment of Reflex Insanity in Women* (Boston: Lee and Shepard, Publishers, 1871), p. 78 [emphasis added].

25. Hollick, *Origins of Life,* p. 369.

26. Jacobi, *Question of Rest,* p. 2; for a discussion of male medical treatment *see* Gail Pat Parsons, "Equal Treatment for All: American Medical Remedies for Male Sexual Problems: 1850–1900," *Journal of the History of Medicine and Allied Sciences,* XXXII (January 1977), pp. 55–71.

27. Catharine Beecher, *Letters to the People on Health and Happiness* (New York: Harper and Brothers, 1855), Appendix, p. 9.

28. Nathaniel Hawthorne, *The Scarlet Letter* (1850), in *The Complete Novels and Selected Tales of Nathaniel Hawthorne,* with an introduction by Norman Holmes Pearson (New York: Random House, 1937), p. 114.

29. Hawthorne, *The Blithedale Romance* (1852), in *Ibid.,* p. 499.

30. Laura Marholm, *Psychology of Women* (London: Grant Richards, 1899), p. 246.

31. Austin, *Perils of American Women,* p. 134.

32. Hayes, *Physiology of Woman,* p. 26; *see also* Moses T. Runnels, M.D., "Physical Degeneracy of American Women," *The Medical Era,* III (April 1886), pp. 297–302.

33. George M. Beard, M.D., *American Nervousness: Its Philosophy and Treatment* (Richmond: J. W. Fergusson and Sons, 1879), p. 2.

34. George M. Beard, M.D., *Sexual Neurasthenia (Nervous Exhaustion) Its Hygiene, Causes, Symptoms, and Treatment,* 5th ed. (New York: E. B. Treat and Company, 1900), p. 15.

35. M. Mitchell Clarke, M.D., *Hysteria and Neurasthenia: A Practitioner's Handbook* (London: John Lane, The Bodley Head, 1904), p. 171.

36. Austin, *Perils of American Women,* p. 143; *see* Ann Douglas Wood, " 'The Fashionable Diseases': Women's Complaints and Their Treatment in 19th Century America," *Journal of Interdisciplinary History,* IV (Summer 1973), pp. 25–52.

its product, its advertising, and its merchandising methods entirely to meet the exigencies of a modern market.[37]

Time had caught up with the Pinkham company. The census of 1920, which for the first time recorded a predominantly urban population, might well have stood as the harbinger of the company's obsolescence. The Vegetable Compound was neither urban nor urbane; it harked back to an era of horse-and-buggy doctors and genteel females. The modern urban housewife , or working woman spurned the Compound as she would a dowdy dress. Women's magazines, which encouraged a devotion to the stylish and modern, did more damage to Lydia Pinkham and her medicine than the muckraking campaigns of Bok and Adams. By poking fun at the Vegetable Compound while extolling the merits of "modern medicine," editors dealt a fatal blow to the company. The name and face which had made the Vegetable Compound proved its unmaking.

Had the Pinkhams responded more astutely to changing times, they might have been able to hold their market or develop new ones. The FTC citation they had greeted so jubilantly because it allowed them to make specific claims regarding menstrual pain and menopausal symptoms hurt them in the long run. It placed them in competition with more effective analgesic drugs and with the modish hormone therapies employed by physicians. If the company had stayed with tonic claims, the Vegetable Compound might have tapped the market that Geritol dominates today.

In its early years the company had been daring and innovative. The success of the Vegetable Compound in the late nineteenth century was due to massive national advertising, a phenomenon unheard of at the time. In the fifties, an era of mass advertising in print and on radio and TV, it was unrealistic to think that the company could hold its market and still keep advertising costs to 50 per cent of the revenue from its dwindling sales. Too many products competed for consumers' attention. If the board of directors had been less interested in keeping profits stable and more interested in building sales, the company might have survived. Instead, as its share of the advertising media declined, so did its sales. Pinkham policy created a vicious downward spiral.

In 1968 the company faced the reality of its shrinking market

266   *Notes (pages 77–84)*

37. Beard, *Sexual Neurasthenia,* p. 27.
38. Charles D. Meigs, M.D., *Females and Their Diseases* (Philadelphia: Lea and Blanchard, 1848), p. 19.
39. Robert B. Carter, quoted in Ilza Veith, *Hysteria, The History of a Disease* (Chicago: University of Chicago Press, 1965), p. 205.
40. Beecher, *Letters to the People,* p. 135.
41. Mary A. Livermore in an introductory letter in Austin, *Perils of American Women,* n. pag.
42. *Ibid.,* p. 158.
43. *Ibid.,* p. 160; *see* P. F. Chambers, M.D., "The Problems Presented to the Gynecologist Twenty-Five Years Ago and Today," *Southern Surgical and Gynecological Transactions,* LXXI (1905), p. 18.
44. Hayes, *Physiology of Woman,* p. 316.
45. Beecher, *Letters to the People,* pp. 5–6; Branca, *Silent Sisterhood,* p. 64; Richard W. TeLinde, M.D., "Prolapse of the Uterus and Allied Conditions," *American Journal of Obstetrics and Gynecology,* XCIV (February 1, 1966), pp. 451–452.
46. Edwin M. Jameson, M.D., *Gynecology and Obstetrics* (New York: Paul B. Hoeber, Inc., 1936), p. 128.
47. Robert Battey, M.D., "Extirpation of the Functionally Active Ovaries for the Remedy of Otherwise Incurable Diseases," *Transactions of the American Gynecological Society,* I (1876), p. 102.
48. *Ibid.,* p. 104; for a discussion of the coercive use of sexual surgery *see* G. J. Barker-Benfield, *The Horrors of the Half-Known Life* (New York: Harper and Row, Publishers, 1976), pp. 120–132.
49. Joseph Taber Johnson, M.D., "Four Cases of Oöphorectomy, with Remarks," *Transactions of the American Gynecological Society,* X (1885), pp. 131–132.
50. Ferdinand Henrotin, M.D., "Conservative Surgical Treatment of Para and Peri Uterine Septic Disease," *Transactions of the American Gynecological Society,* XX)1895), p. 225.
51. *See* Thomas Addis Emmet, M.D., "The Uses of Traction and Morcellation in the Removal of Fibroids *versus* Hysterectomy," *Transactions of the American Gynecological Society,* XX (1895), p. 81; for surgical fees *see* George Rosen, M.D., *Fees and Fee Bills: Some Economic Aspects of Medical Practice in 19th Century America* (Baltimore: The Johns Hopkins Press, 1946), pp. 63 and 81.
52. Elizabeth Blackwell, M.D., *Essays in Medical Sociology* (London: Ernest Bell, 1902), II, pp. 119–120.
53. Mary Putnam Jacobi to Elizabeth Blackwell, December 25, 1888. Thanks to Gina Morantz for this reference from the Blackwell family papers, Manuscript Division, Library of Congress.
54. Matthew Duncan, M.D., quoted in Harold Speert, *Obstetrical and Gynecological Milestones* (New York: The Macmillan Company, 1958), p. 360.
55. For an account of Noeggerath's paper and the discussion which followed *see* Emil Noeggerath, M.D., "Latent Gonorrhea, Especially With Regard to its Influence on Fertility in Women," *Transactions of the American Gynecological Society,* I (1876), pp. 268–300.

56. *See* Clark, *Sex in Education,* pp. 118–161; Gardner, *Conjugal Sins,* p. 182; John S. and Robin M. Haller, *The Physician and Sexuality in Victorian America* (Urbana: University of Illinois Press, 1974), pp. 76–87.

57. Hollick, *Origin of Life,* p. 677.

58. Marholm, *Psychology of Woman,* pp. 248–249; for a recent interpretation of illness as occupation *see* Donald Meyer, *The Positive Thinkers* (New York: Doubleday and Company, 1965), chapter 3.

59. S. Weir Mitchell, M.D., *Fat and Blood: And How to Make Them* (Philadelphia: J. B. Lippincott and Company, 1877), p. 41.

60. Charlotte Perkins Gilman, *The Living of Charlotte Perkins Gilman* (New York: D. Appleton-Century Company, 1935), p. 96.

61. Charlotte Perkins Gilman, *The Yellow Wallpaper* (Old Westbury, New York: Feminist Press, 1973), pp. 9–10. The story originally appeared in *The New England Magazine* (1892).

62. S. Weir Mitchell, M.D., *Doctor and Patient* (Philadelphia: J. B. Lippincott and Company, 1888), p. 11.

63. *See* Emmet, "The Use of Traction & Morcellation," p. 55; Willis E. Ford, M.D., "The Ultimate Result of Trachelorrhaphy," *Transactions of the American Gynecological Society,* XX (1895), p. 299; Barker-Benfield, *Horrors of the Half-Known Life,* pp. 130–132. Dr. Maria Zakrewska indicated in 1891 that some women sought sexual surgery as a means of sterilization in order to avoid unwanted pregnancies. *See* Wood, " 'Fashionable Diseases,' " p. 48.

IV. SELLING THE VEGETABLE COMPOUND

1. "Album of Lydia E. Pinkham," (original formula written in Lydia Pinkham's hand), Vol. 538, LEP SL.

2. Copy of the first Pinkham label, Vol. 463, LEP SL.

3. Lydia Pinkham's copy of King's *Dispensatory* was a tenth edition, dated 1876. Her annotated copy, then, was published a year after the family began to market the Vegetable Compound. It is possible that she took the Compound formula from an earlier edition of the *Dispensatory.* Perhaps she invented it entirely or drew on the formula given to Isaac Pinkham by George Clarkson Todd and only later consulted King. *See* Vol. 546, LEP SL.

4. John King, M.D., *The American Dispensatory,* (10th ed.; Cincinnati: Wilstach, Baldwin and Company, 1876), p. 79.

5. *Ibid.,* p. 768.

6. *Ibid.,* p. 143.

7. Frederic Fluhmann, quoted in Richard W. TeLinde, M.D., "Prolapse of the Uterus and Allied Conditions," *American Journal of Obstetrics and Gynecology,* XCIV (February 1, 1966), p. 452.

8. Lydia E. Pinkham to E. D. Allen, December 27, 1880, in "Medical Directions for Ailments," Vol. 537, LEP SL.

9. Daniel Pinkham's letters, Box 167 (Folder 3117), LEP SL.

10. "Cashbook," Vol. 71, LEP SL.

11. "Cashbook," Vol. 68, LEP SL; for a discussion of early arrangements between advertisers and papers *see* George P. Rowell, *Forty Years an Advertising Agent, 1865–1905* (New York: Franklin Publishing Company, 1926), p. 122.

12. Rowell, *Forty Years,* p. 454.

13. The estimate of commissions may be conservative. Earnest Elmo Calkins, an early advertising agent, noted that commissions sometimes amounted to 50 per cent of the cost of the space. *See* Earnest Elmo Calkins and Ralph Holden, *Modern Advertising* (New York: D. Appleton and Co., 1907), p. 14.

14. Rowell, *Forty Years,* p. 319.

15. *Ibid.*

16. Charles Austin Bates, *Good Advertising* (New York: Holmes Publishing Company, 1896), p. 230.

17. Daniel Pinkham's letters, Box 167 (Folder 3117), LEP SL.

18. Harlan Page Hubbard, "The True Story of Lydia Pinkham," *Fame* I (November 1892), Typescript in Box 164 (Folder 3035), LEP SL.

19. *Ibid.*

20. Daniel Pinkham's letters, Box 167 (Folder 3117), LEP SL.

21. "The Plucky Pinkhams," *Weekly Union,* November 19, 1881, Typescript in Box 163 (Folder 3010), LEP SL.

22. C. F. Cross to Charles H. Pinkham, March 4 and March 11, 1881, Box 167 (Folder 3125), LEP SL.

23. "Partnership Agreement," October 18, 1881, Box 164 (Folder 3043), LEP SL.

24. Hubbard, "True Story," *Fame,* Box 164 (Folder 3035), LEP SL.

25. *Chicago Mirror* to Lydia E. Pinkham Medicine Company, July 25, 1882, Box 84 (Folder 763), LEP SL.

26. "Cashbook," Vol. 71 and balance sheets, Box 84 (Folder 763), LEP SL.

27. Agreement between Charles H. Pinkham and H. P. Hubbard, signed December 27, 1883, Box 84 (Folder 763), LEP SL.

28. Contract with H. P. Hubbard, January 22, 1884, vol. 559, LEP SL.

29. William H. Gove to Charles H. Pinkham, October 17, 1884, Box 168 (Folder 3133a) and "Stock Certificates," Box 164 (Folder 3047), LEP SL.

30. Quoted in Rowell, *Forty Years,* p. 377.

31. Advertisements in "Lydia Pinkham's Scrapbook," Vol. 556, LEP SL.

32. Advertisement, "A Fearful Tragedy," Vol. 556, LEP SL.

33. Frederick Hollick, M.D., *The Origin of Life* (New York: The American News Company, 1878), p. 644.

34. Advertisement, "Life's Woes," Vol. 556, LEP SL.

35. Bates, *Good Advertising,* p. 439.

36. *Ibid.,* p. 441.

37. Mrs. Walter Wilcox to Lydia E. Pinkham Medicine Company, September 26, 1893, Vol. 593, LEP SL.

38. H. P. Hubbard to Charles H. Pinkham, April 24, 1885, Box 84 (Folder 764), LEP SL.

39. Advertisement, "Encouraging Reports," Vol. 556, LEP SL.

40. Advertisement, "Health and Condition of the Working Women of Massachusetts," (n.d.), newsclipping in "Lydia Pinkham's Scrapbook," Vol. 556, LEP SL.

41. Advertisement, "Early Dead," Vol. 556, LEP SL.

42. Lydia E. Pinkham Medicine Company to H. P. Hubbard, January 29, 1884, Vol. 559, LEP SL.

43. Testimonial from Mrs. Annie Custer in advertisement, "Encouraging Reports," Vol. 556, LEP SL.

44. Testimonial "from a lady writing from Elmira," in *Ibid.*

45. Correspondence in "Medical Directions for Ailments," Vol. 537, LEP SL.

46. Advertisement, "Nerve Strain," Vol. 556, LEP SL.

47. Advertisement, "Mrs. Lydia E. Pinkham of Lynn, Mass.," Vol. 556, LEP SL.

48. Advertisement, "Nerve Strain," Vol. 556, LEP SL.

49. *Ibid.*

50. Lydia E. Pinkham Medicine Company to H. P. Hubbard, May 2, 1885, Vol. 588, LEP SL.

51. Charles H. Pinkham to H. P. Hubbard, August 21, 1885, Vol. 588, LEP SL.

52. "A Seasonable Request," *Printers' Ink,* I (August 1, 1888), p. 49.

53. "Cashbook," Vol. 71, LEP SL and "A Seasonable Request," *ibid.,* p. 49.

V. SENSATIONAL PRUDERY

1. Newspaper clipping from the *Boston Herald,* n.d., Box 158 (Folder 2913), LEP SL.

2. Pettingill and Company was reputed to handle the largest volume of newspaper advertising in the country. *See Printers' Ink,* XIII (December 4, 1895), p. 46. For a history of the development of the agency *see* S. M. Pettingill, "Reminiscences of the Advertising Business," *Printers' Ink,* XIII (December 24, 1890), pp. 686–90.

3. "A Well Known Face," interview with Charles H. Pinkham in the *Boston Herald,* n.d., Box 163 (Folder 3020), LEP SL.

4. The shift toward respectability in advertising is documented in Earnest Elmo Calkins and Ralph Holen, *Modern Advertising* (New York: D. Appleton and Company, 1907), pp. 167–170.

5. Quoted in George Presbury Rowell, *Forty Years an Advertising Agent* (New York: Franklin Publishing Company, 1926), p. 401.

6. "Cashbook," Vol. 71, and "Profit and Loss Statements 1890–1899," Vol. 246, LEP SL.

7. Rowell, *Forty Years,* p. 404.

8. "Profit and Loss Statements 1890–1899," Vol. 246, LEP SL.

9. "Lydia E. Pinkham's Familiar Face," *Kansas City World,* n.d., Vol. 556, LEP SL.

10. Anonymous letter, Jan. 23, 1897, Box 167 (Folder 3116), LEP SL.

11. Advertisement, "A Life's Experience," Vol. 345, LEP SL.

12. Lydia E. Pinkham Medicine Company to Mr. Fred A. Dettloff, May 11, 1898, Vol. 571, LEP SL.

13. Advertisement, "Lydia E. Pinkham's Vegetable Compound Cures Irregularity, *etc.,*" Vol. 345, LEP SL.

14. For a discussion of the treatment of hysteria in the Victorian era *see* Ilza Vieth, *Hysteria, The History of a Disease* (Chicago: University of Chicago Press, 1965), pp. 199–220.

15. Booklet, "Health, Vigor, and Strength" (1900), p. 21 in Vol. 382, LEP SL.

16. Advertisement, "Woman's Influence," Vol. 348, LEP SL.

17. Advertisement, "Pretty and Attractive Women," Vol. 348, LEP SL.

18. Ray Vaughn Pierce, *The People's Common Sense Medical Adviser in Plain English; Or, Medicine Simplified,* 69th ed. (Buffalo, N.Y.: World's Dispensary Printing Office, 1895).

19. Manuscript, "Lydia E. Pinkham's Guide to Health, A Private Textbook," n.d., Box 123 (Folder 2494), LEP SL.

20. Booklet, "My Lady Beautiful" (1901), p. 12, in Vol. 379, LEP SL.

21. *Ibid.*

22. Testimonial from Mary A. Stahl, Watsontown, Pa., in booklet, "Yours for Health" (1901), p. 32, in Vol. 379, LEP SL.

23. Testimonial from Mrs. W. F. Sawyer, Vermont, in booklet, "Women's Letters" (1914), p. 32, in Vol. 385, LEP SL.

24. Lydia E. Pinkham Medicine Company to Carl Rudolph, June 26, 1896, Vol. 563, LEP SL.

25. Laura B. Hunt to James T. Wetherald, May 27, 1897, Vol. 567, LEP SL.

26. William H. Gove to Charles H. Pinkham, March 31, 1890, Box 168 (Folder 3133a), LEP SL.

27. Advertisements, "Can I Assist You, Madam?" and "Why Are You Sick?," Vol. 345, LEP SL.

28. "Lydia E. Pinkham's Familiar Face," Vol. 556, LEP SL.

29. Booklet, "Guide to Health and Etiquette" (1890), p. 38, in Vol. 380, LEP SL.

30. Booklet, "To the Women of America" (1899), p. 2, in Vol. 345, LEP SL.

31. Booklet, "Yours for Health" (1901), p. 18, in Vol. 379, LEP SL.

32. Booklet, "My Lady Beautiful" (1971), p. 24, in Vol. 379, LEP SL.

33. Booklet, "Silent Places" (1907), pp. 1 and 14, in Vol. 383, LEP SL.

34. Booklet, "The Ages of Woman" (1905), p. 43, in Vol. 382, LEP SL.

35. Booklet, "Treatise on the Diseases of Women Dedicated to the Women of the World" (1904), p. 59, in Vol. 382, LEP SL.

36. *Ibid.*

37. Advertisement, "Will Women's Rights Bring Happiness?," Vol. 345, LEP SL.

38. *Ibid.*

39. Booklet, "Wisdom for Women" (1912), p. 59, in Vol. 384, LEP SL.

40. Booklet, "Secrets of Happiness" (1910), p. 25, in Vol. 384, LEP SL.

41. Booklet, "Lydia E. Pinkham's Private Text Book" (1907), p. 14, in Vol. 381, LEP SL.

42. Booklet, "Secrets of Happiness" (1910), p. 25, in Vol. 384, LEP SL.

43. Charles Knowlton M.D., *Fruits of Philosophy, An Essay on the Population Question* (2nd New Ed.; London: Free Thought Publishing Company, n.d.).

44. Charles Pinkham [Jr.], *Advertising* (Lynn, Mass.: published by the Lydia E. Pinkham Medicine Company, 1953), p. 93, listed as Vol. 328, LEP SL.

45. Booklet, "The New Woman" (1903), n. pag., in Vol. 380, LEP SL; for a discussion of the relationship between douching as a birth control measure and douching as a hygienic practice, *see* James W. Reed, *From Private Vice to Public Virtue: The Birth Control Movement and American Society Since 1830* (New York: Basic Books, Inc., 1978), pp. 10–11.

46. Pinkham, *Advertising*, p. 117, Vol. 328, LEP SL.

47. Lydia E. Pinkham Medicine Company to Mrs. Nathaniel Seaver, March 23, 1897, Vol. 566, LEP SL.

48. "Lydia E. Pinkham's Familiar Face," Vol. 556, LEP SL.

49. "Profit and Loss Statements 1898–1899," Vol. 246, LEP SL.

50. Booklet, "Treatise on the Diseases of Women" (1901), p. 4, in Vol. 382, LEP SL.

51. Booklet, "Yours for Health" (1899), p. 2, in Vol. 381, LEP SL [emphasis added].

52. Booklet, "Throwing the Life Line" (Spring 1902), p. 16, in Vol. 379, LEP SL.

53. Booklet, "Facts With Proof" (1897), p. 31, in Vol. 380, LEP SL.

54. Advertisement, "Women! Remember This," Vol. 345, LEP SL.

55. Anonymous letter, n.d., Box 168 (Folder 3142), LEP SL.

VI. "UP TO OUR NECKS IN TROUBLE"

1. Laura B. Hunt to J. H. McKinnon, March 2, 1900, Vol. 577, LEP SL; Frank Blair, "The Proprietary Association, Its History Since the Founding in 1881," *Standard Remedies,* Vol. 19 (June 1932), pp. 4–7.

2. [Mark Sullivan], "The Patent Medicine Conspiracy Against Freedom of the Press," *Collier's* (November 4, 1905), reprinted in Samuel Hopkins Adams, *The Great American Fraud* (Chicago: The American Medical Association, n.d.), pp. 145–165; James Harvey Young, *The Toadstool Millionaires* (Princeton: Princeton University Press, 1961), pp. 107–108.

3. Charles H. Pinkham to Noyes Bros., March 9, 1895, Vol. 393, LEP SL.

4. Laura B. Hunt to J. H. McKinnon, March 2, 1900, Vol. 577, LEP SL; David J. Pivar, *Purity Crusade: Sexual Morality and Social Control, 1868–1900* (Westport, Connecticut: Greenwood Press, Inc., 1973), pp. 212–214.

5. James T. Wetherald to Richard Evans, April 7, 1900, Box 168 (Folder 3132), LEP SL.

6. Laura B. Hunt to T. Oliver Fine, March 2, 1900, Vol. 577, LEP SL.

7. Laura B. Hunt to Samuel B. Hartman, March 26, 1900, Vol. 577, LEP SL; "Howells Counterfeiting Case, 1900," Box 169 (Folders 3171–3175), LEP SL.

8. Diary of Arthur W. Pinkham, 1900, "Brief History of the Pinkham-Gove Controversy," Box 171 (Folder 3223), LEP SL.

9. "Obituary, Charles Hacker Pinkham," newsclipping in Box 157 (Folder 2907), LEP SL; Charles Nelson Sinnett, *Richard Pinkham of Old Dover, New Hampshire and His Descendants East and West* (Concord, New Hampshire: Rumford Printing Co., 1908), pp. 231–235.

10. Laura B. Hunt to T. Oliver Fine, November 8, 1900, Vol. 579, LEP SL.

11. Aroline Pinkham Gove to Charles Pinkham, January 12, 1896, Box 177 (Folder 3322), LEP SL.

12. Aroline Gove, quoted in "Brief History," Box 171 (Folder 3223), LEP SL.

13. William H. Gove to Jennie B. Pinkham, January 25, 1901, and January 31, 1901, Vol. 580, LEP SL.

14. "Brief History," Box 171 (Folder 3223), LEP SL; "Delmac Liver Regulator," Box 169 (Folder 3180), LEP SL.

15. "Partnership Agreements," Box 164 (Folder 3044), LEP SL.

16. "Brief History," Box 171 (Folder 3223), LEP SL.

17. "United States Gross Sales, News Advertising, General Advertising, Profit or Loss, 1887–1934," Vol. 246, LEP SL.

18. Edward Bok, *The Americanization of Edward Bok: The Autobiography of a Dutch Boy Fifty Years After* (New York: Charles Scribner's Sons, 1923), p. 162.

19. "The Curtis Code," quoted in Earnest Elmo Calkins, *The Business of Advertising* (New York: D. Appleton and Company, 1907), p. 4.

20. Harvey Washington Wiley, *An Autobiography* (Indianapolis: Bobbs-Merrill Co., 1930), pp. 215–220.

21. Mark Sullivan, *Our Times* (New York: Charles Scribner's Sons, 1927), II, 525–528; [Sullivan], "Patent Medicine Conspiracy," in Adams, *Great American Fraud,* p. 165.

22. Bok, *Americanization,* pp. 342–343; Edward Bok, "The 'Patent Medicine' Curse," *Ladies' Home Journal,* Vol. 21 (May 1904), pp. 18 and 215–220; Mark Sullivan, *The Education of an American* (New York: Doubleday, Doran and Co., 1938), pp. 184–185.

23. Sullivan, *Education,* pp. 186–191; [Sullivan], "Patent Medicine Conspiracy," in Adams, *Great American Fraud,* pp. 149 and 154–155; Pinkham advertising contract with *Alliance Weekly,* June 26, 1895, Box 85 (Folder 769), LEP SL.

24. Bok, *Americanization,* p. 344; Sullivan, *Education,* p. 191.

25. Samuel Hopkins Adams, "The Nostrum Evil," *Collier's* (October 7, 1905), reprinted in Adams, *Great American Fraud,* p. 3.

26. Quoted in Arthur and Lila Weinberg, eds., *The Muckrakers* (New York: Simon and Schuster, 1961), p. 176.

27. "Profit or Loss Statement, 1906," Vol. 246, LEP SL; Bok, *Americanization*, p. 341; Sullivan, *Education*, 187–188; Sullivan, *Our Times*, II, 512–513; Edward Bok, "Pictures That Tell Their Own Stories," *Ladies' Home Journal*, XXII (September 1905), p. 15.

28. Samuel Hopkins Adams, "The Fundamental Fakes,"*Collier's* (February 17, 1906), reprinted in Adams, *Great American Fraud*, p. 59.

29. Edward Bok, "How the Private Confidences of Women Are Laughed At," *Ladies' Home Journal*, XXI (November 1904), p. 18.

30. Booklet, "Treatise on the Diseases of Women," (1901), p. 4, in Vol. 382, LEP SL.

31. Bok, "Private Confidences," p. 18.

32. Sullivan, *Education*, p. 187.

33. Laura B. Hunt to C. C. Ellis, February 25, 1896, Vol. 562, LEP SL.

34. Mark Sullivan, "The Inside Story of a Sham," *Ladies' Home Journal*, XXIII (January 1906), p. 14.

35. Laura B. Hunt to Kate Yoder, March 28, 1902, Vol. 587, LEP SL.

36. Laura B. Hunt to Laura Fixen, March 28, 1902, Vol. 587, LEP SL.

37. Advertisement, "The Turn of Life," Vol. 347, LEP SL.

38. Laura B. Hunt to James T. Wetherald, October 21, 1897, Vol. 569, LEP SL.

39. Charles H. Pinkham to W. O. Osborne, November 8, 1894, Vol. 593, LEP SL.

40. Quoted in Sullivan, "Inside Story," p. 14.

41. *Ibid.*

42. Edward Bok, "A Few Words to the W.C.T.U.," *Ladies' Home Journal*, XXI (September 1904), p. 16; "Lawn Party on Mrs. Pinkham's Grounds," newsclipping in Box 158 (Folder 2913), LEP SL; Laura B. Hunt to J. H. McKinnon, May 31, 1899, Vol. 575, LEP SL.

43. Samuel Hopkins Adams,*The Health Master* (Boston: Houghton Mifflin Co., 1913), p. 112; Samuel Hopkins Adams, "Peruna and the Bracers,"*Collier's* (October 28, 1905), reprinted in Adams, *Great American Fraud*, p. 17.

44. Booklet, "Truth" (Spring 1906), centerfold, n. pag., in Vol. 583, LEP SL.

45. Booklet, "Guide to Health" (1893), p. 4, in Vol. 380, LEP SL.

46. Harvey Washington Wiley, quoted in Young,*Toadstool Millionaires*, p. 243.

47. Theodore Roosevelt, quoted in Sullivan, *Our Times*, II, p. 531; *see* James G. Burrows,*AMA, Voice of American Medicine* (Baltimore: Johns Hopkins Press, 1963), pp. 67–85.

48. Oscar E. Anderson, Jr.,*Health of A Nation: Harvey W. Wiley and the Fight for Pure Food* (Baltimore: Johns Hopkins Press, 1963), chapter 4; Young, *Toadstool Millionaires*, pp. 238.

49. Sullivan, *Our Times*, II, pp. 531–550; Young, *Toadstool Millionaires*, pp. 240–242; Anderson, *Health of A Nation*, pp. 185–194.

50. *U.S. Statutes at Large*, XXXIV (Part I), pp. 768–772.

51. Arthur J. Cramp, "Pinkham's Vegetable Compound," *Hygeia* (November

1935), pp. 1013–1015, clipping in Pinkham file, Department of Propaganda, American Medical Association, Chicago [hereafter cited as AMA].

52. Samuel Hopkins Adams, "Patent Medicines Under the Pure Food Law," *Collier's* (June 8, 1907), reprinted in Adams, *Great American Fraud*, p. 184.

53. Frank J. Cheney, quoted in Young, *Toadstool Millionaires*, p. 243.

54. Harvey Washington Wiley, quoted in James Harvey Young, *The Medical Messiahs: A Social History of Quackery in the Twentieth Century* (Princeton: Princeton University Press, 1967), p. 43.

55. "Information on Drugs," *Standard Remedies*, XII (May 1926), p. 95.

56. Samuel Hopkins Adams, "Patent Medicines, The Law and The Public," *Collier's* (January 20, 1912), reprinted in Adams, *Great American Fraud*, p. 128.

57. Samuel Hopkins Adams, quoted in George Creel, "The Press and Patent Medicines," *Harper's Weekly*, LX (February 13, 1915), p. 155.

58. Advertisements, "Stop! Women, and Consider," "Lydia E. Pinkham's Vegetable Compound," "Perfect Womanhood," "Health of Women," Vol. 348, LEP SL.

59. Booklet, "Treatise on the Diseases of Women Written for the Women of the World" (1908), p. 7, in Vol. 380, LEP SL.

60. Booklet, "Letters to a Young Housewife" (1909), n. pag., in Vol. 348, LEP SL.

61. Reading notices, reprinted in Charles Pinkham, *Advertising*, p. 154, Vol. 328, LEP SL.

62. *Ibid.*

63. Bok, "The 'Patent Medicine' Curse," p. 18.

64. Bok, *Americanization*, p. 168.

65. Upton Sinclair, quoted in Weinberg (eds.), *The Muckrakers*, p. 205; Mark Sullivan, with a certain professional jealousy, insisted that Sinclair could not be considered a muckraker. "The 'Muckrakers'—Lincoln Steffens, Miss Ida Tarbell, Ray Stannard Baker, and others—were utterly different from Sinclair in their methods. They put out their product as *fact*, and asked the public to accept it and test it as such." Sullivan, *Our Times*, II, pp. 478–479 fn.

66. Quoted in Young, *Medical Messiahs*, p. 36.

67. United States v. Johnson, 221 U.S., 497 (1911).

68. "As a Physician Sees Women," *Ladies' Home Journal*, XXIV (March 1907), p. 16.

VII. THE TEETH OF THE LAW

1. George Creel, "Poisoners of Public Health," *Harper's Weekly*, LX (January 2, 1915), p. 4.

2. "United States Gross Sales, News Advertising, General Advertising, Profit or Loss, 1887–1934." Vol. 246, LEP SL; Charles Pinkham, *Advertising*, p. 149, Vol. 328, LEP SL.

3. George Creel, "The Law and the Drug Sharks," *Harper's Weekly*, LX (February 6, 1915), p. 136.

4. Creel, "Poisoners of Public Health," p. 5.

5. *See* James G. Burrow, *AMA: Voice of American Medicine* (Baltimore: Johns Hopkins Press, 1963), pp. 27–51.

6. "Deaths—Arthur J. Cramp," *Journal of the American Medical Association*, CXLVII (December 29, 1951), p. 1773; James Harvey Young, *The Medical Messiahs* (Princeton: Princeton University Press, 1967), p. 129.

7. Arthur J. Cramp, ed., *Nostrums and Quackery*, 2nd rev. ed. (Chicago: American Medical Association Press, 1921), p. 6; Samuel Hopkins Adams, *The Great American Fraud* (Chicago: American Medical Association Press, n.d.), advertisement in back, n. page.

8. Cramp, *Nostrums and Quackery*, pp. 160–163.

9. "Lydia E. Pinkham's Vegetable Compound," *British Medical Journal* (July 1, 1911), clipping in Pinkham file, Department of Propaganda, American Medical Association, Chicago, Illinois [hereafter cited as Propaganda Department, AMA]; Arthur J. Cramp to Treasury Department, September 23, 1913, Pinkham file, Propaganda Department, AMA; for discussion of Peruna see George Creel, "Doc Munyon and His Pals," *Harper's Weekly*, LX (January 16, 1915), pp. 54–55. The Pinkham company had difficulty measuring precisely the percentage of alcohol contained in the Vegetable Compound. The difficulty accounts for the fact that chemical analysis frequently showed percentages in excess of or below the 18 per cent printed on the label.

10. "Pharmacological and Clinical Research," Vol. 411, p. 9, LEP SL.

11. W. H. Osborn to William H. Gove, March 21, 1914, and William H. Gove to W. H. Osborn, March 25, 1914, Box 34 (Folder 224), LEP SL; Charles Pinkham, *Advertising*, p. 149, Vol. 328, LEP SL.

12. W. H. Osborn, quoted in "Pharmacological and Clinical Research," Vol. 411, p. 9, LEP SL.

13. W. H. Osborn, quoted in Arthur J. Cramp to Dr. W. T. Sharpless, June 29, 1914, Pinkham file, Propaganda Department, AMA.

14. Cramp, *Nostrums and Quackery*, p. 163.

15. Charles Pinkham, *Advertising*, p. 150, Vol. 328, LEP SL.

16. Quoted in Cramp, *Nostrums and Quackery*, p. 163.

17. "U.S. Gross Sales, 1887–1934," Vol. 246, LEP SL; Memo from Daniel R. Pinkham to Arthur W. Pinkham, December 9, 1937, Box 168 (Folder 3149), LEP SL.

18. Morris Fishbein, *A History of the American Medical Association 1847–1947* (New York: W. B. Saunders Company, 1947), pp. 235–236 and 865–886.

19. Quoted in Young, *Medical Messiahs*, pp. 58–59.

20. George Creel, "Mr. Patten Sues," *Harper's Weekly*, LX (February 27, 1915), pp. 206–207; Fishbein, *History of the AMA*, pp. 495–498; Burrow, *AMA*, pp. 124–125.

21. "Government Citations," Box 142 (Folder 2662), LEP SL.

22. Lyman F. Kebler to Carl L. Alsberg, February 17, 1915. Office of the Solicitor, Department of Agriculture (closed case files), Food and Drug Case 6550, Record Group 16, Archives Branch, Washington National Records Center, Suitland, Maryland [hereafter cited as RG16, WNRC].

23. The analysts reported that the Compound contained 17.9 per cent alcohol and 0.56 per cent solid substances. Food and Drug Case 6550 (Notice of Judgment 4995), Records of the Bureau of Chemistry, Record Group 97, National Archives Building, Washington, D.C. [hereafter cited as RG97, NA].

24. Tower, Talbot, and Hiller, attorneys for the Lydia E. Pinkham Medicine Company, to U.S. Attorney George W. Anderson, October 1, 1915 (closed case files), F&D 6550, RG16, WNRC.

25. See Oscar E. Anderson, Jr., Health of a Nation: Harvey W. Wiley and the Fight for Pure Food (Baltimore: Johns Hopkins Press, 1963), p. 200.

26. W. P. Jones to Acting Solicitor W. C. Henderson, November 22, 1915 (closed case files), F&D 6550, RG16, WNRC.

27. Assistant U.S. Attorney Daniel A. Shea to the Solicitor, Department of Agriculture, October 23, 1916 (closed case files), F&D 6550, RG16, WNRC.

28. Cramp, Nostrums and Quackery, p. 162.

29. Charles Pinkham, Advertising, p. 150, Vol. 328, LEP SL.

30. Mr. Cooley to Walter G. Campbell, September 21, 1918, General Correspondence, Bureau of Chemistry, RG97, NA.

31. Young, Medical Messiahs, p. 41; Creel, "Law and the Drug Sharks," p. 270.

32. "U.S. Gross Sales, 1887–1934," Vol. 246, LEP SL.

33. Charles Pinkham, Advertising, p. 60, Vol. 328, LEP SL.

34. Dr. Finley Ellingwood's revisions of "Lydia E. Pinkham's Private Textbook," Box 168 (Folder 3149), LEP SL.

35. Booklet, "Beauty Hints" (Spring 1925), p. 10 in Vol. 386, LEP SL.

36. Creel, "Poisoners of Public Health," p. 4.

37. George Creel, "How the Drug Dopers Fight," Harper's Weekly, LX (January 30, 1916), pp. 110–111.

38. Cramp, quoted in Burrow, AMA, p. 256.

39. Harvey Washington Wiley, An Autobiography (Indianapolis: Bobbs-Merrill Company, 1930), pp. 302–306; Anderson, Health of a Nation, pp. 259–261.

40. "Letters of Inquiry," 1917, Pinkham file, Propaganda Department, AMA.

41. Dr. P. J. Finnigan to Lydia E. Pinkham Medicine Company, October 2, 1922, Box 169 (Folder 3179), LEP SL.

42. "Journal, June 1920–July 1922," Vol. 25, LEP SL; "Brief History," Box 171 (Folder 3223), LEP SL.

43. Booklet, "Recreation" (April 1917), p. 12 in Vol. 386, LEP SL.

44. Frank Blair, "The Proprietary Association, Its History Since the Founding in 1881," Standard Remedies, XIX (June 1932), pp. 7 and 24.

45. Editorial, "The Era of the Trade Organization," Standard Remedies, XI (May 1975), pp. 9–13; "Brief History," Box 171 (Folder 3223), LEP SL; "Profit or Loss Statements, 1920–1929," Vol. 246, LEP SL.

46. Ernest P. Lane to the Proprietary Association, August 27, 1920, Box 142 (Folder 2659), LEP SL.

47. Paul H. Dunbar, quoted in Harvey Washington Wiley, *The History of A Crime Against the Food Law* (Washington, D.C.: published by the author, 1929), p. 376.

48. John S. Jamieson, "The Food and Drugs Act," *Standard Remedies,* XI (June 1925), pp. 12–13 and 105.

49. Wiley, *History of A Crime,* pp. 374 and 396; Anderson, *Health of A Nation,* p. 272.

50. "Government Citations," Box 142 (Folder 2662), LEP SL.

51. Arthur J. Cramp, "Pinkham's Vegetable Compound," *Hygeia* (November 1935), p. 1014, clipping in Pinkham file, Propaganda Department, AMA.

52. "Information on Drugs," *Standard Remedies,* XII (May 1926), pp. 94–96.

53. William H. Gove to *Chicago Tribune,* August 29, 1916, newsclipping in Pinkham file, Propaganda Department, AMA.

54. I would like to thank Isabella K. Rhodes, Muriel R. Burr, and Katharine D. Frankenstein, Smith 1907, for sharing with me their recollections of Lydia Pinkham Gove.

55. Arthur W. Pinkham, *Reminiscences,* pp. 40–70, Vol. 531, LEP SL.

56. "Bill of Complaint: Jennie B. Pinkham *et als.* v. Lydia E. Pinkham Medicine Company, Supreme Judicial Court of Maine, 1921," Box 179 (Folder 3354), LEP SL.

57. "Stockholders' Records," Box 179 (Folder 3349), LEP SL; "By-laws of the Lydia E. Pinkham Medicine Company," Box 164 (Folder 3068), LEP SL.

58. Arthur W. Pinkham to Frank Blair, March 20, 1922, Box 193 (Folder 3419), LEP SL.

59. Charles Pinkham, *Advertising,* pp. 170–172, Vol. 328, LEP SL.

60. William P. Gove, quoted in Daniel R. Pinkham to Arthur W. Pinkham, February 18, 1924, Box 193 (Folder 3420), LEP SL.

61. "Lydia E. Pinkham Medicine Company v. Aroline P. Gove *et. al.,* Preliminary Judgment, July 8, 1937," Box 174 (Folder 3278), LEP SL.

62. Advertisement, "Do You Know As Much As Your Cat?" Vol. 352, LEP SL.

63. "U.S. Gross Sales, 1887–1934," Vol. 246, LEP SL.

VIII. THE NEW WOMAN ... THE SAME OLD MEDICINE

1. Booklet, "Pinkham Pioneers," pp. 10–16 in Vol. 387, LEP SL.

2. John Higham, "American Culture in the 1890's," in *Writing American History, Essays on Modern Scholarship* (Bloomington, Indiana: Indiana University Press, 1970), pp. 82–83; John S. and Robin M. Haller, *The Physician and Sexuality in Victorian America* (Urbana, Illinois: University of Illinois Press, 1974), pp. 174–187; "Daisy Bell," words and music by Henry Dacre.

3. In the following discussion of the Gibson Girl as femme fatale I am greatly

indebted to Martha Kingsley's essay, "The Femme Fatale and Her Sisters," in Thomas B. Hess and Linda Nochlin, eds., *Woman as Sex Object* (New York: Newsweek, 1972), pp. 183–1205; *see also* Fairfax Downey, *Portrait of an Era as Drawn by C. D. Gibson* (New York: Charles Scribner's Sons, 1936); Charles Dana Gibson, *Drawings* (New York: R. H. Russell and Son, 1895).

4. *See* Barbara Welter, "The Cult of True Womanhood, 1820–1860," *American Quarterly*, XVIII (Summer 1966), pp. 151–174.

5. For statistics on marriage and employment *see* Daniel Scott Smith, "Family Limitation, Sexual Control, and Domestic Feminism in Victorian America," in Mary Hartman and Lois W. Banner, eds., *Clio's Consciousness Raised* (New York: Harper and Row, 1974), pp. 121–122.

6. *See* John R. McGovern, "The American Woman's Pre-World War I Freedom in Manners and Morals," in Jean E. Friedman and William G. Shade, eds., *Our American Sisters*, 2nd ed. (Boston: Allyn and Bacon, Inc., 1976), pp. 345–365.

7. Rheta Childe Dorr, *A Woman of Fifty* (New York: Funk and Wagnalls Company, 1924), p. 19.

8. William Henry Chafe, *The American Woman* (New York: Oxford University Press, 1972), p. 55.

9. Dorr, *Woman of Fifty*, pp. 107 and 122.

10. John Martin, quoted in Gwendolyn Salisbury Hughes, *Mothers in Industry* (New York: New Republic, Inc., 1925), pp. 2–3; John Martin, "The Mother in Industry," *Survey*, XXXV (March 18, 1916), p. 722.

11. Edward Bok, *The Americanization of Edward Bok* (New York: Charles Scribner's Sons, 1923), pp. 345–351.

12. John C. Burnham, "The Progressive Revolution in America Attitudes Toward Sex," *Journal of American History*, LIX (March 1973), pp. 885–908; David J. Pivar, *The Purity Crusade* (Westport, Connecticut: Greenwood Press, 1973), pp. 204–280.

13. The phrase "repeal of reticence" appeared in Agnes Repplier's article of that title in *Atlantic Monthly*, CXIII (March 1914), pp. 297–304.

14. William T. Foster, quoted in Burnham, "Progressive Era Revolution," p. 902.

15. "Sex O'Clock in America," *Current Opinion*, LV (August 1913), p. 113–114.

16. *See* Nathan G. Hale, Jr., *Freud and the Americans* (New York: Oxford University Press, 1971), pp. 259–267; Paul Robinson, *The Modernization of Sex* (New York: Harper and Row, 1976), pp. 1–41.

17. H. Havelock Ellis, *Studies in the Psychology of Sex*, 2nd rev. ed. (Philadelphia: F. A. Davis Company, 1922), III, pp. 246 and 20.

18. Theodore Roosevelt, quoted in John M. Blum, *The Republican Roosevelt* (New York: Atheneum, 1969), p. 106.

19. Ellis, *Studies in Psychology of Sex*, VI, p. 486.

20. *Ibid.*, p. 481.

21. Margaret Deland, "The Change in the Feminine Ideal," *Atlantic Monthly*, CV (March 1910), pp. 291 and 293.

22. Robert Herrick, *Together* (New York: Grosset and Dunlap, 1908), p. 321; *see also* Christopher Lasch, *The New Radicalism in America* (New York: Alfred A. Knopf, 1965), pp. 38–46.

23. Beatrice M. Hinkle, "Women and the New Morality," in Freda Kirchwey, ed., *Our Changing Morality* (New York: Albert and Charles Boni, 1930), pp. 235–249.

24. Dorothy Dix, quoted in McGovern; "The American Woman's Pre-World War I Freedom," in Friedman and Shade, *Our American Sisters*, p. 351.

25. *Ibid.*, p. 350.

26. H. L. Mencken, "The Flapper," *Smart Set*, XLV (February 1915), pp. 1–2.

27. F. Scott Fitzgerald, *The Crack-Up* (New York: New Directions Paperback, 1956), p. 133.

28. Ben B. Lindsey and Wainwright Evans, *The Revolt of Modern Youth* (New York: Boni and Liveright, 1925), pp. 157–159.

29. Dorothy Dix, quoted in McGovern, "The American Woman's Pre-World War I Freedom," in Friedman and Shade, *Our American Sisters*, p. 348.

30. Robert S. Lynd and Helen Merrell Lynd, *Middletown* (New York: Harcourt, Brace and World, 1929), pp. 140, 135, 143.

31. Lindsey and Evans, *Revolt of Modern Youth*, pp. 56–65; for a discussion of the impact of expertise on the American family *see* Christopher Lasch, *Haven in A Heartless World, The Family Besieged* (New York: Basic Books, Inc., 1977), pp. 12–21.

32. Lindsey and Evans, *Revolt of Modern Youth*, p. 34.

33. Ads for the film version of *Flaming Youth* are quoted in Lynd and Lynd, *Middletown*, p. 266.

34. Samuel Hopkins Adams [pseudonym Warner Fabian], *Flaming Youth* (New York: Boni and Liveright, 1923), p. 336; for a sardonic look at Adams' "research" *see* Lillian Hellman, *An Unfinished Woman* (Boston: Little, Brown and Company, 1969), pp. 42–47.

35. Elsie Clews Parsons, "Changes in Sex Relations," in Kirchwey, *Our Changing Morality*, p. 39.

36. Florence Guy Seabury, "Stereotypes," in *Ibid.*, p. 222.

37. *Ibid.*, p. 231.

38. Booklet, "The New Woman" (Spring 1903), n. pag., in Vol. 381, LEP SL.

39. Booklets, "Needle Art and Health Book" (Summer 1923), p. 5, in Vol. 385, LEP SL; "How Phyllis Grew Thin" (1924), p. 8 and "War-Time Cook and Health Book" (March 1918), p. 16, in Vol. 386, LEP SL.

40. *See* Erwin H. Ackerknecht, M.D., *Therapeutics From the Primitives to the 20th Century* (New York: Hafner Press, 1973), pp. 128–146; for a more popular view *see* Paul de Kruif, *Microbe Hunters* (New York: Blue Ribbon Books, 1926).

41. J. L. Bubis, M.D., *Women Are My Problem* (New York: Comet Press Books, 1953), pp. 11 and 70.

42. Franklin H. Martin, M.D., *Fifty Years of Medicine and Surgery* (Chicago: The Surgical Publication Company, 1934), p. 195.

43. Palmer Findley, *Story of Childbirth* (Garden City, New Jersey: Doubleday, Doran and Company, 1933), p. 327.

44. Bubis, *Women Are My Problem*, p. 11; *see also* Louis S. Reed, *Midwives, Chiropodists, and Optometrists, Their Place in Medical Care* (Chicago: University of Chicago Press, 1932), pp. 20–22.

45. *See* Nathan G. Hale, Jr., *Freud and the Americans* (New York: Oxford University Press, 1971), pp. 462–480.

46. Abraham Myerson, M.D., *The Nervous Housewife* (Boston: Little, Brown, and Company, 1927), pp. 75, 238, and 239–240.

47. Alan Gregg, *Challenges to Contemporary Medicine* (New York: Columbia University Press, 1956), pp. 12–13.

48. *See* Gertrude Atherton, *Black Oxen* (New York: A. L. Burt Company, 1923); for a discussion of Steinach's early experiments *see* Eugen Steinach, *Sex and Life: Forty Years of Biological and Medical Experiments* (New York: Viking Press, 1940), pp. 129–185.

IX. RULE OR RUIN?

1. James T. Wetherald to Arthur W. Pinkham, February 16, 1926, Box 192 (Folder 3400), LEP SL.

2. "Motion for a Temporary Injunction and Appointment of a Receiver: Jennie B. Pinkham, *et als.* v. Lydia E. Pinkham Medicine Company, Supreme Judicial Court of Maine, 1927," Box 179 (Folder 3354), LEP SL.

3. "Directors' records," Vol. 555, LEP SL.

4. Arthur W. Pinkham to Robert H. Gross, October 3, 1927, Box 193 (Folder 3447), LEP SL.

5. "U.S. Gross Sales, 1887–1934," Vol. 246, LEP SL.

6. Lydia Pinkham Gove to Arthur W. Pinkham, February 10, 1932, Box 127 (Folder 2532), LEP SL; for a discussion of Getchell's test copy *see* Charles Pinkham, *Advertising*, pp. 190–196, Vol. 328, LEP SL.

7. "Northeastern Advertising Agency," Box 127 (Folder 2530), LEP SL.

8. "Hearing, April 29, 1932: Burnham v. Gove, Supreme Judicial Court of Massachusetts," Box 175 (Folder 3292), LEP SL.

9. "Hearing, March 15, 1932: Burnham v. Gove, Supreme Judicial Court of Massachusetts," Box 175 (Folder 3292), LEP SL.

10. "Master's Report, December 4, 1936: Lydia E. Pinkham Medicine Company v. Aroline P. Gove *et als.*, Supreme Judicial Court of Massachusetts," Box 178 (Folder 3325), LEP SL.

11. *Ibid.*

12. "In Memoriam: Lydia Pinkham Gove," Box 160 (Folder 2947), LEP SL.

13. "U.S. v. Certain Quantities of Lydia E. Pinkham Tablets," Office of the Solicitor, Department of Agriculture (closed case files), Food and Drug Cases 30714 and 30578-80, RG 16, WNRC. The government seized the Pinkham merchandise

in the summer of 1933, after the Food and Drug Administration objected to Lydia's copy, which read "Persistent Use Brings Permanent Relief." After much delay, the case came before the court in 1935. The Pinkham company, which by then had changed its formula and its advertising, mounted no defense and the judge ordered the seized goods destroyed.

14. "Bill of Complaint: Lydia E. Pinkham Medicine Company v. Aroline P. Gove *et als.*, Supreme Judicial Court of Massachusetts, February 5, 1936," Vol. 555, LEP SL.

15. "Bill of Complaint: Aroline P. Gove *et als.* v. Lydia E. Pinkham Medicine Company, Supreme Judicial Court of Maine, February 26, 1936," Box 173 (Folder 3266), LEP SL.

16. "Master's Report," Box 178 (Folder 3325), LEP SL.

17. "Lydia E. Pinkham Medicine Company v. Aroline P. Gove *et als.*," 298 Mass., 62 (1937).

18. "Lydia E. Pinkham Medicine Company v. Lydia P. Gove," 305 Mass., 217 (1940).

19. "Lydia E. Pinkham Medicine Company v. Aroline P. Gove *et als.*," 303 Mass., I (1939).

20. "Lydia E. Pinkham Medicine Company v. Commissioner of Internal Revenue," Box 175 (Folder 3290), LEP SL.

21. Lydia Pinkham Gove to Gove Family Relatives, January 9, 1938, Box 160 (Folder 2948), LEP SL.

22. "Hearing, November 23, 1940: Lydia Pinkham Gove v. Lydia E. Pinkham Medicine Company, Supreme Judicial Court of Maine," Box 175 (Folder 3289), LEP SL.

23. *Ibid.*

24. Quoted in Jean Burton, *Lydia Pinkham Is Her Name* (New York: Farrar, Straus and Company, 1949), p. 269.

25. "Findings, February 17, 1941: Lydia Pinkham Gove v. Lydia E. Pinkham Medicine Company, Supreme Judicial Court of Maine," Box 176 (Folder 3302), LEP SL.

26. *See* James Harvey Young, *The Medical Messiahs* (Princeton: Princeton University Press, 1967), pp. 158–180.

27. Advertisement, "The Whispering Campaign That Never Stopped," Vol. 354, LEP SL.

28. E. J. Adams to Lydia E. Pinkham Medicine Company, August 15, 1938, Box 171 (Folder 3212), LEP SL.

29. Dr. Charles W. Green, quoted in Charles Pinkham, *Advertising,* p. 214, Vol. 328, LEP SL.

30. Federal Trade Commission Stipulation 02702, January 15, 1941, cited in "Clinical and Pharmacological Research," Vol. 411, LEP SL.

31. Charles Pinkham, *Advertising,* pp. 238 and 272, Vol. 328, LEP SL.

32. Calvin L. Butler to Dr. Robert P. Herwick, October 11, 1951, Vol. 550, LEP SL.

33. *See* Burton, *Lydia Pinkham Is Her Name,* pp. 275–277.

34. Copy, Certificate of Death, Lydia Pinkham Gove, February 24, 1948, Town Clerk, Marblehead, Massachusetts.

35. Charles Pinkham, *Advertising,* p. 311, Vol. 328, LEP SL.

36. *Ibid.,* p. 318.

37. "A Survey of Marketing Activities for the Lydia E. Pinkham Medicine Company," submitted by Barrington Associates, February 15, 1957, p. 15, Vol. 417, LEP SL.

38. "Lydia Pinkham Plant Closing After 87 Years," *Washington Post,* November 20, 1973.

CONCLUSION: THE BUSINESS OF WOMEN'S MEDICINE

1. Joseph F. Kett, *The Formation of the American Medical Profession: The Role of Institutions, 1780–1860* (New Haven: Yale University Press, 1968), p. 108.

2. Rosemary Stevens, *American Medicine and the Public Interest* (New Haven: Yale Uviversity Press, 1971), p. 24.

3. *See* Mary Roth Walsh, *Doctors Wanted: No Women Need Apply* (New Haven: Yale University Press, 1977), pp. 1–34.

4. *See* Gerald E. Markowitz and David K. Rosner, "Doctors in Crisis: A Study of the Use of Medical Education Reform to Establish Modern Professional Elitism in Medicine," *American Quarterly,* XXV (March 1973), pp. 83–107; Stephen J. Kunitz, "Professionalism and Social Control in the Progressive Era: The Case of the Flexner Report," *Social Problems,* XXII (October 1974), pp. 16–27.

5. C. Rufus Rorem and Robert P. Fischelis, *The Costs of Medicines, Publications of the Committee on the Costs of Medical Care: No. 14* (Chicago: University of Chicago Press, 1932), p. 100.

6. *Ibid.,* pp. 157 and 196.

7. James L. Goddard, "The Medical Business," in *Life and Death in Medicine: A Scientific American Book* (San Francisco: W. H. Freeman and Company, 1973), p. 121.

8. Ellen Goodman, "The Cure for Hysterics," *The Boston Globe,* May 17, 1977.

9. Erwin H. Ackerknecht, *Therapeutics From the Primitives to the 20th Century* (New York: Hafner Press, 1973), p. 145.

10. *See* Stevens, *American Medicine:* Thomas Szaz, *The Myth of Mental Illness* (New York: Harper and Row, 1961); and Ivan Illich, *Medical Nemesis* (New York: Pantheon Books, 1976) for examples of contemporary criticism of the medical profession.

Essay on the Sources

The Lydia E. Pinkham Medicine Company was the first patent medicine concern to make available to historians its archives and financial records. The Pinkham collection at the Arthur and Elizabeth Schlesinger Library on the History of Women in America, Radcliffe College, contains some 194 boxes and 600 volumes pertaining to Pinkham family history and the development of the Lydia E. Pinkham Medicine Company. From this extensive collection comes the bulk of my research on the Pinkham company.

The Pinkham records prove most valuable in their comprehensive catalog of company advertising. With the exception of advertisements placed before 1879, the collection contains examples from each advertising campaign. In addition there is a complete collection of the printed pamphlets, bottle books, and textbooks distributed by the company.

Lydia Pinkham's personal scrapbooks and journals, while few in number, provide access to the woman who developed the Vegetable Compound. Other family records include the privately published reminiscences of Arthur W. Pinkham, personal correspondence between Charles H. Pinkham and his wife, and the letters written by Daniel Rogers Pinkham to his brother Will in the 1870's, when the company was struggling to build its market. The family feud between the Pinkhams and the Goves is evident in the collection, which contains a disproportionate amount of Pinkham material and relatively few items which illuminate the Gove's side of the story. The correspondence relating to litigation between the Pinkham directors and the Goves, for example, deals primarily with the Pinkhams' case.

Unfortunately for the contemporary social historian, the hundreds of thousands of letters written to Lydia Pinkham by women seeking advice on their medical problems were destroyed by the Pinkhams, probably in 1940 when the company discontinued its correspondence department to conform with tighter regulation of medical advice by the Post Office Department. A few individual letters remain in Lydia Pinkham's personal "Medical Directions for Ailments," and the glimpse into the lives of ordinary women in the 1870's and 1880's these letters afford serves to make the loss of the bulk of the collection all the more disappointing. Some evidence of women's medical concerns can be gleaned from printed testimonials, but these must be read with the warning that the company frequently doctored testimonials to conform to its advertising needs and to delete embarrassing references and correct mistakes in spelling and grammar. As a result, the printed testimonials are more homogeneous and less interesting than the originals.

Much of the material contained in the Pinkham collection relates to the financial aspect of the business and is of interest primarily to the business historian. Day books, purchase records, tax forms, and ledger accounts do, however, yield significant items for the social historian. Only by culling these sources is it possible to determine the extent to which the company relied on paid brokers to procure testimonials, the effect of Prohibition on freight damages, and other pieces of interest to a general audience.

For years the Pinkhams ran a museum in the plant where they preserved important documents in the company's history. From this source have come significant materials relating to advertising and clinical research. Charles H. Pinkham, Jr., Lydia Pinkham's grandson, authored a volume on the company's advertising history which, while it glosses the family's internal feud, presents an important account of the firm's advertising policies from its inception to 1952. Company-compiled studies of the pharmacological and clinical research undertaken during the thirties provide important information on formula research and government regulation.

The National Archives and its Washington National Records Center at Suitland, Maryland, provide records of the Pinkham company's dealings with the Bureau of Chemistry and Food and Drug Administration. Of particular interest are the Department of Agriculture's food and drug closed case files in Record Group 16.

Arthur J. Cramp's files at the Department of Propaganda of the American Medical Association, Chicago, Illinois, contain information which sheds light on the close association between the AMA and government regulatory agencies, as well as letters of inquiry from patent medicine users who tell their stories candidly.

The National Library of Medicine, Bethesda, Maryland, is of great use in locating periodical medical literature of the nineteenth century. The Surgeon General's Index, an exhaustive topical listing of books and articles dealing with medicine, provides a valuable tool and the library's generous interlibrary loans of journal articles enable a good deal of research to be carried on at long distance.

The Archives of the Yale Medical Library contain many rare medical books, among them Benjamin Rush's lectures and texts, as well as a sizeable collection of nineteenth-century medical books and articles.

Work on Lydia Pinkham has aimed at a popular audience. The earliest biography of Lydia Pinkham, authored by Elbert Hubbard, was distributed by the company as a promotional device. *Lydia E. Pinkham* (East Aurora, N.Y.: The Roycrofters, 1915) is a typical Hubbard panegyric. Robert Collier Washburn's *Life and Times of Lydia Pinkham* (New York: G. P. Putnam's Sons, 1931), gives a sketchy view of Lynn history and Lydia Pinkham's life, perhaps because Lydia Pinkham Gove limited Washburn's access to company records and expurgated unfavorable remarks from his manuscript. Jean Burton's later biography, *Lydia Pinkham Is Her Name* (New York: Farrar, Straus and Company, 1949), provides a fuller account of Lydia Pinkham and the business she founded, but reads too much like a piece of company advertising. E. Lee Strohl in "Ladies of Lynn—Emphasis on One," *Surgery, Gynecology and Obstetrics* CV (December 1957), pp. 769–75, simply goes over ground already covered by others.

A less flattering portrait of Lydia Pinkham emerges in writings dealing with medical quackery. Eric Jameson in *The Natural History of Quackery* (London: Michael Joseph, 1961) presents a particularly unsympathetic view of Lydia Pinkham and her Vegetable Compound. Stewart Holbrook's *The Golden Age of Quackery* (New York: The Macmillan Company, 1959) tries to place the Vegetable Compound in the context of the therapeutic stalemate of the nineteenth century, but suffers from the note of hilarity so often found in books dealing with patent medicines. The medical profession's critique of the Vegetable Compound is best presented in Arthur J. Cramp's monumental *Nostrums and Quackery,* 3 vols. (Chicago: The Press of the American Medical Association, 1911, 1921, and 1936).

The muckrakers give a good accounting of themselves in the pages of

The Ladies' Home Journal and *Collier's*. Samuel Hopkins Adams' "Great American Fraud" series in *Collier's*, along with several articles authored by Mark Sullivan, are collected in *The Great American Fraud* (Chicago: Press of the American Medical Association, n.d.). *The Americanization of Edward Bok* (New York: Charles Scribner's Sons, 1923) is a particularly revealing autobiography in which Bok clearly evidences his ambivalence toward his audience of middle-class women. Mark Sullivan's *The Education of an American* (New York: Doubleday, Doran & Company, 1938) gives a balanced view of the muckrakers' role in food and drug reform. Harvey Washington Wiley's articles in *Good Housekeeping* and his *Autobiography* (Indianapolis: Bobbs-Merrill, 1930) illuminate his place as a muckraker and reformer.

As yet no definitive history of American advertising exists, although Frank Presbrey's *The History and Development of Advertising* (Garden City, N.Y.: Doubleday, Doran & Company, 1929) and Otis Pease's *The Responsibilities of American Advertising: Private Control and Public Influence 1920–1940* (New Haven: Yale University Press, 1958) together cover a good deal of advertising history. More recently, Stuart Ewen has explored American advertising from a critical perspective in *Captains of Consciousness: Advertising and the Social Roots of the Consumer Culture* (New York: McGraw-Hill Book Company, 1976). For a glimpse at advertising from an early adman's point of view, George P. Rowells' *Forty Years an Advertising Agent* (New York: Franklin Publishers, 1926) is invaluable, as is the periodical he edited, *Printers' Ink*.

James Harvey Young, in *The Toadstool Millionaires* (Princeton: Princeton University Press, 1961) and *The Medical Messiahs* (Princeton: Princeton University Press, 1967), presents a lucid and scholarly study of the history of patent medicines and government regulation. Young's thorough research stands as a model to scholars in the field. Of lesser importance is James Cook's *Remedies and Rackets* (New York: W. W. Norton & Company, 1958). Oscar E. Anderson, Jr., discusses regulation in the context of the life of Harvey Washington Wiley in his *Health of a Nation: Harvey W. Wiley and the Fight for Pure Food* (Chicago: University of Chicago Press, 1958).

Medical history has too often been written by doctors intent on portraying the march of medical science. Two recent works add a necessary balance: William G. Rothstein's *American Physicians in the Nineteenth Century* (Baltimore: The Johns Hopkins Press, 1972) and Martin Kaufman's *Homeopathy in America: The Rise and Fall of a Medical Heresy* (Baltimore: The Johns Hopkins Press, 1971). Gert H. Brieger's edited selections from the medical literature of the nineteenth century in *Medical America in the Nineteenth Century* (Baltimore: The Johns Hopkins Press, 1972) provide a valuable reference. The writings of Richard Harrison Shryock, which include *The Development of Modern Medicine* (New York: Alfred A. Knopf, 1947), *Medicine and Society in America 1660–1860* (New York: New York University Press, 1960), and *Medicine in America: Historical Essays* (Baltimore: The Johns Hopkins Press, 1966), are wide-ranging and provide a standard history of modern medicine. Madge Pickard and R. Carlyle Buley in *The Midwest Pioneer, His Ills, Cures and Doctors* (Crawfordsville, Indiana: R. E. Banta, 1945) write a lively and remarkably helpful work on popular medicine in rural America.

The professionalization of American medicine is treated in a number of excellent works, most notably Joseph F. Kett's *The Formation of the American Medical Profession: The Role of Institutions 1780–1860* (New Haven: Yale University Press, 1968). Rosemary Stevens, in *American Medicine and the Public Interest* (New Haven: Yale University Press, 1971), carries the story to the present. Gerald Markowitz and David Rosner in "Doctors in Crisis: A Study of the Use of Medical Education Reform to Establish Modern Professional Elitism in Medicine," *American Quarterly,* XXV (March 1973) pp. 83–107, provide a provocative analysis of the roots of medical conservatism. And Mary Roth Walsh in *Doctors Wanted: No Women Need Apply* (New Haven: Yale University Press, 1977), points to the barriers against women in the medical profession.

The best understanding of nineteenth-century medicine can be gained from the popular and professional medical books of the period. Benjamin Rush's *Six Introductory Lectures* (Philadelphia: M. and J. Conrad and Company, 1801) outlines Rush's monistic system, while Samuel Thomson's *New Guide to Health Prefixed by a Narrative of the Life and Medical Discoveries of the Author* (Boston: E. G. House, 1825, 2nd. ed.) poses an empiric monistic system to rival that of Rush. Sylvester Graham's *Lectures on the Science of Human Life* (New York: Fowler and Wells Publisher, 1883) presents the essence of Graham's popular health movement. Samuel Hahnemann's *Organon of Homeopathic Medicine* (Philadelphia: North American Academy of Homeopathic Healing Art, 1836) is the standard work of the homeopathic sect.

Medical literature dealing with women is so extensive that it is possible here to mention only the most significant works. Charles Meigs in *Females and Their Diseases* (Philadelphia: Lea and Blanchard, 1848) set the tone for nineteenth-century gynecology by claiming a woman's sexual organs dictated her nature. William Acton's *Functions and Disorders of the Repro-*

ductive Organs (London: John Churchill and Sons, 1865, 4th ed.) is notable for its allegation that women have no sexual desires. Edward H. Clarke wrote *Sex in Education, or a Fair Chance for Girls* (Boston: Robert Brothers, 1873) to convince educators that female periodicity posed an insurmountable obstacle to coeducation. Augustus K. Gardner's *Conjugal Sins* (New York: J. S. Redfield, Publishers, 1870) provides a classic argument for marital restraint. And G. L. Austin in *The Perils of American Women, a Doctor's Talk with Maiden, Wife and Mother* (Boston: Lea and Shepard, 1883) sounds a familiar theme. For quick reference, see Ronald G. Walters, ed., *Primers for Prudery, Sexual Advice to Victorian America* (Englewood Cliffs, N.J.: Prentice-Hall, 1974) for a sampling of advice literature from the nineteenth century.

The women physicians Elizabeth Blackwell and Mary Putnam Jacobi offer thoughtful rebuttals to the notion of woman as invalid in Blackwell's *The Human Element in Sex* (London: J. and A. Churchill, 1894) and Jacobi's brilliant response to Edward Clarke, *The Question of Rest for Women During Menstruation* (New York: G. P. Putnam's Sons, 1877).

The past decade has seen an increasing number of secondary works dealing with women and medicine in the nineteenth century, primarily as a result of the new feminism. Among the books and articles which I have found most valuable in sharpening my focus and confirming my estimate of the relationship between medical practice and patent medicine are the works of Carrol Smith-Rosenberg and Charles Rosenberg, most notably "The Female Animal: Medical and Biological Views of Woman and Her Role in Nineteenth-Century America," *Journal of American History*, VI (September 1973), pp. 332–356, and the provocative work of G. J. Barker-Benfield, culminating in *The Horrors of the Half-Known Life: Male Attitudes Toward Women and Sexuality in Nineteenth-Century America* (New York: Harper and Row, 1976). Ann Douglas Wood's " 'The Fashionable Diseases': Woman's Complaints and Their Treatment in Nineteenth-Century America," *Journal of Interdisciplinary History*, IV (Summer 1973), pp. 25–52, and the rejoinder by Regina M. Morantz, "The Perils of Feminist History," *Journal of Interdisciplinary History*, IV (Spring 1974), pp. 649–660, point to some of the interpretational disputes that exist in the field. Among the more popular treatments of women and medicine are John S. and Robin Haller, *The Physician and Sexuality in Victorian America* (New York: W. W. Norton & Company, 1974) and Barbara Ehrenreich and Deirdre English, *For Her Own Good: 150 Years of the Experts' Advice to Women* (Garden City, New York: Doubleday/Anchor Press, 1978).

Women and women's sphere in the nineteenth century has been the subject of several excellent books and articles, beginning with Barbara Welter's classic piece, "The Cult of True Womanhood 1820–1860," *American Quarterly,* XVIII (Summer 1966), pp. 151–174, and Gerda Lerner's "The Lady and the Mill Girl: Changes in the Status of Women in the Age of Jackson," *Midcontinent American Studies Journal,* X (Spring 1969), pp. 5–15. Among the best of the recent studies are Nancy Cott's *The Bonds of Womanhood: "Woman's Sphere" in New England, 1790–1835* (New Haven: Yale University Press, 1977) and Ann Douglas' *The Feminization of American Culture* (New York: Alfred A. Knopf Inc., 1977).

Studies on women in the early twentieth century have not been as numerous, nor of as high a quality as the work done on the earlier period. Among the best of the secondary works is John R. McGovern's "The American Woman's Pre-World War I Freedom in Manners and Morals," available in Jean E. Friedman and William G. Shade, eds., *Our American Sisters,* (Boston: Allyn and Bacon, Inc., 1976), pp. 345–365. Rheta Childe Dorr's *A Woman of Fifty* (New York: Funk and Wagnalls Company, 1924) is an excellent autobiography which helps to illuminate the New Woman.

For a look at changes in sexual mores, see John C. Burnham, "The Progressive Revolution in American Attitudes Toward Sex," *Journal of American History,* LIX (March 1973), pp. 885–908; Paul Robinson's *The Modernization of Sex* (New York: Harper and Row, 1976); and Nathan G. Hale, Jr.'s excellent book, *Freud and the Americans* (New York: Oxford University Press, 1971).

Histories of the birth control movement in America also provide insight into changing attitudes toward female sexuality. David Kennedy's *Birth Control in America: The Career of Margaret Sanger* (New Haven: Yale University Press, 1970), Linda Gordon's *Woman's Body, Woman's Right: A Social History of Birth Control in America* (New York: Grossman Publishers, 1976), and James W. Reed's *From Private Vice to Public Virtue: The Birth Control Movement and American Society Since 1830* (New York: Basic Books, Inc., 1978) are markedly different in their interpretations and merit close scrutiny.

Finally, in my study of gynecological practice in the twentieth century, I found two autobiographies by doctors of particular help: J. L. Bubis, *Women Are My Problem* (New York: Comet Press Books, 1953) and Franklin H. Martin, *Fifty Years of Medicine and Surgery* (Chicago: The Surgical Publication Company, 1934).

Index